MW01128479

★ # DC BABY

REVISED SECOND EDITION

FSC

Mixed Sources
Product group from well-managed
forests, controlled sources and
recycled wood or fiber

Cert no. SW-COC-2062
www.fsc.org
© 1996 Forest Stewardship Council

★DC BABY

REVISED SECOND EDITION

by Sarah K. Masterson

To subscribe to the free monthly e-newsletter or the blog alerts email
list, go to www.dc-baby.com

Printed at Kirby Lithographics, Arlington, VA

for Noah, Ava, and Charlie

and for Mimi,
whose loving care of my children makes my work possible

Table of Contents

PREFACE

I wrote the first edition of this book in 2005, after making a cross-country relocation from Texas to DC with my husband and baby daughter, who celebrated her first birthday right about the time we landed in Washington. I had lived in DC once before – for a period of about three years while working on my (never dissertated) doctoral degree in English and Women's Studies at the University of Maryland, College Park. But in those days I was unmarried and child-free. So when my husband accepted a new job in the spring of 2005 that would bring me back to Washington as a parent, I had a bit of a panic. We'd be leaving family and friends behind for uncharted territory. I knew my way around DC for sure, but not with a young child!

So I did what academic/journalist/writers do best, to manage their neurotic anxieties as best they can: I researched. I got online, I joined DC parents' listservs, and I read everything I could get my hands on. I made a few email friends and acquaintances among Washington-area mothers, who kindly shared their wisdom. I amassed a huge cache of information that did, in fact, make our move and our adjustment easier.

As we began settling into our new life with a baby in DC, it occurred to me that I might not be the only parent in need of the great heaping piles of local research I had collected over the previous months. It occurred to me that in preparation for the move, I had searched in vain for a resource book that was current and specifically geared toward DC newcomers with kids and first-time parents in Washington. It occurred to me – especially as I was in a professional transition and trying to carve out my next career move – that such a book needed to be written. And that there was nothing, really, to stop me from being the one to write it. So I did. My husband and I founded our own publishing company, outsourced what we needed to, and did the rest ourselves. We learned a lot about publishing the hard way, but it's been a fun ride.

Since the first edition of the book sold out in 2006, I've been working on a heavily revised and expanded second edition. The manuscript has been through countless visitations. Huge chunks of my writing have been lost in at least two major computer meltdowns over the past year. But so much has changed on the local scene since 2005, and I've learned so much as a local parent, and have met many wonderful parents and local business owners and service providers since that first edition, I have somehow convinced myself to persevere toward a second edition. Through a tough second pregnancy, medical complications, bed rest, and now a newborn son, I've kept pushing forward. And at long last, this book is done!

Some things you, as my readers, should know. By nature, the content in a resource like this is forever in flux. Businesses open and close all the time. They change phone numbers and locations. New service providers come on the scene. Support groups start up and shut down. But I've done my best – with the help of a small army of dedicated readers of the first edition of my book, my blog, and the monthly e-newsletter – to send to press a book that is as relevant and "of the moment" as possible. As always, visiting the website or giving a new-to-you spot a call is a good idea. Also a good idea: Visiting www.dc-baby.com regularly and subscribing to the free monthly e-newsletter, where I will share updates to book content.

Finally, a note about methodology. Every now and then a question comes up about who gets included in this book, and how, and why. It's really very simple: This book is one woman's account of pregnancy and parenting young children in and around Washington, DC. Its content is based upon personal experiences my husband and I have had, as well as those of our neighbors, friends, and the many parents whom I've never met in person but who have generously shared their reviews and recommendations with me over the past three-plus years. (Too many to name in this space, and certainly too many to quote in the book, but you know who you are – and I appreciate you.)

Naturally, it would be impossible to represent every business and service provider in the DC area catering to families of young children. Yet I've worked hard to be as comprehensive as possible, within reasonable constraints of time and space. It would be equally impossible to give all the programs and businesses I cover in this book "equitable attention." Some businesses and service providers are reviewed in greater depth, because I have extensive personal experience with them. And just because a business or program gets a shorter review in this book than another with which I have greater familiarity doesn't make it any less worthy. I encourage you to use the information in the book as a springboard for finding the places and people YOU love!

When all's said and done, the integrity of this project stems from the fact that recommendations come from first-hand experience, uninfluenced by advertising dollars. In other words, no pay for play. I received no compensation from any business or service provider featured in this book. Not a word on these pages has been "bought."

Thanks again to all of you who have shared your knowledge with me over the past few years. Thanks to my husband and publishing business partner Noah for his hard work on this project. Thanks to photographer Elizabeth Dranitzke of PHOTOPIA (www.photopiadc.com) for taking a great author photo of moi with my daughter. And thanks to all of you for reading!

Happy DC parenting,
Sarah Klein Masterson
September, 2008
www.dc-baby.com

CHAPTER 1
Pregnancy, Birth, & Postpartum

SUPPORT FOR FERTILITY ISSUES

RESOLVE of the Mid-Atlantic Region
www.resolve.org
A national nonprofit organization based out of Bethesda, MD, RESOLVE
has a very active local chapter. RESOLVE provides support programs and
information to women and couples experiencing infertility.

DC'S FAVORITE OB/GYNS

Dr. Susanne Bathgate
George Washington University Hospital/Office at 2150 Pennsylvania Ave.
NW
202.994.4357, www.gwu.edu/~resobgyn/faculty.html

Dr. Russell Bridges
Sibley Hospital/Office at 2440 M St., Suite 416
202.223.3006, www.robertrussellbridgesmd.com

Dr. Thu Tran at Capital Women's Care Rockville office
Shady Grove Adventist Hospital
301.424.1696, http://marylandobgyn.com

Drs. Bergin & Powers at Chevy Chase Ob/Gyn
5550 Friendship Blvd., Suite 200, Chevy Chase, MD
301.986.9390, www.chevychaseobgyn.com

Dr. Joan Loveland at Reiter & Hill
Sibley Memorial Hospital / Offices in DC, Chevy Chase, & Falls Church
301.654.5700, 202.331.1740, 703.533.9211
www.rhj-obgyn.com

> *"Dr. Joan Loveland is my favorite… She's very professional and also very open and communicative. Plus, hip and fun!"*
>
> *- Carla*

Dr. Nancy Gaba at GW Medical Faculty Associates
202. 994.4357, www.gwdocs.com

Dr. Lorraine Gillian
Washington Hospital Center/Offices at 106 Irving St. NW, Suite 4700 and 11721 Woodmore Rd., Suite 100, Mitchellville, MD
202.723.9100, 202.877.DOCS

Dr. Melody Abraham at Reiter & Hill, PLLC
Sibley Memorial Hospital and Georgetown University Hospital
Offices in DC, Chevy Chase, & Falls Church
301.654.5700, 202.331.1740, 703.533.9211
www.rhj-obgyn.com

Dr. Richard Footer (solo practice)
2440 M St., Suite 718, Georgetown, NW DC
202.659.4917

> *"I really preferred having an ob/gyn in solo practice, which is why I chose Dr. Footer for my second baby. He's great, and I disliked the larger practices where you see a different person every time and can't be sure who will be with you at delivery. I also have a friend who had two babies with Dr. Virginia Thompson in solo practice, and she had a good experience."*
>
> *- Anonymous DC mama*

Dr. Virginia Thompson (solo practice)
2440 M St., Suite 420, Georgetown, NW DC, 202.296.7963
Foxhall Ob/Gyn
NW DC, www.foxhallobgyn.com

Dr. Jean-Gilles Tchabo
Arlington, 703.558.6591

> **author's note:**
> Dr. Tchabo, who delivers at Virginia Hospital Center in
> Arlington, has a strong reputation as a talented, progressive-
> minded, caring ob/gyn who specializes in complicated births,
> including VBACs and breech babies. Dr. Tchabo is widely
> respected among local birth doulas and midwives, and over
> the past two years I have heard nothing but glowing reviews
> from patients and colleagues alike.

Drs. Fern Grapin & Dr. Marc Siegal at Physicians for Women
4660 Kenmore Ave., Suite 1100, Alexandria
703.370.0400, www.physiciansforwomen.net

Physicians & Midwives Collaborative
Two locations in Alexandria (4660 Kenmore Ave, Suite 902 and 2616
Sherwood Hall Ln., Suite 208)
Also in Lake Ridge (12508 Lake Ridge Dr.)
www.physiciansandmidwives.com

> **author's note:**
> On the recommendation of so many of our readers, we
> went with Physicians & Midwives for our second pregnancy.
> This is one of the very few area practices where certified
> nurse-midwives do hospital deliveries and where ob/gyns
> and midwives work together as a team. During what turned
> out to be a difficult pregnancy, we received excellent care
> and support from the midwives, as well as from Dr. Denise
> Cunningham. Midwife Liz Itote was with us for the fast and
> furious delivery of our son, and she handled a potential
> emergency situation with absolute calm and skill. We liked
> that P&M has its own lab for blood work, refers to the
> Perinatal Diagnostic Center at Alexandria Hospital when
> needed, has friendly front-desk staff, and offers nice perks
> such as a midwife-guided, small-group hospital tour and
> informal Q&A during the jittery third trimester. We valued
> P&M's unique approach – They were the perfect fit for us!

Simmonds & Simmonds
19241 Montgomery Village, Gaithersburg - 301.948.3600
77 Thomas Johnson Dr., Frederick – 301.620.7144
11301 Rockville Pike, North Bethesda – 240.514.0140
26005 Ridge Rd., Damascus – 301.414.2300

> *"Our ob/gyn is the greatest ever! Dr. [Anne] Shrout at Simmonds & Simmonds. She even puts up with my 'witty' comments!"*
>
> *- Andrew, founder/owner of Andy's Parties*

Drs. Nancy Saunders & Janet Schaffel at Women Ob/Gyn Physicians
NW DC
http://womenob-gyn.com

Virginia Women's Health Associates
Vienna, Reston
www.vwha.yourmd.com

Women Physicians of Northern Virginia
Fairfax, Reston, Ashburn
www.womenphysicians.org

CESAREAN AWARENESS

NoVa ICAN Chapter: Regular meetings, open to all. Visit www.icanofnova.org or contact Lori Cooper, lskcooper@icanofnova.org
Baltimore-area ICAN Chapter: Regular meetings, open to all. Contact Barbara Stratton, ICANofBaltimore@comcast.net
National ICAN website: www.ican-online.org
Childbirth Connection website: www.childbirthconnection.org

DC'S FAVORITE MIDWIVES

Nurse-Midwives at Fairfax Ob/Gyn Associates
Karen Foster-Anderson, Elizabeth Goodiel, Janee Mao Leong, CNMs
Fairfax & Woodbridge, www.fairfaxobgyn.com

Peggy Franklin RN, ND, CPM, LM
202.494.6476, www.birthbydesign.org
Specializes in: Home births, water births, VBACs

UPDATE ON MIDWIFERY CARE IN VIRGINIA

"Virginia has started licensing Certified Professional Midwives (CPMs). The law changed on July 1, 2005, to allow for the regulation of CPMs (A Certified Professional Midwife is a knowledgeable, skilled and professional independent midwifery practitioner who has met the standards for certification set by the North American Registry of Midwives (NARM) and is qualified to provide the midwifery model of care. The CPM is the only international credential that requires knowledge about and experience in out-of-hospital settings.)

A research study published by the British Medical Journal in June 2005 concluded that 'Planned home birth for low risk women in North America using certified professional midwives was associated with lower rates of medical intervention but similar intrapartum and neonatal mortality to that of low risk hospital births in the United States.'

There are now 17 LMs serving Virginia. Northern Virginia has two LMs serving the area: myself, Tammi McKinley (Arlington) and Peggy Franklin (Gainesville)."

- Tammi McKinley, Arlington mama & licensed midwife

BirthCare & Women's Health
1501 King St., Old Town Alexandria
703.549.5070
www.birthcare.org
BirthCare is a practice of certified nurse-midwives (CNM) who support home births, as well as in their freestanding birth center in Old Town. They also provide well-woman gynecological care. A longtime local favorite for low-risk women who want a low-intervention birth in a non-hospital setting.

> *"Connor was born at home with the BirthCare midwives. Erin attended the birth and Audrey Fletcher was my birth assistant. Both Audrey and Erin definitely helped make my dream birth come true. Through the miracle of lactation consultant Pat Shelly from the Breastfeeding Center, who came to my home Friday night just hours after Connor's birth, and met with me again the following Monday, Connor is now an exclusively breastfed baby."*
>
> *- Elaine*

Family Health & Birth Center

17th St. NE, DC
202.398.2007 or 202.398.5520
www.developingfamilies.org/dcbc.html
Family Health and Birth Center (formerly the DC Birth Center) is staffed by four midwives (CNMs), with continuity of care provided by pediatric nurse-practitioners (PNPs). The midwives provide prenatal, labor and delivery, postpartum and well-woman gynecological services. They attend births at the Center and at the Washington Hospital Center, where they have a consulting relationship with the ob/gyn staff. The Center now accepts private insurance!

> *"I took a group tour of the DC Birth Center after they did a big remodeling/renovation, and it was really nice. I think it would be especially convenient for people like me, who live on Capitol Hill and want a low-intervention alternative to a hospital birth. I was able to briefly meet one of the midwives, and I liked her a lot."*
>
> *- Holly*

Loudoun Community Midwives

Leesburg, VA
www.lcmidwives.com
Specializes in: Loudon Hospital Birthing Center births

> *"Margie Branquist, the [Loudon Community] midwife on-call when I went into labor, was great. She gave positive encouragement throughout my labor. During the pushing stage she helped me focus and coached me through techniques that helped my labor and delivery along. She respected our wishes and helped us make informed decisions without any pressure."*
>
> *- Melanie*

Midwifery Care Associates
Bethesda, www.midwiferycareassociates.com
The certified nurse-midwives (CNMs) of Midwifery Care Associates (MCA) attend births at Shady Grove Adventist Hospital, as part of Simmonds & Simmonds (a collaborative practice of ob/gyn physicians, midwives, and physician assistants (PAs). They provide the full scope of well-woman gynecological care, prenatal care, birth, and postpartum.

> **author's note:**
> MCA was founded in May 2007 in response to the closing of several area midwifery practices, including the freestanding birth center at The Maternity Center in Bethesda, where the MCA midwives previously practiced. Since Shady Grove Adventist Hospital plans to open a new tower in fall 2007 featuring private postpartum rooms and "other amenities supporting family-centered care," the MCA midwives' practice will be an even more appealing option for low-risk expectant moms.

Tammi McKinley, CPM, LM
NoVa
240.539.4501, www.naturalbeginnings.org
Specializes in: home births and other out-of-hospital births, water births, VBAC

Physicians & Midwives Collaborative
Two locations in Alexandria (4660 Kenmore Ave, Suite 902 and 2616 Sherwood Hall Ln., Suite 208)

Also in Lake Ridge (12508 Lake Ridge Dr.)
www.physiciansandmidwives.com

> *"I had a great experience delivering my second baby at INOVA Alexandria with one of the midwives from Physicians and Midwives. The labor and delivery staff was very accommodating and supportive of my birth choices."*
>
> *- Melody*

For more midwifery info:
DC childbirth educator Susan Messina maintains an excellent website chock-full of local resources. Check the site for up-to-date information on midwives practicing throughout the DC metro area:
http://www.susanmessina.com/midwives.html

ACNM (American College of Nurse-Midwives)
www.acnm.org
MANA (Midwives Alliance of North America)
www.mana.org
NARM (North American Registry of Midwives)
www.narm.org
MidwifeInfo.com
www.midwifeinfo.com

LOCAL LISTSERVS FOR PREGNANCY

DC Expectant Moms
http://health.groups.yahoo.com/group/dcexpectantmoms
This list, founded and moderated by Melody Kisor, childbirth educator, doula, and founder of The Baby Duck, the DC Expectant Moms list is open to pregnant women and new moms from throughout the DC metro area. The active (but not overwhelming) list shares information and empathy on everything from health issues and medical care to shopping, classes, and playgroups. Childbirth educators, doulas, and lactation specialists are also members of the list and can offer helpful resources and referrals. Members sometimes organize social meet-ups in DC and the suburbs, both before and after their babies are born.

Childbirth Education

http://groups.yahoo.com/group/childbirth-ed

NoVa doula and childbirth educator Amara DalPezzo is the founder and moderator of the Childbirth Education listserv, which aims to support expectant parents who want to learn more about their pregnancy, the birth of their child and how to plan for the birth they want. The list discusses a wide range of topics, some of which are controversial. Amara says, "This list focuses on truthful information about pregnancy and birth... It is up to each individual family to decide which information is right for them."

MORE PRENATAL INFO & SUPPORT

Expectant Parents Classes at Parenting Playgroups

www.parentingplaygroups.com

Parenting Playgroups in Alexandria, founded by developmental psychologist Dr. Rene Hackney, offers an eight-hour Expectant Parents Class, typically meeting on three week-night evenings. Diverse topics include temperament, attachment, the role of fathers, babyproofing and safety, newborn health, family stress and transition, infant massage, and the use of sign language with babies. For more info, contact Rene at 703.922.0044 or rene@parentingplaygroups.com.

Sidelines Support Network

www.sidelines.org

The Sidelines National Support Network is a national network of support groups for women experiencing complicated or high-risk pregnancies. The national website's resource page lists links to companies, support groups, federal agencies, and info related to complications in pregnancy. It also has articles, letters, email support, and local chapter contacts. The contact person for Washington, DC, Maryland, and Virginia is Anne Simmons-McGroarty. You can reach her at sidelinesofva@webtv.net or 540.891.5292.

SPAL Support Group

Local mother Carolyn Mara facilitates a network bringing together women who are pregnant again after experiencing the loss of a baby: the SPAL (Subsequent Pregnancy After a Loss) Support Group. SPAL meets once a month in Falls Church and is a safe, supportive environment in which to talk about concerns and fears, as well as to meet other women who understand what you have been through. For more info, contact Carolyn at 703.754.5836.

Birth Options Alliance (formerly the Takoma Park Birthing Circle)
NEW blog & website: www.BirthOptionsAlliance.blogspot.com
To join the listserv:
http://health.groups.yahoo.com/group/takomabirthing
The Takoma Park Birthing Circle has headed in a new direction, in the wake of the closing of the long-respected Maternity Center in Bethesda and the beloved practice of the Takoma Park midwives. A nonprofit organization, the Birth Options Alliance (BOA) now "assists expectant women and families in the capital area by providing evidence-based information about pregnancy, childbirth, and parenting, and advocating for accessibility of a full range of caregiver and birth location options." They operate a Yahoo listserv, host monthly birth salons (free and open to the public), conduct community outreach and education, advocate for legislation supportive of birth options, and have the longer-term goal of creating a freestanding birth center in suburban MD/DC.

Birthing Circle of Frederick, Maryland
www.birthingcircle.org
A member-supported organization "dedicated to promoting normal birth through public education." The Birthing Circle represents healthcare providers, educators, birthing mothers, and their advocates in supporting women's rights to make informed decisions about their pregnancy and birth options. The organization also supports the Mother-Friendly Childbirth Initiative put forth by the Coalition for Improving Maternity Services (CIMS), www.motherfriendly.org. And they are strong advocates of midwifery. The Birthing Circle offers a newsletter to members, as well as access to their lending library. Business memberships are also available. And they host an Annual Birth Festival.

BirthMatters Virginia
www.birthmattersva.org
Birth Matters Virginia provides information and support with the goal of educating women and families about evidence-based models of maternity care and supporting care providers who practice mother- and

baby-friendly care. They hold monthly "coffee talks" throughout the state of Virginia, open to the public. Check the website for NoVa meetings.

Childbirth Solutions (Middleburg, VA)
www.childbirthsolutions.com
Childbirth Solutions is a resource center in NoVa hosting a variety of classes and events for pregnant women and prospective and new parents. They also have a full resource library and the website features message boards and online chats. Also a newsletter available.

Magic of Motherhood
www.magicofmotherhood.com
Founded by local mother and prenatal educator Jill Chasse, Magic of Motherhood provides a number of resources for expectant mamas and their partners, including pregnancy support, prenatal counseling, and information on pre-birth bonding and early learning. They also provide online parenting/pregnancy/learning classes for busy DC families, and bereavement and grief support for parents who have lost a baby.

DC'S FAVORITE BIRTH DOULAS
Word to the wise: Doulas are in exceptionally high demand in the DC area, and the number of clients each doula can accept is limited. They book up many months in advance, so it's never too early to make the calls.

> **author's note:**
> What can you expect to pay for a trained, fully-certified birth doula? The going rate in the Washington, DC area is $800 to $1,300, which typically includes several prenatal visits, continuous support throughout your labor and birth, and at least one postpartum follow-up. Doulas-in-training, who have completed educational requirements but are still accruing births to complete the certification process, typically charge less than the full market rate. So if you are on a strict budget, you don't have to rule out doula support.

Channing Armell
540.856.2525, armell@shentel.net
Serves: NoVa and DC metro area

Channing is trained through both CAPPA (for labor) and DONA (for postpartum). Channing is also an experienced grandmother of EIGHT!

Dawn Star Borchelt
largercircle@verizon.net, www.largercircle.blogspot.com
Serves: DC metro area
Dawn is a Birthing from Within mentor and doula providing both birth and postpartum doula services. She has 10 years of experience working with mothers and their families in community settings, in addition to childbirth education and doula experience. She especially enjoys working with a diverse clientele. Dawn is based in southern Maryland but is "willing to travel anywhere in the DC region, south of the top of the Beltway."

Heidi Bachman, CD
202.832.6923, hbachman@aol.com
Serves: DC and metro area
Heidi is a DONA-certified birth doula, experienced with both hospital and non-hospital birth settings. She attends births at all DC metro-area hospitals and birthing centers. Heidi is also a Lamaze childbirth educator offering private and group classes in DC, as well as leading groups for new moms.

Beautiful Journeys Doula Services, Julie Sites
703.627.0554, metrodcdoula@aol.com
Serves: DC metro area
DONA-trained and –certified. Also provides breastfeeding support.

Birthbliss, Laura Marks, HBCE, CHT
301.467.8725, www.birthbliss.com
Offers doula services as well as childbirth education and hypnobirthing instruction.

Birthing Hands of DC
202.236.1764, www.birthinghandsdc.com
Serves: DC metro area
Birthing Hands is a team of professional English- and Spanish-speaking doulas and midwife birth assistants, providing services in hospital, birth

center and home birth settings. They offer birth doula and postpartum doula services, individualized childbirth and pregnancy classes, breastfeeding instruction and support, and more. Founder Claudia Booker is a DONA-certified birth doula, an ICTC-certified Full Circle doula, an experienced midwife birth assistant, a CAPPA-certified childbirth educator, La Leche League International certified breastfeeding peer counselor, and is a student of midwifery.

> *"Claudia's calm, good-humored, and gentle support during our short but intense labor with our second son was priceless. Claudia took the time beforehand to get to know us and our wishes for the birth, so she was able to provide exactly the support we were looking for."*
>
> *- M.M.*

BirthPartners Birth Assisting
Audrey Fletcher, 703.830.4199, a4mom@aol.com
Pam Llewellyn: 301.776.8785, npllewellyn@verizon.net
Lori Stillwagon: 301.290.5188, birthingyourway@comcast.net
These three doulas work as a team, supporting the clients of BirthCare & Women's Health in Old Town Alexandria, as well as non-BirthCare clients when their schedules allow. All three are on the BirthCare staff as birth assistants.

Birth Diva
202.271.3240, www.birthdiva.com
Offers a variety of services for couples who are planning toward a natural childbirth – including Bradley Method classes, labor and postpartum doula support, prenatal massage...and even prenatal bellydance classes.

Elena Caraballo
703.731.7381, ummilyas2000@yahoo.com
www.birthservice.com
Serves: DC metro area
DONA- and CAPPA-trained as a birth doula. Also a student midwife, birth assistant, and postpartum doula.

Child Birth Care
www.childbirthcare.com
Serves: DC metro area
Provides labor and postpartum doula services and referrals.

Confident Birth Services, Lara Maupin
703.237.9857, confidentbirth@verizon.net
Serves: NoVa, DC metro area
DONA-trained and -certified. Lara is also a Lamaze-certified childbirth educator.

Aimee LaBuy Crane
703.440.5888, www.birthblessings.com
Serves: DC metro area
ALACE-trained and -certified. Also a childbirth educator and lactation consultant.

> *"Thank you does not even begin to cover how grateful we are to have had Aimee with us for every step of a challenging 40-hour labor. Nature does it best, but Aimee is our runner-up."*
>
> *- Sarah & Matt*

Dreambirths, directed by doula Amara DalPezzo
571.344.0438, amara@dreambirths.com
www.dreambirths.com
Amara is an ALACE-trained and certified birth doula, as well as a childbirth educator serving women who give birth in NoVA and DC, in settings ranging from hospitals to homebirths. Her childbirth education classes meet in Manassas. Amara's background also includes training/experience with DONA, BirthWorks, hypnobirthing, and natural childbirth. She also now leads an expanded birth doula program through Dreambirths, LLC, which matches clients to doulas using helpful profiles. Amara says, "For clients this is beneficial because they are set up on interviews with doulas who know they can provide what they need. For doulas, this is nice because the clients they service are more likely to match their preferred style of birthing. This results in wonderfully fulfilling birthing experiences."

> *"Amara's support was invaluable and provided us with the tools and self-confidence we needed to ensure labor and delivery went as we hoped it would. It was truly a dream birth!"*
>
> *- Anonymous DC mama*

Kat Haines, CD
diamou@earthlink.net
Serves: Capitol Hill neighborhood, DC

Allison Harris, Kairos Birth Support Services
oasishealingarts@starpower.net
www.kairosdoulas.net
Serves: DC metro area
Allison and the other Kairos doulas are DONA-trained and –certified.

> *"Our experience with Allison Harris as our doula was wonderful... Having Allison there to explain what was happening, to coach us through our fears and pain...kept the mood in the room for everyone light and even jubilant and made this an unforgettably happy birthing experience..."*
>
> *-Sherian*

Holy Cross Hospital's Birth Doula Program
http://www.holycrosshealth.org/svc_maternity_doula_faq.htm
An optional program for women birthing at Holy Cross Hospital, providing doula support for labor and birth. The program includes prenatal meetings with a doula, a non-emergency prenatal doula warm-line, open house events allowing you to meet all the doulas working at the hospital, and 24-hour on-call doula staffing.

Katie Horner
703.304.6146, mrskatehorner@hotmail.com
Katie is DONA_trained and certified. She has had successful and positive experiences attending hospital births, and would be a good match for any birth setting.

Liz Kaufman

202.446.4400, birthchedva@aol.com
Serves: DC metro area
Liz is an ALACE-trained birth doula and is a birth assistant with BirthCare & Women's Health in Old Town and the Birth Center in NE DC. She offers both birth and postpartum doula support.

Love 'N Care, Lois Ecker

410.284.8355, loisecker@aol.com
www.lovencaredoula.com
Serves: Maryland, DC, and Nova
This agency is led by certified postpartum doula and lactation counselor Lois Ecker, certified through UCLA, NAPCS, and Healthy Children, with over 30 years of infant experience. The agency offers doulas for all stages, baby nurses, lactation consultants, classes, and more.

Cecilia Racine, MSW

202.486.9545, alaboroflovedc@aol.com
www.alaboroflovedc.com
Serves: DC, suburban Maryland, and NoVa, all birth settings, including hospital, home, and birth center.
Cecilia is DONA-trained doula who is also a social worker in the field of maternal mental health. She has a special skill in working with birthing women who are survivors of sexual abuse and women who have experienced postpartum depression (PPD) or other perinatal mood disorders. She is familiar with a variety of childbirth methods, including Bradley, hypnobirthing, and Lamaze. Cecilia also has a special interest in working with international families and helping them connect to bilingual doulas who speak Spanish, French, German, or Italian. Her website is even viewable in Spanish, at www.alaboroflovedc.com/spanish/index.htm.

> *"Thanks to Cecilia for being such an integral part of our baby's birth. The experience definitely surpassed our expectations! And Cecilia was a critical and amazing support person for me."*
>
> *- Kerri*

Mindee Mosher
mindar4@aol.com, 301.617.8585
Serves: Suburban Maryland, DC metro area
DONA-trained and -certified. Specializes in VBACs (vaginal birth after cesarean).

Mind Body Births, Alana Rose
Serves: DC metro area
www.mindbodybirths.com
Alana Rose is a birth doula offering services throughout the DC metro area. She also teaches hypnobirthing childbirth ed classes in DC and Arlington.

Momease (Alexandria & GW University Hospital)
www.momease.com
Momease has a respected doula program, in addition to offering the support of baby nurses, breastfeeding counselors, and breastfeeding equipment. They also offer wide variety of prenatal, childbirth prep, and parenting classes at George Washington University Hospital and in Alexandria, VA.

Mother & Baby Matters
703.787.4007, motherbaby_office@juno.com
www.motherandbabymatters.com
This NoVa-based agency provides a range of support services for birthing women and their families throughout metro DC. As the first-of-its-kind doula agency in the Washington area, founded in 1991, they have a longstanding reputation in the community. Among the services they offer: Birth doulas, postpartum doulas, overnight help during the postpartum period, family care assistants, and breastfeeding support.

"My doula from Mother & Baby Matters, Donna Winsor, was fabulous! Donna quietly and unobtrusively offered me the perfect amount of labor help, while letting my husband be the primary support person. She also worked beautifully, as a team, with my labor and delivery staff and my midwives, all

> *of whom commented on how helpful and professional she was during the birth."*
>
> *- Melody*

> **author's note:**
> We hired Donna Winsor from M&B Matters for the birth of our second child. Couldn't have been happier! Donna spent quality time getting to know us in the weeks before the birth, helped us work through a birth plan that addressed our needs and wants, and provided helpful resources and suggestions as we prepared for the big day. Donna's calm and reassuring presence during labor was a lifesaver. Her strong but unaggressive manner helped me to focus my energies and safely deliver our son. Thank you, Donna!

Nurtured Beginnings:
Paula Levin-Alcorn, Mary Beth Miller MacKinnon, & Pamela Huffman
www.nurtured-beginnings.com
Serves: NoVa, DC, and suburban Maryland (close-in to DC).
Specializes in all birth settings, including hospital, freestanding birth centers, and homebirths. All are DONA-certified. Each of the doulas previously worked individually in private practice, but Nurtured Beginnings has been an active collaborative since spring 2004. Paula is also an LCSW with significant experience in maternal-child health, and is a mother of two. Mary Beth is raising her two sons and worked in high-tech before becoming a doula. Pamela is also the mother of two girls. The Nurtured Beginnings doulas offer a unique perk – Monthly gatherings at which past, current, and prospective clients are welcome. They meet at the Falls Church Community Center in NoVa, and all babies/children are welcome. It's a great way to network with other expectant and new parents, or find out more about the experience of having a doula.

> *"We had no idea what to expect from a doula and were blown away by Pamela's support, professionalism, capabilities and personal consideration throughout pregnancy and birth. Having her involved made the birth so*

> *much more manageable and comfortable than it could have been."*
>
> *- Lindsay*

Heidi Streufert, CD

301.624.2439 (home), 240.601.5312 (mobile)
heidi@transitionsdoula.com
http://transitionsdoula.com
Heidi is a Birthworks-certified doula serving the Baltimore and DC metro areas and their surrounding suburbs, based out of Frederick County, MD (60-mile travel radius). She has been certified through Birthworks since 2004, attending births and offering breastfeeding support since 1992. Heidi has a great deal of knowledge about optimal fetal positioning and has attended the Spinning Babies workshop with Gail Tully. Her interests include "helping women desiring VBAC, homebirth, birth center birth, and those desiring a safe, natural, gentle birth in a hospital setting."

> *"Hiring Heidi as my doula was the best decision of my pregnancy! She provided unwavering support, a wealth of information, and confidence in me, my baby and the birth process, allowing me to have a perfect homebirth."*
>
> *- Amy*

RuthCarol Touhey, CD

202.546.2614, rstouhey@comcast.net
Serves: DC, NoVa, and suburban Maryland.
Specializes in supporting all birth settings, including hospital, birth center, and home. DONA-trained and -certified.

> *"RuthCarol Touhey was a wonderful doula through my 26-hour labor. She helped make the day wonderful. We will always remember our son's birthday as one of peaceful*

> *anticipation as she was the kindest, most patient, best*
> *support person we could have asked for."*
>
> *- Amy*

Transitions Birth Doulas:
Lori Cooper, CD & Margaret Eldridge, CD
www.transitionsbirthdoulas.com
Serving: DC, NoVa, Suburban Maryland, all birth settings.
DONA-trained and -certified. Lori also serves as the Northern Virginia coordinator for ICAN (International Cesarean Awareness Network) and has trained as a birth assistant with BirthCare in Old Town Alexandria. Margaret has also trained as a Bradley childbirth educator and has a special interest in natural birth.

> *"Our Transitions doula was able to support me emotionally*
> *and provide a sense of comfort to both my husband and me.*
> *I'm amazed at her ease with the whole process. She was so*
> *calm and respectful. It exceeded all expectations and*
> *experiences from that of my previous two births."*
>
> *- Julie*

Heather Wilson
202.360.1138, heatherannewilson@gmail.com
Heather is DONA-trained and -certified.

Robin White, CD
301.320.5061, mother_matters@yahoo.com
Serves: DC, NoVa, & suburban MD
Robin, a Bethesda mom of a young son, has provided doula support to more than 75 families throughout the metro area. DONA-trained and -certified, she has served as the DONA MD/DC Representative since 2005. Robin supports families according to their terms in all birth settings, including hospital, birth center, and home in both medicated and unmedicated births. Her birth doula package includes a complimentary interview, two prenatal visits, continuous emotional and physical support during labor, and a follow-up postpartum visit.

> *"Robin truly loves the miracle of childbirth and wants you to have the most fulfilling experience possible. Having her attend that day was one of the best decisions I ever made. She helped make it possible for us to deliver without any medication or other interference."*
>
> *- Jenifer*

> *"Robin's knowledge and calm presence were a constant source of support, comfort, and encouragement. Robin does a great job working with the hospital staff and doctors, too... She was wonderful – very professional and organized, and it's obvious she cares a lot about her clients. I would definitely use her again!"*
>
> *– Sonya, Bethesda mama*

Sarah Wholey, CD
703.855.0324, doulasarahw@yahoo.com
Serves: DC metro area.
Specializes in working with clients in all birth settings, including hospital. DONA-certified. Emotional and physical support 24/7 during pregnancy, continuous labor support, and free loan of a birth ball.

Wise BirthWays, Birthing from Within-trained mentors
Susan Lucas & Priscilla McGee
www.wisebirthways.com
Serving: Metro DC and Maryland.
Offering prenatal and labor support in all birth settings, with both unmedicated and medicated births. Both Susan and Priscilla have trained with the *Birthing from Within* program. They also offer childbirth education classes and postpartum support.

> *"Susan's emotional support was invaluable before, during, and after the delivery. She was always calm and professional, yet openly enthusiastic about the entire process. Susan*

> *quelled any anxieties by explaining each procedure and staying focused on my needs."*
>
> - Anonymous DC mama

Finding more birth doulas:
DC childbirth educator Susan Messina maintains an excellent website chock-full of local resources. Check the site for up-to-date recommendations on both veteran and novice doulas (many of whom offer reduced rates during their certification process):
www.susanmessina.com/doulas.html
DONA (Doulas of North America), www.dona.org
ALACE (Association of Labor Assistants & Childbirth Educators), www.alace.org
CAPPA (Childbirth & Postpartum Professional Association), www.cappa.net
ICEA (International Childbirth Education Association), www.icea.org
BirthWorks, www.birthworks.org
Birthing from Within, http://birthingfromwithin.com
The Baby Duck, www.thebabyduck.com

DC'S FAVORITE CHILDBIRTH EDUCATORS

First-time expectant parents are sometimes unaware how many choices there are in childbirth education. Hospital-based classes are one option, and some are taught by excellent instructors. But it's also important to understand that hospital instructors are constrained by the corporate policies of their employers to teach in certain ways, and with certain information. Most hospital-based classes are less than 12 hours total, and they don't always have enough time for clients to practice techniques and positions that can be crucial for labor comfort (whether or not you plan to use medication). Some hospitals shy away from discussing their rates of cesarean section or the particulars of their policies, and some discourage women from making a "birth plan" or hiring a doula for support. So, we encourage expectant women to take preparation into your own hands. Do the research on your options, learn about the different philosophies and approaches, and then make the best choice for YOU.

Heidi Bachman, Lamaze-trained educator
202.832.6923, hbachman@aol.com, www.lamaze.org
Serves: DC, NoVa, & MD
Heidi is a Lamaze-certified childbirth educator providing group and private classes. She has experience teaching at Sibley and George Washington University Hospitals, and offers classes in her DC home, client homes, and other locations in the metro area. Heidi is also a DONA-certified birth doula experienced with hospital and non-hospital birth settings.

Birthbliss, Laura Marks, HBCE, CHT
301.467.8725, www.birthbliss.com
Offers childbirth education, including hypnobirthing – as well as doula services.

Birth Diva
202.271.3240, www.birthdiva.com
Offers a variety of services for couples who are planning toward a natural childbirth – including Bradley Method classes, labor and postpartum doula support, prenatal massage...and even prenatal bellydance classes.

Birthing Hands of DC
202.236.1764, www.birthinghandsdc.com
Serves: DC metro area
Birthing Hands is a team of professional English- and Spanish-speaking doulas and midwife birth assistants, providing services in hospital, birth center and home birth settings. They offer birth doula and postpartum doula services, individualized childbirth and pregnancy classes, breastfeeding instruction and support, and more. Founder Claudia Booker is a DONA-certified birth doula, an ICTC-certified Full Circle doula, an experienced midwife birth assistant, a CAPPA-certified childbirth educator, La Leche League International certified breastfeeding peer counselor, and is a student of midwifery.

Tiffany Collins, RN, CD
Birth Savvy: Labor Prep for Modern Parents
703.599.2837
Serves: NoVa & DC metro area

37

Amara DalPezzo, ALACE-trained educator
571.344.0438, amara@dreambirths.com
www.dreambirths.com, www.alace.org
Serves: NoVa
Amara is an ALACE-trained and certified birth doula and childbirth educator whose seven-class childbirth prep sessions meet at the George Mason University campus in Manassas, VA. (For more about Amara, see the listing for Dreambirths under "Birth Doulas.")

Susan Gunn, AAHCC, Bradley-trained educator
www.naturalbirthdc.com, www.bradleybirth.com
Serves: Washington, DC
Susan teaches Bradley Method natural childbirth classes in Adams Morgan and Capitol Hill, DC.

> *"Although my wife has never said as much, I'm sure my contribution to our first birth amounted to nothing short of an emotional drain on her. After taking the Bradley class with Susan Gunn, the birth of our second child was a completely different experience. I was an integral part of the process; so much so that after our son was born, our midwife inquired, with a hint of amazement, who our instructor was."*
>
> *- Ken*

Birth FLOW Classes, Larissa Guran, Lamaze-trained educator
301.891.7452, larissa@northstarbirth.com
www.northstarbirth.com, www.lamaze.org
Serves: Silver Spring, MD
Larissa is a Lamaze-trained childbirth educator, as well as a public health professional specializing in perinatal health and healthcare access, and a DONA-certified birth doula. Larissa's classes are designed to be engaging, interactive, and personalized, with a focus on practical coping and decision-making skills for labor and birth. She is adept at helping you navigate the healthcare system in a way that gets you what you need while building positive relationships with your care team.

> *author's note:*
> Susan Messina is, truly, beloved among childbirth educators!

> Since working on the first edition of this book in 2005, we've heard countless glowing reviews. Students in Susan's classes, which meet in the Palisades neighborhood of NW DC, say her approach made all the difference in their experience of pregnancy and birth – whether it all went "as planned" or took unexpected twists and turns along the way.

Susan Messina Birthworks-trained educator

Serves: Washington, DC, www.birthworks.org
www.susanmessina.com

> *"I have been recommending this class to all of my friends. Susan has wonderful energy and I felt very comfortable asking any and all of my questions. I liked the Birthworks approach because it was progressive, while still being open to people's individual choices."*
>
> *-Stephanie*

Mind Body Births, Alana Rose

Serves: DC & Arlington
www.mindbodybirths.com
Alana Rose offers hypnobirthing childbirth ed classes. Want to gather a small group and host the class in your home? You can receive a "hostess" discount on your own class tuition. Mind Body Births also offers birth doula services throughout the DC metro area.

Momease

www.momease.com
Serves: Washington, DC & Alexandria, VA
Classes are available for couples and single moms, as well as special offerings targeted just to dads and a sibling class for kids expecting a new baby brother or sister. Momease also does workshops on parenting with pets, prenatal massage, infant massage, CPR/first aid, prenatal nutrition, and pregnancy fitness and yoga.

Lori Pendergast, Birthworks-trained educator
703.779.2945, klaerj@verizon.net, www.birthworks.org
Serves: Leesburg, VA

Rose Quintilian, HCHI, Hypnobabies-trained educator
240.631.8177, rose@mygentlebirth.com
www.mygentlebirth.com
Serves: Montgomery County, MD (Classes held in Gaithersburg)

Sharon Stevenson, Hypnobirthing, Mongan Method-trained educator
703.971.7305, sharon@yogabirthandbeyond.com
www.yogabirthandbeyond.com
Serves: NoVa (Classes held in Alexandria and Springfield)
Sharon has served at the National Center for Homeopathy for 19 years
and is currently its executive director. She offers a series of
hypnobirthing-certified classes, as well as a three-hour "Empowering
Couples" workshop, aimed at empowering partners. She is also a birth
doula and teaches prenatal and postpartum yoga classes, Itsy Bitsy Yoga,
and infant massage classes.

Trisha Stotler, CHT, Hypnobirthing, Mongan Method-trained educator
703.585.9364, trisha@insightlifeservices.com
www.insightlifeservices.com, www.hypnobirthing.com
Serves: NoVa (Classes held in downtown Vienna)
Trisha offers a five-week series of hypnobirthing classes. She is a CHT in
private practice and was trained by Marie Mongan, M.Ed., M.Hy., creator
of the Hypnobirthing method and director of the Hypnobirthing Institute.

Ursula Sukinik, Bradley-trained educator
usukinik@comcast.net, 301.231.5122, www.bradleybirth.com
Serves: Bethesda
Ursula offers a 10-week session of group Bradley Method classes, but also
private crash-course-style classes for the time-challenged among us. She
also teaches relaxation workshops for expectant mamas/couples and is a
certified doula.

Emily Wang, Hypnobirthing educator
www.amazing-birth.com, emily@amazing-birth.com
Serves: Suburban MD, DC metro area

Emily is a Hypnobirthing Certified Educator and a Ph.D. Certified Hypnotist.

> "I love the philosophy; I love [Emily's] teaching manner. Thanks to Hypnobirthing, the support and encouragement I received, my baby's birth was wonderful. I was confident and free of fear."
>
> - Kristin

Wise BirthWays, Birthing from Within-trained mentors
Susan Lucas & Priscilla McGee
www.wisebirthways.com
Serving: Metro DC & MD
Both Susan and Priscilla have trained with the Birthing from Within program. In addition to their standard six-week session, they also offer weekend intensives, private classes, and "Birthin' Again" for parents who are having their second (or third, or fourth!) child. Susan and Priscilla also provide prenatal and labor support as doulas in all birth settings, with both unmedicated and medicated births, as well as postpartum support.

> "I feel the [Birthing from Within] classes allowed me to actively participate in the labor process. I really felt connected and that I played an important part in bringing Jacob into the world. Furthermore, I felt mentally prepared for everything that happened during labor and was able to stay present. This really put all my fears to rest."
>
> - Jonah

More Info & Referrals:
ALACE-certified instructors, www.alace.org
"Birthing from Within" mentors, www.birthingfromwithin.com
BirthWorks-certified instructors, www.birthworks.org
Bradley Method-certified instructors, www.bradleybirth.com
CAPPA-trained instructors, www.cappa.net
Hypnobirthing instructors, www.hypnobirthing.com
Lamaze-certified instructors, www.lamaze.org

The Baby Duck, www.thebabyduck.com
Our Kids, www.our-kids.com (under "Classes")

DC'S FAVORITE PREGNANCY MASSAGE

Pregnancy massage is appropriate after the first trimester and with the written approval of your prenatal healthcare provider.

Birth Diva
202.271.3240, www.birthdiva.com
Offers a variety of services for couples who are planning toward a natural childbirth – including prenatal massage.

Kelly Bowers, CMT
Eye Street Massage, Farragut West Metro, NW DC
Also does in-home appointments for homebound clients in DC and NoVa.
www.bowershours.com, www.eyestreet-massage.com

> "Kelly's massages helped me to cope with a difficult pregnancy, and then allowed me to keep working and have a healthy pregnancy. I also enjoyed massage post-pregnancy, and it made me feel like a new woman."
>
> - Anonymous DC mama

Mary Beth Hastings, CMT
202.276.3661
Mary Beth does private pregnancy massage appointments, as well as offering a labor massage class for expectant mothers and their spouses/coaches. (Formerly held at the now-defunct Maternity Center in Bethesda.) These classes are focused on empowering birth partners to give relief and support during labor, covering relaxation and visualization techniques, use of sensitive touch, contraction distraction techniques, dos and don'ts of labor massage, specific techniques for back labor, and reflexive/zone therapy approaches for use during labor.

Electra Liatos & Robin Brownstein at MINT Day Spa
Adams Morgan, DC
202, 328.6468, www.thespaatmint.com

Maryland Massage Therapy Center
Bethesda
301.913.0345, www.mdmassage.com

James Montgomery
Woodley Park, DC
202.288.4911 www.massagedc.net

Jennifer Moore, Moore Than Yoga
Arlington
703.671.2435, www.moorethanyoga.com
Jennifer is a reflexologist and Reiki practitioner who also teaches a (highly recommended) prenatal and postpartum yoga class. We can personally attest to her fabulous massage skills!

Missy Nolan at Designing Image Day Spa
Downtown Bethesda (in the Air Rights Building)
301.961.8640, www.designingimage.net

Old Town Massage Center, Jette Hansen
Old Town Alexandria
703.518.8484, www.oldtownmassagecenter.com
Jette also does in-home appointments for pregnant women on bedrest, with written authorization from a doctor.

> *author's note:*
> We met Jette – and saw her in action at the massage table with pregnant clients – at the Beltway Babies event in spring 2006. (And I got a soothing chair massage from one of her talented partners.) Jette is a former birth doula who really understands the changes a woman goes through – both physically and emotionally – during pregnancy and postpartum. And she has a wonderfully soothing, calming nature that puts clients at ease.

Claudette Plater, RN, NCMT at Tranquil Moment
Loudon/Fairfax
703.724.4210, www.tranquilmoment.com

Claudette welcomes expectant dads to be in the room during pregnancy massage, to learn techniques for home use.

Tri-Therapeutic Massage
Vienna
703.752.4078, www.trimassage.com

The Teal Center
At Randolph Towers & Virginia Hospital Center
703.522.7637 or 703.588.5454 , www.tealcenter.com

Kerem Karpinski, CMT
Takoma Park & Silver Spring
202.263.7265, relaxwithkerem@yahoo.com

Sugar House Day Spa
Old Town Alexandria
703.549.9940, www.sugarhousedayspa.com

> **author's note:**
> Sugar House is a luxuriously pampering environment for treating yourself to a massage, and we've had good experiences with a few different therapists there. The attentive service, nice changing rooms and soothing massage waiting areas are lovely, in a restored historic Old Town setting. Heavenly.

Dina Weiss, CMT
Silver Spring
301.622.5855, www.healing-connections.net

DC'S FAVORITE PHYSICAL THERAPISTS & CHIROPRACTORS SPECIALIZING IN PREGNANCY & POSTPARTUM

Susan Guardardo, Physical Therapist at VSG P.T.
Chevy Chase, MD
301.718.2820 (office) or 301.706.3841 (cell)
http://vsgpt.com

Susan says, "The new demands of lifting and caring for a newborn, coupled with the hormonal and physical changes which occur during pregnancy, make new mothers susceptible to a variety of musculoskeletal injuries, ranging from low back pain to write pain, neck pain, and feet pain." These are the discomforts she specializes in treating and relieving.

Dr. Anthony Noya, Chiropractor
NW DC, near Tenley
www.noyachiropractic.com
Dr. Noya specializes in prenatal chiropractic, and is also experienced in working with postpartum moms and children.

> *"I highly, highly, highly recommend Dr. Anthony Noya. Pregnant moms and children are his niche!"*
>
> *- Robin White, Bethesda mama & DONA-certified birth doula*

DC'S FAVORITE PRENATAL FITNESS

Also check with your local Parks & Recreation Dept. and YMCA branch, since they regularly offer prenatal yoga – and water aerobics classes that are perfect low-impact aerobics workouts for pregnancy.

Christy Dostal, personal trainer at MINT Mind-Body Studio
Adams Morgan, DC
www.mintfitness.com

18th & Yoga
Adams Morgan, DC
www.18thandyoga.com

Birth Diva
202.271.3240, www.birthdiva.com

Body in Balance Center
Alexandria/Slaters Ln. corridor
www.bodyinbalancecenter.com

> **author's note:**
> Tucked away in an unobtrusive space near the delectable
> Buzz coffee shop and bakery, the new Body in Balance
> Center offers a prenatal fitness class for women in all stages
> of pregnancy – as well as fusion flow classes for moms and
> babies, infant massage classes, children's creative movement
> and yoga, and a range of adult yoga classes. We have
> personal experience with the children's creative movement
> – and loved it!

Boundless Yoga
U St., DC
www.boundlessyoga.com

Capitol Hill Yoga
Capitol Hill, DC
www.capitolhillyoga.com

Circle Yoga
Chevy Chase, DC
www.circleyoga.com

Flow Yoga Center
Logan Circle, DC
www.flowyogacenter.com

Georgetown Yoga
Georgetown, DC
www.georgetownyoga.com

> **author's note:**
> Georgetown Yoga's prenatal yoga instructor Kara Sullivan
> has been practicing yoga since 1995 and teaching since 2004.
> She also became a mama in early 2006, so her appreciation
> of pregnancy's many challenges is recent and personal.

Hot Mama Fitness Studio
Bethesda
www.hotmamafitnessstudio.com

> *author's note:*
> Longtime DC personal trainer Vionna Jones opened Hot
> Mama Fitness Studio in summer 2008 – and it's soaring. Hot
> Mama is delivering a new and appealing approach to
> prenatal and postpartum fitness, serving both first-time
> moms and veterans who are looking to get their groove
> back. The centrally-located Bethesda studio offers fitness
> and yoga classes, nutrition and wellness counseling and
> workshops, personal training...and did I mention on-site
> childcare?

Mind the Mat Yoga & Pilates
Del Ray, Alexandria
www.mindthemat.com

> *author's note:*
> New kid on the block in 2008 is Mind the Mat, located along
> Del Ray's gloriously walkable Mt. Vernon Ave. shopping and
> dining district. They offer prenatal yoga, Mommy & Me yoga
> and pilates, kids' yoga and creative movement classes, infant
> massage instruction, and child and adult nutrition classes
> and consulting. A welcome – and welcoming - destination for
> Alexandria mamas and families.

Moore Than Yoga
Arlington
703.671.2435, www.moorethanyoga.com

> *author's note:*
> Jennifer is a thoughtful, gentle teacher with a feisty sense of
> humor. After taking a Mother's Day workshop with her, we
> understood first-hand why her prenatal and postpartum
> classes are so loved, and why she works so well with children
> and families. She has such a nurturing way about her,

encouraging students to nurture themselves. We also recommend Jennifer as a reflexology practitioner, during pregnancy and far beyond – best "foot massage" ever!

Pure Prana Yoga
Old Town Alexandria
www.pureprana.com

author's note:
Pure Prana's prenatal yoga classes are consistently recommended by Alexandrian moms. The studio offers prenatal and postpartum yoga, as well as special pregnancy and postpartum workshops led by holistic health counselors, doulas, and other professionals in the field. And as an added bonus, they're in a lovely location right upstairs from the fabulous Mischa's coffee shop.

Sacred Well Yoga
Falls Church
www.swys.net

Sun & Moon
Arlington & Fairfax
www.sunandmoonstudio.com

Studio Serenity Yoga
Dupont Circle, DC
www.studioserenity.com

Tranquil Space Yoga
Dupont Circle, Bethesda
www.tranquilspace.com

Unity Woods Yoga Center
Bethesda, Arlington, Woodley Park, Tenleytown
www.unitywoods.com

Yoga Birth & Beyond, Sharon Stevenson
Alexandria
www.yogabirthandbeyond.com

Willow Street Yoga
Takoma Park & Silver Spring
www.willowstreetyoga.com

SARA LAVAN: Nourishing moms (& kids) on the local scene
www.nourishingmoms.com
We recently had the chance to get to know a new (and extraordinary) Washingtonian serving pregnant and postpartum moms, babies, and children. Sara Lavan, transplanted from NYC to Alexandria in 2006 with her spouse and young children, is a holistic health counselor, pilates instructor (including pre- and postpartum pilates), and dancer with years of experience teaching creative movement for kids. She's also the co-publisher of Nourishing Moms, an online resource for expectant and new moms with an emphasis on whole foods nutrition and mind/body health. Check out their teleclasses and the free Nourishing Moms e-newsletter, where you'll find quick and inspiring reads, recipes, and more. Also check out Sara's classes at Body in Balance and Mind the Mat. Our daughter took a summer creative movement class with Sara and fell head over heels in love!

MONICA CORRADO: Simply Being Well in Takoma Park
www.simplybeingwell.com
Wellness chef and educator Monica Corrado, founder of Takoma Park-based Simply Being Well, teaches private and group classes on topics such as cooking for wellbeing, using flower essences and essential oils, and holistic health. She's a passionate local advocate for sustainable and local food, farming, and the healing arts. Contact Monica at simplybeingwell@aol.com or 240.988.8312.

KIM RUSH LYNCH: Cultivating Health

www.cultivating-health.com

Holistic health counselor and food educator Kimberly Rush Lynch focuses on helping moms and dads to improve the eating habits and overall health and wellbeing of their children. She offers private consultations and group classes on topic such as finding the right foods for children and families, balancing food choices, and finding balance in everyday family life. Before becoming a health counselor, Kim was the program director at the Washington Youth Garden at the national Arboretum, where she helped kids and families learn where our food comes from, how to grow it organically, and how to cook it in tasty, healthy ways. She's a member of the American Association for Drugless Practitioners and is one of the founding members of the Greenbelt Farmers Market. Contact Kim at kimberly@cultivating-health.com or 301.356.4731.

DC'S FAVORITE MATERNITY SHOPPING

9 Maternity

12246 Rockville Pike, Rockville, 301.468.2022

www.9maternity.com

author's note:

9 Maternity is a locally-owned boutique founded in 2003 by a local mama who had become fed up with the lack of options for smart, upscale pregnancy clothing. In addition to chic clothes, they also stock lingerie, accessories, and books. You can join the mailing list at their website to receive news of sales and special promotions.

NEW: **Ann Taylor Loft Maternity**

www.anntaylorloft.com

Yes, it's true! A.T. Loft now offers (cute and competitively priced) maternity chic. To date, available online only. But it won't be long before the maternity line is in selected Ann Taylor Loft stores.

A Pea in the Pod
Pentagon Center, Tyson's Galleria
www.apeainthepod.com

Apple Seed
Old Town Alexandria
www.appleseedboutique.com

> *"Apple Seed is an adorable Old Town maternity boutique with a fabulous selection of items for expectant mothers, new mothers, and infants. The shop owners are two charming young women who make every visit a pleasure."*
>
> *-Erica*

author's note:
A stroll past Apple Seed's window display makes me want to be pregnant again. (Well, almost.) The clothing, accessories, and gifts they carry are hip and fun, but not overly trendy. For pregnancy they carry everything from designer jeans to (cute – seriously!) swimsuits, business-appropriate to dressy-dresses to everyday casual. Lovely baby and toddler clothes and gifts. And we love that they have plenty of nicely-appointed dressing rooms. The service is friendly and attentive. They host special events and sales throughout the year. Gives us reason to gush.

Gap Maternity
Fair Oaks Mall
www.gapmaternity.com

Mimi Maternity
Mazza Gallerie, White Flint Mall, Fairfax Corner
www.mimimaternity.com

Motherhood Maternity
Pentagon Center, Montgomery Mall, Wheaton Plaza, Prince George's Plaza, Tyson's Corner, Landmark Mall, Lake Forest Mall, Springfield Mall, Fair Oaks Mall, Dulles Town Center, Columbia Mall
www.motherhood.com

Old Navy Maternity
Springfield Commons, Potomac Yard (Alexandria), Bailey's Crossroads, Tyson's Corner Center, Rivertowne Commons (Oxon Hill), Prince George (Hyattsville), Montgomery (Bethesda), Westfield (Wheaton), St. Charles (Waldorf), Bowie Town Center, Dulles Town Center, Parkridge Center (Manassas), Arundel Mills (Hanover)
www.oldnavy.com

Target Maternity
In VA: Alexandria (Potomac Yard & Hybla Valley), Falls Church (Skyline & Arlington Blvd.), Springfield Mall, Chantilly, Fairfax & Fair Lakes Shopping Center, Leesburg, Manassas, Springfield, Sterling, Woodbridge
In MD: Hyattsville, Bowie, Lanham, Columbia, Glen Burnie, Gaithersburg, Germantown, Largo, Frederick, District Heights, Waldorf, Wheaton, Laurel, Silver Spring, Rockville
www.target.com

NEED HELP? GET A BABY CONCIERGE!
DC mama Kimberly Shore Levin founded Nursery Know-it-All for Washington's busy expectant parents, who just don't have enough time to do it all themselves. Kim — a veteran mother, with three children under the age of five — provides personalized services such as helping you complete a baby registry, locating quality stores to purchase furniture, deciding on a stroller purchase, planning a bris/baby naming/christening, completing birth announcements and thank-you notes, shopping childcare and selecting nanny candidates. Kim sees her job as "making pregnancy as stress-free and fun as possible, without sweating over the details." Visit www.nurseryknowitall.com.

Capitol Moms Motherhood Resource Service, founded by Arlington mama Teia Collier, is a full-service pregnancy, baby, and motherhood concierge service. They do the research, track trends, and call upon relationships with the companies who provide products and services. You sit back and relax. Teia and team offer personal shopping, product and service referrals, event planning and management, baby and new parent registry, maternity leave management, nursery design, and corporate and personal gift selection. To schedule a personal consult or to get more info, contact Teia at info@capitolmoms.org or 571.723.3304. Visit www.capitolmoms.org/motherhood.html. Also check out Teia's maternity blog, Capitol Moms 2 Be, at http://capitolmoms2be.blogspot.com.

SUPPORT FOR PERINATAL DEPRESSION & ANXIETY

Postpartum Support International (PSI)
www.postpartum.net
In addition to the helpful information on their website, PSI also hosts free weekly information sessions for women – as well as concerned family members and friends – via a toll-free conference call phone line. Limited to the first 15 callers, these sessions provide information about postpartum depression and other perinatal mood disorders, and give participants an opportunity to ask questions and get input from PSI healthcare professionals. Sessions last about one hour. The calls are not meant to take the place of visits to healthcare providers and do not provide therapy. Participants must call 1.800.944.8766 five minutes before the call begins. For more details, go to **http://postpartum.net/info-sessions.html**.

Postpartum Support Virginia
www.postpartumva.org, **info@postpartumva.org**
After many months of hard work and planning, our friend and longtime PPD advocate Adrienne Griffen launched a new not-for-profit organization serving women and families in NoVa and beyond. Postpartum Support Virginia offers one-on-one support and groups, resources and info for expectant and new mothers and their partners and families, and outreach to local communities. Adrienne, an Arlington mother of three, suffered from severe postpartum depression (PPD) after

53

the birth of her second child. After struggling to find help and eventually getting her groove back, she vowed to improve resources and support for women in the DC area going through similar experiences. If you are suffering from symptoms of depression and/or anxiety during pregnancy or in the first year after having a baby, visit the website for more information and reach out for help – it's available!

DC Peer Support Group:
Meets the second and fourth Wednesday evening of each month in the Palisades neighborhood of NW DC. Open to any new mom or pregnant woman in the DC-area who is experiencing depression or anxiety. For more info or to attend, contact Lynne McIntyre, lynne@lynnemcintyre.com or 202.744.3639.

Arlington Peer Support Group:
Meets the second and fourth Wednesday mornings of each month at Virginia Hospital Center. Open to any new mom or pregnant woman in the DC area who is experiencing depression or anxiety. For more info or to attend, contact Adrienne Griffen, griffens@comcast.net or 703.243.2904.

Fairfax Peer Support Group:
Meets the first and third Thursday evenings of each month at Kings Park Library in Fairfax. Open to any new mom or pregnant woman in the DC-- area who is experiencing depression or anxiety. Contact Benta Sims, 703.536.9469 or j-bsims@comcast.net.

Gaithersburg Support Group:
This group meets on the second Thursday evening of each month at 16220 S. Frederick Rd., Suite 502 in Gaithersburg. Contact PSI Maryland coordinator Sara Evans at sarajevans@gmail.com or at 240.401.8045.

Loudon County Peer Support Group:
Meets the second and fourth Monday evenings of each month at Loudon Hospital. Open to any new mom or pregnant woman in the DC area who is experiencing depression or anxiety. Contact Natalie Griffin, 703.858.8941 or ndgriffin@verizon.net.

Support in Montgomery County, MD:
Contact PSI Maryland coordinator Sara Evans, 301.869.6886 or
sarajevans@gmail.com.

Support in Annapolis & Baltimore, MD:
For support and information about Peer Support Groups in the
Annapolis/Baltimore area, contact Rebecca Levin, 410.620.7808 or
rebecca@leafgarden.net.

DC'S FAVORITE BREASTFEEDING SUPPORT

Classes, Support Groups, & Consultants

Breastfeeding Center of Greater Washington
2141 K St. NW DC, 202.293.5182
www.breastfeedingcenter.org
The Center is a nonprofit organization providing a wide range of free
breastfeeding preparation classes and support groups, groups on
returning to work as a nursing mom, weaning, and breast pump basics.
Their lactation consultants also do private consultations at the Center,
and are even known to make home visits on occasion. They are also a
one-stop-shop for breastfeeding equipment. Other classes, offered at
competitive prices, include infant massage, babywearing and
breastfeeding, and introducing solid foods.

author's note:
Pat Sheliy, a.k.a. "The Breast Whisperer," is in a league of her
own. I long ago lost count of the number of women I've
heard from who credit their breastfeeding success to her
wisdom and assistance. Pat founded and now directs the
Center. She holds a bachelor of science in nursing and a grad
degree in healthcare management. She's an RN, an
International Board Certified Lactation Consultant (IBCLC), a
certified infant massage instructor, and an ASPO-certified
Lamaze instructor whose diverse work has taken her to
military hospitals, home visits, corporate and community
outreach, private practice, Columbia Hospital for Women

and INOVA Alexandria hospital. Pat's wisdom has been a
godsend to many a struggling nursing mom.

INOVA Lactation Consulting & Breastfeeding Moms Groups
www.inova.org
Some INOVA locations in Virginia offer weekly support groups for
breastfeeding moms. Cost is approximately $5 per meeting. Call ahead to
find out about the group nearest you, or to make a private appointment
with an INOVA lactation consultant.

Geraldine Fitzgerald, CPNP, IBCLC
301.946.0167 or 301.946.2448, ghfitz94@aol.com

ILCA-Certified lactation consultants:
International Lactation Consultant Association (ILCA)
www.ilca.org, click on "Find a lactation consultant"

La Leche League of Maryland, Delaware, & DC
www.lllofmd-de-dc.org

La Leche League of Virginia & West Virginia
www.lllusa.org/VA

Momease
www.momease.com
Serves: Washington, DC & Alexandria, VA
This respected agency specializing in childbirth education classes, doula
services, and parenting classes, also offers breastfeeding equipment and
support.

Mother & Baby Matters
12001 Market St., Suite 301, Reston
703.787.4007, motherbaby_office@juno.com
www.motherandbabymatters.com, click on "Breastfeeding Program"
Mother & Baby Matters' comprehensive breastfeeding program offers
ongoing support and information during the prenatal and postpartum
periods. They offer pre-delivery counseling, post-delivery consultation by
phone or at the hospital, at-home instruction and support (provided on
an ongoing basis as part of a full-service postpartum care plan), lactation

specialists for private consultations about breastfeeding problems, and Board Certified Lactation Consultants (BCLC) for private in-home visits.

Northern Virginia Lactation Center
Fairfax Medical Arts Building, Fairfax, 703.425.2229
www.northernvirginialactation.com
The Center offers private consultations with lactation consultants in their office or via home visits, classes on working and breastfeeding, as well as childbirth preparation classes and infant massage. They also provide breast pump rentals and purchases.

Breast Pump Rentals & Sales

Babies 'n Business
8218 Wisconsin Ave., Bethesda
301.656.2526
www.worksitelactation.com
Authorized dealer of Medela products, including accessory kits, supplies, and replacement parts. Also rents Medela pumps. Offers corporate lactation support for employers and individual support for mothers, and one-on-ones with lactation consultants. Serves Montgomery County and DC.

Breastfeeding Center of Greater Washington
2141 K Street NW, 202..293.5182
Virginia office: 703.978.2000
www.breastfeedingcenter.org
(For more info on the Center, see listing under "Classes, Support Groups, & Lactation Consultants.")

Cheryl's Health Boutique
15200 Shady Grove Rd., Suite 106, Rockville
301.330.1084
Sales and rental of Medela pumps and accessories. Knowledgeable advice and support for breastfeeding mothers.

Foer's Pharmacy
818 18th St. NW & H St. NW (Foggy Bottom/Farragut Square)

202.775.4400
Small but quality selection, friendly service.

Georgetown University Hospital (Parenting Services Office)
3800 Reservoir Rd NW & 38th St. NW
202.444.6455
www.georgetownuniversityhospital.org
Sales and rental of hospital-grade Ameda pumps at good prices. One-on-one instruction on how to use the pump; available for questions.

INOVA Hospitals in Northern VA
www.inova.org
Short- and long-term rental of breast pumps. Lactation consultation/support by appointment on weekdays.

Momease
www.momease.com
Serves: Washington, DC & Alexandria, VA
Breastfeeding equipment and support. (For more about this organization's other services and classes, see their listings under "Birth Doulas" and "Childbirth Educators.")

Mother & Baby Matters
12001 Market St., Suite 301, Reston
703.787.4007, motherbaby_office@juno.com
www.motherandbabymatters.com, click on "Breastfeeding Program"
Sales and rental of Medela pumps and supplies. Accessories for the Medela "Pump in Style." Also offer Supplemental Nursing System (SNS) products, including shells, shields, double pumping kits, soothies, and gel pads. Lactation consultants available for private appointments.

Northern Virginia Lactation Consultants
10560 Main St., Fairfax, 703.425.2229
www.northernvirginialactation.com
Medela and Ameda sales and rental, including parts and accessories, with one-on-one instruction in how to use products. No deposit for rentals. They offer free phone follow-up for clients who have purchased or rented a pump and a free weekly weigh-in for breastfeeding babies. Also carry

discount maternity and nursing bras. Private appointments with lactation consultants.

Preston's Pharmacy
5101 Lee Hwy. & N. Edison St., Arlington
703.522.3412
Can call in advance to reserve one of their hospital-grade pumps for rental. Offer a variety of products and very friendly service.

Breastfeeding Hotline

La Leche League U.S. Breastfeeding Helpline
Toll-free, 24-hour breastfeeding advice and info
1.877.4LA.LECHE
www.lllusa.com

Online Pump Rental & Sales

Medela, Inc., www.medela.com
My Breast Pump, www.mybreastpump.com

Web-Based Support

KellyMom.com
www.kellymom.com
Breastfeeding info, resources, database of lactation consultants, products, and books.

Motherwear
www.motherwear.com
Clothing (including sleepwear, bras, etc.) for nursing mamas. Their website also provides free, educational breastfeeding information.

NEW: Motherwear's Breastfeeding Blog
http://breastfeeding.blog.motherwear.com

Pumping Moms
www.pumpingmoms.org

http://health.groups.yahoo.com/group/pumpmoms
Website, listserv with almost 3,000 members. Helpful for info, feedback
from experienced breastfeeding mothers, and support.

DC'S FAVORITE POSTPARTUM DOULAS

Word to the wise: As with birth doulas, postpartum doulas are in high
demand in the DC area. Many families who wait until after a baby's birth
to look for a postpartum doula find themselves out of luck. Ideally, you
should interview candidates well before your due-date.

And Then Comes Baby, Peggy Burt Edwards
703.674.7707, andthencomesbaby@mac.com

Birth Diva
202.271.3240, www.birthdiva.com
Offers a variety of services for couples who are planning toward a natural
childbirth – including Bradley Method classes, labor and postpartum
doula support.

Birthing Hands of DC
202.236.1764, www.birthinghandsdc.com
Serves: DC metro area
Birthing Hands is a team of professional English- and Spanish-speaking
doulas and midwife birth assistants, providing services in hospital, birth
center and home birth settings. They offer birth doula and postpartum
doula services, individualized childbirth and pregnancy classes,
breastfeeding instruction and support, and more.

Dawn Star Borchelt
largercircle@verizon.net, www.largercircle.blogspot.com
Serves: DC metro area
Dawn is a Birthing from Within mentor and doula providing both birth
and postpartum doula services. She has 10 years of experience working
with mothers and their families in community settings, in addition to
childbirth education and doula experience. She especially enjoys working
with a diverse clientele. Dawn is based in southern Maryland but is

"willing to travel anywhere in the DC region, south of the top of the Beltway."

Elena Caraballo
703.731.7381, ummilyas2000@yahoo.com
www.birthservice.com
Serves: DC metro area
Postpartum doula who is also DONA- and CAPPA-trained as a birth doula, works as a birth assistant and is training as a student midwife.

Child Birth Care
www.childbirthcare.com
Provides postpartum doula services and referrals.

Pam Ferinde, & Jennifer Sharp, Postpartum Doulas & Baby Nurses
Family Transitions, www.doula2.com
mpferinde@aol.com, jennifersharp87@hotmail.com
Pam has 15 years of experience in obstetrics, newborn nursery, and pediatrics. She is also certified by Dr. Harvey Karp's "Happiest Baby on the Block" program, has experience with multiples and preemies, and is a lactation specialist. Jennifer trained with Pam and has three years of newborn and infant care experience, as well as infant safety and CPR training at Shady Grove Hospital. Jennifer is a college student working on a degree in early childhood.

> *"Jennifer Sharp has been with us for about five weeks and also has been a wonderful gift to our family, providing loving care for the babies and giving us the opportunity to get in some solid blocks of sleep. Can't say enough good things about Pam and Jennifer's services. They have given us a wonderful start to life with twin infants."*
>
> *- Kristen*

Julie Carroll, DONA-trained
860.510.3905, ppdoulava@yahoo.com
Serves: NoVa & DC metro area
Julie is DONA-trained and -certified as a postpartum doula. Julie specializes in helping the new family adjust to having a baby, providing

basic newborn needs, supporting breastfeeding, as well as helping with errands, cleaning, cooking, helping with older children, and letting new mamas get a chance to sleep/shower/rest.

Kairos Birth Support Services
oasishealingarts@starpower.net
www.kairosdoulas.net
Serves: DC metro area
The Kairos birth and postpartum doulas are DONA-trained and -certified.

> *"Our [Kairos Birth Support Services] postpartum doula, Rochelle, was wonderful... The transition into motherhood without her would have been difficult. My husband and I were both insecure about our parenting skills at first, so it was such a relief to have Rochelle come in every day to discuss concerns we had, and to know that we had her help..."*
>
> *- Vivian*

Liz Kaufman
202.446.4400, birthchedva@aol.com
Serves: DC metro area
Liz is an ALACE-trained birth doula and is a birth assistant with BirthCare & Women's Health in Old Town and the Birth Center in NE DC. She offers both birth and postpartum doula support.

Margie Lidoff
202.270.6893, marvonne@peoplepc.com
Provides services in-home, in-hospital, or at place of client's choosing. Help with newborn care, moral support, breastfeeding issues, cooking, light cleaning, running errands, accompanying to appointments, and more.

Mother & Baby Matters
12001 Market St., Suite 301, Reston
703.787.4007, motherbaby_office@juno.com
www.motherandbabymatters.com, click on "Postpartum Doulas" and "Overnight Help"

MotherKind Postpartum Support, Kendra Ragland
301.587.0851, motherkind@comcast.net

Liz Riddle
202.744.3977, lizriddle@verizon.net
Serves: DC metro area

> **POSTPARTUM DOULA VS. BABY NURSE?**
> If you get confused about the difference, you're not alone.
> Generally speaking, a postpartum doula takes care of
> supporting the mother and the household, so that mama can
> focus her energy and attention on the newborn. The
> postpartum doula is a wealth of information about this
> period and baby care, but she is hired primarily to free YOU
> up to take care of your infant. A baby nurse, on the other
> hand, will take care of the baby. She does things like bathe,
> dress, change diapers, bring to you for nursing or give
> bottles, rock and cuddle, etc. Many couples hire a baby
> nurse for nighttime stay-overs when sleep deprivation is
> taking a toll.

DC'S FAVORITE BABY NURSES

Babiease LLC, Meredith Ball
410.274.9329
www.babiease.com
Meredith specializes in working with multiples and preemies, and she can
provide "around the clock" care, night care, or consulting. Night care
includes feedings, bathing, bottle preparation, laundry, etc., as well as
working with babies to follow a feeding schedule (logging along the way)
and encouraging them to sleep longer stretches. Meredith's care also
focuses on supporting breast- and/or bottle-feeding, observing problems
and discussing them with parents (reflux, developmental, etc.), sharing
basic knowledge of health and care of newborns and preemies, and
training nannies and/or family help. She has an understanding of how
apnea monitors work and is accustomed to working with other medical

equipment and special challenges. She's also reportedly GREAT with nursery organization and helping you get organized!

> *"Meredith Ball arrived when [our twin daughters] were three weeks old and was invaluable in helping us understand our babies' evolving needs and how we could best meet them. I appreciated the excellent care she gave them at night – helping them get on the right track and giving us a bit of rest – but especially the many conversations I had with her in which we discussed how I could continue their positive sleeping and eating… She offered us myriad useful suggestions for making many aspects of caring for twins much more efficient and manageable. She also spent time with our nanny and helped her understand and adopt our philosophy with regard to caring for our daughters."*
>
> *-Christa*

Nannies & More (nanny agency that also has baby nurses)
www.nanniesandmore.com

Potomac Home Health Care Services (a nonprofit joint venture of Sibley Memorial Hospital and Suburban Hospital)
http://www.sibley.org/services/h_healthcare.tmpl
Serves: MD and Washington, DC

DC'S FAVORITE BABYWEARING RESOURCES

Trish Thackston, The Baby Hammock
www.thebabyhammock.com
The fabulous Trish Thackston, Alexandria mama and founder of small business The Baby Hammock, offers a low-cost babywearing workshop and demonstrations on the first Saturday morning of each month. Cost is just $10 to hold your RSVP, and can be applied toward any product purchase from The Baby Hammock's inventory. Trish demonstrates how to use a large range of baby carrier types – and you get the opportunity to try them out yourself. No obligation to buy, no pressure, but it's a nice change to see and feel the many different kinds of soft carriers in person before you make a product decision. Trish is very knowledgeable about

the wraps and slings she carries – including Maya Wraps, New Native Baby Carriers, HotSlings pouches, Baby Trekker, Belle Baby Carrier, Moby Wrap, EllaRoo Wrap, Mei Tai, Mei Hip, and the ERGO Carrier. If you find something you like, you can purchase it on the spot.

NINO Babywearing Group

This is the "Nine In Nine Out" (NINO) group for the Washington, DC metro area. They meet once a month or more and are interested in the premises of anthropologist Ashley Montagu's work on babywearing. NINO group members use slings, wraps, or other soft carriers for the first nine months or more after giving birth. For more info or to join the listserv, go to http://groups.yahoo.com/group/nino_dc-md-va.

DC'S FAVORITE POSTPARTUM FITNESS

Baby Boot Camp
Instructors throughout metro Washington
www.babybootcamp.com

Body in Balance Center
Alexandria/Slaters Ln. corridor
www.bodyinbalancecenter.com

Bounce Back with Baby
At the Jewish Community Center of Greater Washington (JCC)
www.jccgw.org

Capitol Hill Yoga
Capitol Hill, www.capitolhillyoga.com
Offers a Baby & Me class incorporating yoga postures with infant massage and baby movement.

Hot Mama Fitness Studio
Bethesda
www.hotmamafitnessstudio.com

Mind the Mat Yoga & Pilates
Del Ray, Alexandria
www.mindthemat.com

Mommy Mall Walkers
Potomac Mills & Springfield Mall
http://members.tripod.com/heather372-
ivil/mommymallwalkers/index.html
Listserv at http://groups.yahoo.com/group/mommymallwalkers/

Postpartum Yoga at Moore Than Yoga
Arlington
703.671.2435, www.moorethanyoga.com

See Mommy Run
www.seemommyrun.com
Chapters throughout the DC area – Or start your own!

Stroller Strides
Instructors offering classes throughout metro Washington.
www.strollerstrides.net

> *"I'm a huge fan of Stroller Strides classes on Capitol Hill, on the Capitol grounds and at Lincoln Park. They helped me get back into shape after my daughter was born and meet some wonderful women."*
>
> *-Jennifer*

Postnatal Yoga at Tranquil Space
Dupont Circle & Bethesda
301.654.9642, www.tranquilspace.com

DC'S FAVORITE INFANT MASSAGE INSTRUCTION

Georgetown University Hospital
Birth & Family Education Classes, 202.342.2400
www.georgetownuniversityhospital.org

Holy Cross Hospital
Silver Spring
www.holycrosshealth.org

Moore Than Yoga
Arlington
703.671.2435, www.moorethanyoga.com

Potomac Massage Training School
202.686.7046, www.pmti.org

Capitol Hill Yoga
Capitol Hill, www.capitolhillyoga.com
Offers a Baby & Me class incorporating yoga postures with infant massage and baby movement.

Hela @ The Collection
Chevy Chase, www.helaspa.com

Trish Stone, CIMI, MOT, OTR/L
301.946.2486, trish.stone@yahoo.com
www.iaim.ws/benefits.html
Trish Stone is a certified infant massage instructor, as well as an occupational therapist and developmental specialist. She teaches private individual and group classes in suburban Maryland and the DC metro area.

Tranquil Space
Dupont Circle & Bethesda
301.654.9642, www.tranquilspace.com

Old Town Massage Center
Old Town Alexandria
703.518.8484, www.oldtownmassagecenter.com

LITTLE BABY, B-I-G ANNOUNCEMENT
www.sunshinestorks.com, 301.437.3506
Sunshine Storks, a Maryland-based firm, specializes in announcing your new baby's arrival in a big way. Their rentals of six-foot-stork birth announcements for your lawn, and baby bundle door signs, are a fun way to share the news with friends, family and neighbors.

MORE SUPPORT FOR NEW MAMAS

Mamistad (Pregnant & New Moms Meetup Group)
www.mamistad.com
Mamistad was founded by a Falls Church mom to bring pregnant women and new mothers from NoVa, DC, and the Maryland suburbs together. The Meetup group includes a one-time membership fee of $15. For more info (especially while their website is still under construction), send email to cynthia@mamistad.com.

Metro DC Multiples Moms
This listserv of 100+ members links up new mothers of twins or other multiples. Members come from throughout the DC metro area. For more info or to join their listserv, go to http://groups.yahoo.com/group/metrodcmultiplesmoms.

Mothers & Babies Support Group at the Adele Lebowitz Center for Youth & Families
This group, professionally facilitated by a local therapist at the Lebowitz Center in Friendship Heights, provides new moms (with their babies, newborn to 12 months) with an opportunity to learn about themselves and their children, as well as to make connections with other mothers. They meet mid-day during the week, and sliding scale fees are available to families with financial need. To enroll or to get more info, contact Megan Telfair or Peggy Tilghman at 202.537.6050.

New Parents Group at DC Jewish Community Center

The New Parents Group at the DCJCC (located on 16th St. NW) is professionally facilitated by Sarah Gershman, a social worker and Jewish Education Associate at the DCJCC. Bring your baby and meet other new parents for a warm and informal group discussion. They discuss the joys and struggles of being a new family, as well as topics like creating family traditions for holidays and everyday life. DCJCC members get a discount on registration cost. For more info, contact Sarah Gershman at sarahg@dcjcc.org or 202.777.3237.

New Moms Group at Georgetown University Hospital

This FREE social group for new moms meets weekday mornings at Georgetown Hospital's "family room" in the maternity/postnatal department (second floor of the main hospital building's north wing). Informal discussions have covered topics like baby-calming strategies, issues related to breast- and bottle-feeding, and sleep strategies. They are a laid-back, welcoming group! For more info, contact local mom and founder of the group Shelley Ducker at shelley.ducker@digene.com or call Lactation Parenting Services at Georgetown, 202.444.6455.

New Moms Groups at Inova Hospitals, Northern VA

www.inova.org

Contact the Inova Hospital nearest you for the current schedule of New Moms Groups and Breastfeeding Support Groups.

> *"When my first was born, I went to the infant support group that Fairfax Hospital offers to new moms for several weeks to get out of the house, learn how to care for my baby, and meet other moms. Eight of us ended up bonding, and five years later we still meet every Tuesday."*
>
> *- Stephanie*

New Moms Group at Parenting Playgroups in Alexandria

Hourly topics are led by developmental psychologist Dr. Rene Hackney, covering topics like temperament, attachment, role of fathers, sleep issues, mealtimes, and potty training. Groups meet on weekdays. For more info, contact Rene at 703.922.0044 or go to www.parentingplaygroups.com.

New Moms Support Group in Bethesda
www.dccounseling.com
Professionally facilitated by Nancy Markoe, MSW, LICSW and Deborah
Horan, MSW, LGSW of Counseling Associates of Metro Washington, this
group for first-time moms and their babies (up to age six months) meets
on weekday mornings in Bethesda. The group addresses the issues
confronted by mothers of babies and toddlers, with an emphasis on
practical parenting. It allows new moms to meet other women facing the
challenges of new motherhood who wish to discuss their concerns and
feelings in a safe and supportive environment. For more info or to
register, contact Nancy at 202.494.6840 or nmarkoe@dccounseling.com
or Deborah at 301.325.3052 or dlhoran@dccounseling.com.

New Moms Support Group in Chevy Chase/Tenleytown
Licensed clinical social workers Jen Kogan and Allison Fellowes Comly
professionally facilitate a support group for new moms and their babies in
NW DC. Groups are available on weekday mornings as well as weekday
evenings at their office on Wisconsin Ave. The groups focus on exploring
your changing self as you grow as a parent, reflecting on the relationship
you have with your baby and others, sharing practical ideas and solutions
to feeding/sleeping/soothing baby, nurturing yourself as a part of good
parenting, and developing friendships with other new moms. For more
info or to register, contact Jen Kogan, LICSW at 202.215.2790 or Allison
Fellowes Comly, LICSW at 202.841.3697.

PACE
www.pacemoms.org
Parent and Community Education (PACE) is a support group for new
mothers with infants up to six months of age. They meet for eight
sessions of two hours each, with groups in DC, Montgomery County, and
NoVa. Topics include eating, sleeping, emotional attachment, safety,
relationships, and parenting issues. Many groups continue as active
playgroups after the formal PACE program concludes. Special groups are
available for new moms, second-time moms, and for workplace settings.

> *"PACE held my hand when I was new to motherhood and
> new to Washington."*
>
> *- Kay*

Shalom Baby program at Jewish Federation of Greater Washington
www.shalomdc.org (Click "Shalom Baby" icon)
The Shalom Baby program is intended to welcome parents, their newborns, and newly-adopted children into the local Jewish community. For interested families they provide a gift bag containing info on parenting, coupons, Jewish resources for parents and families, and goodies for baby (hand-delivered by a Shalom Baby "ambassador" volunteer), as well as ongoing support from caring volunteers and an opportunity to make new friendships with other Jewish parents in the DC area. To participate and receive a gift packet, contact Francie Kranzberg at 301.770.4848.

Kim West, "The Sleep Lady"
www.sleeplady.com
info@sleeplady.com, 410.974.1600
DC parents swear by Kim West, a.k.a. "The Sleep Lady." Based out of her Annapolis office, West offers a phone class on newborn sleep, private consultations, and phone coaching sessions for the parents of young children. She's seen it all, she knows what she's doing, and she's fearless.

"FIRST OUTINGS" FOR NEW MAMAS & BABIES

So there you are... joyous and in love with your new baby, but also sleep-deprived, disheveled, and craving a change of scenery. You just need somewhere pleasant to go beyond your own four walls – where you won't get dirty looks when the baby starts to wail or needs a diaper change. I remember it well. A few suggestions:

"Baby Pictures"
Fairfax Corner 14 Cinema de Luz
www.nationalamusements.com (go to "Programs," click "Kids & Families" and the "Baby Pictures")
This Fairfax, VA theater offers a weekly morning movie just for new moms (or dads) and their babies. Lights are dimmed (but not totally dark) and the sound level is reduced. Gymboree also offers on-site play sessions before the movie, at 9 a.m. They set up a baby-changing station and there is a snack cart for purchasing drinks and breakfast eats. Heads up: You

can't bring strollers into the theater, but they offer a complimentary "stroller check" in the lobby. A great way to get out and about among other adults (who know what you're going through in the postpartum months).

"Majestic Movie Moms"
Majestic 20 Theater, Silver Spring
www.consolidatedmovies.com (go to "Movie Mom's Club")
Call 301.565.8884 for showtimes.
Majestic 20 offers a weekly Wednesday movie just for new moms (or dads) and their babies. Showtimes vary from week to week, but are usually late morning, around 11 or 11:30 a.m. – Movie titles and showtimes are announced two to three weeks in advance on the website. Lights are dimmed (but not totally dark) and the sound level is reduced. Their website says they wholeheartedly welcome breastfeeding, fussy babies, diaper changes...you name it! So no worries; you'll be in good company.

"Mommy & Me Movies"
Arlington Cinema & Drafthouse
www.arlingtondrafthouse.com
The Drafthouse launched this great program in spring 2007, hosting new moms (or dads) and their babies every Tuesday at 1:30 p.m for "second run" movies. The lights are dimmed (but not totally dark), the sound level is reduced, and you can bring your stroller inside the theater. They also offer some items from their menu during the movie, so you can have a late lunch or snack while you're at it. This is a great way for new parents to get out of the house and catch a movie in a baby-friendly setting. You might even make a new friend who has a lot in common with your new lifestyle. Be sure to check the website or call ahead to confirm show times.

Union Station
www.unionstationdc.com
There are several reasons why I like Union Station for an outing with a new baby. For one thing, it's a good option no matter what the weather. In the heat of summer and the cold of winter, you can spend a few hours at Union Station without having to brave the elements – You can metro directly into the station or park in the covered garage. It's a beautiful

setting where you can do as little or as much as you want, and spend as little or as much as you want. Sit with the baby and people-watch while you sip coffee, or meet your partner or a girlfriend for lunch at one of the nice restaurants in the Main Hall. You can shop if you like, and when the weather cooperates you can take a nice stroll around the fountain out front. If you're new to DC, you and baby might even want to catch one of the Washington tour-mobiles that depart from the front drive of the station (Gray Line, Old Town Trolley, and Tourmobile). During the non-summer months, these tours are not ridiculously crowded, and typically the driver/tour guides are friendly and can help with your stroller when you board the bus. You can get on and off at various locations around the city. If baby's game, you can even catch a movie in Union Station's theater (located on the bottom level next to the food court). And during the winter holidays, the décor makes the station a beautiful place to stroll.

National Mall
www.nps.gov/nama
When the weather is nice, the Mall is a great place to stroll with a baby. You can toss a blanket on the grass for a picnic or a stretch, people-watch, and step into any of the (free admission) museums of the Smithsonian Institution. For a nice but not formal or overpriced lunch, I highly recommend the self-serve-style cafe inside the National Museum of the American Indian – fabulous, with so many yummy choices! And babies will love sitting with you next to the huge windows overlooking the stone waterfall. Another good choice is the café in the National Gallery of Art's sculpture garden, next to the large fountain.

Fairfax New Moms Luncheon
Rochelle Goldberg, 703.273.5593
www.event-builders.com (Click "New Moms Luncheon" for schedule and upcoming speakers)
This group of new moms and their babies (newborns to eight months) meets every Wednesday from 10:30 a.m. to 12 noon at The Sweet Life Café on Chain Bridge Rd. in Fairfax. Each week a different speaker covers a topic of interest – ranging from early child development and health to parenting challenges, from how to find and use children's consignment shops to scrapbooking. The group is professionally facilitated by Rochelle Goldberg at Event Builders, and reservations are required in advance.

Cost is $20 for an individual luncheon or $75 for any four luncheons. (Makes a nice gift certificate for an expectant or new mom who lives in the Fairfax area.)

> **author's note:**
> I've attended the New Moms Luncheon group in Fairfax, and I was impressed! Lovely setting, good food, insightful guest speakers, and the chance to have a 'grownup' meal in a nice, 'sit-down' restaurant without having to get a sitter. Fussy babies and feedings are welcome here, and it's a good way for Fairfax-area moms to meet new friends, form playgroups or make playdates, find out about local resources, etc. And while it's tempting to think that you could easily organize your own lunch outings with other new moms rather than paying a little extra to attend a professionally managed group... If you ask me, it's worth every penny to have someone else coordinating the room with the restaurant, handling the logistics of speakers, and taking the phone calls/emails/RSVPs from attendees each week. What new mom has the time and energy to deal with that? In this case you really do get what you pay for, and then some.

Strolling the Mt. Vernon Trail
Access from several locations, including the GW Parkway and Old Town Alexandria
www.nps.gov/gwmp/mvtmap.html
Over 17 miles long, the Mt. Vernon trail stretches along the Potomac River from Roosevelt Island to George Washington's Mt. Vernon estate south of Old Town. The segment between Old Town and Mt. Vernon is really pretty, with plenty of small lots to park your car, prime spots to stop for a picnic or a stretch in the grass, and plenty of shade. The surface is almost entirely paved, which makes it manageable for strollers. While you can expect lots of bike and foot traffic on the trail during the weekends, weekdays are much quieter. On a nice day, it's a lovely walk along the water. Safety reminder: Always stay to the right with your stroller, allowing bikers and joggers to pass on the left. And as tempting

as it is to chill out with an iPod, be sure you can hear your baby and everything going on around you at all times.

Strolling the Capital Crescent Trail
Access from several locations, including downtown Bethesda and Georgetown
www.cctrail.org
Recorded info at: 202.234.4874
This scenic trail for bikers, joggers, and walkers has plenty of shade and is accessible to baby strollers. During the weekends it can get quite crowded, but weekdays are quieter. The entrance to the trail in downtown Bethesda (adjacent to the Barnes & Noble store) is a good place to start if you need a place to park your car – In addition to the meters on the street, there are nearby public garages and lots. If you want to get on the trail in Georgetown, go to the western end of Water St. NW (underneath the Whitehurst Freeway and Key Bridge). Those first few miles have beautiful views along the Potomac and the C&O Canal. Safety reminder: Always stay to the right with your stroller, allowing bikers and joggers to pass on the left. And keep the iPod turned off, so you can hear your baby and everything going on around you at all times.

CHAPTER 2
Babysitters, Childcare, & Preschools

FINDING A BABYSITTER

Arlington-Area Babysitting Co-Op
www.geocities.com/Heartland/Meadows/6989/
This well-established babysitting co-op for families in Arlington and the surrounding communities is a network of parents who trade babysitting services on the "barter" system.

American University JobCorps
http://jobcorps.ausg.org/about
The JobCorps website for AU students is a great place to find college student babysitters if you live in Tenley, Glover Park, Georgetown, or a surrounding neighborhood. The site is sponsored by the AU Student Government and is free for both students and community members.

Babysitters.com
www.babysitters.com
This is a national, web-based referral program with listings for sitters in DC, NoVa, and suburban Maryland. Sitters pay an annual fee to join, and parents search for free. A quick search for the Alexandria area code of 22314 turned up a list of 15 possible candidates, each with an extensive roster of information.

Chevy Chase Babysitting Co-Op
The Chevy Chase Babysitting Co-Op has been around since the early 1960s. Families living in the Chevy Chase neighborhood exchange child care with each other, coordinated each month by volunteers on a rotating basis. For more information or to apply for membership, contact Chevy Chase parent Nedra Weinstein at 301.654.2419.

Hillzoo
www.hillzoo.com

Many DC parents – especially those who live on Capitol Hill - say they found a good sitter through Hillzoo. Many of the candidates are Hill staffers looking to supplement their too-meager salaries or save for grad school. Using Hillzoo is free.

MONA Babysitting Co-Op
www.monamoms.org
One of the many perks of MONA (Mothers of North Arlington) membership is the organization's babysitting co-op. Members trade babysitting on the "barter" system. To find out more about MONA membership, send email to: info@monamoms.org.

Uptown Babysitting Co-Op
The Uptown Babysitting Co-Op is a group of parents who live in Woodley Park, Cleveland Park, Chevy Chase, Tenley, and Friendship Heights. It can accept up to 20 families at a time and is a great network of friends and neighbors supporting each other by trading sitting help. To find out more about how it works and possible membership, send email to mdatch@starpower.net.

Sittercity
888.211.9749
www.sittercity.com
Thousands of Washington babysitters are networked through this national, web-based program. From the main site, enter your zip code to find listings nearest you. The sitters register for free, while the parents subscribe for a sign-up fee of about $35, plus about $10 monthly fee.

Student-Sitters.com
www.student-sitters.com
One mother told me she found her best babysitter ever through this web-based service. You can sort through the resumes of college students who are interested in babysitting and select those you're interested in interviewing. UMD students are known to frequent the list. The service requires a paid membership – about $25 for three months – slightly less for subsequent renewal periods. Sitters are paid an average of $10 an hour, with $8 an hour as the absolute minimum allowable. Pay goes directly to the babysitter, not the agency.

Wee Sit
703.764.1542
weesit@aol.com
www.weesit.net
Wee Sit is a family-owned babysitting service for families in NoVa and DC. It was founded by a local mama in 1984, and their average babysitter has been with the agency for five years. All sitters are over age 21 and are pre-screened and CPR certified. Wee Sit can provide sitters not just for in-home care, but also for churches, clubs, large family gatherings, and at DC-area hotels for visitors. Rates range from $15 to $18 an hour with a four-hour minimum.

TRAINING FOR TEENAGE BABYSITTERS
The Red Cross offers a babysitter training course for 11- to 15-year-olds. Check the website for locations and dates in your area. Also at the Red Cross website: The Red Cross Babysitter Training Handbook, a babysitter's self-assessment tool, safety tips for sitters, and blank forms you can specialize for your household (complete with local emergency numbers). Go to:
www.redcross.org/services/hss/courses/babyindex.html

FINDING A NANNY

The National Association for Nanny Care (www.nannycredential.org) suggests asking these questions of any nanny placement agency you are considering working with:

About the Screening Process:
What does the agency look for in a nanny candidate, and what qualifications do they require? Do they perform a background check, and what does that include? Will all the screenings be completed before the nanny begins work? Do they verify and check all references, including non-childcare employment references?

About the Placement Process:
How long will it take you to find a nanny through the agency? How many candidates will they present to you? Will they match candidates to your

specific job description, or will they send you all available candidates and let you decide who to interview? What information will you receive about each candidate? What is their placement fee, and what is their guarantee period? If the nanny leaves or is fired during the guarantee time, do they offer a full refund, a pro-rated refund, or a replacement nanny?

About the Agency:
Will they provide you with references from local parents who have used the agency? Do they provide training and support for their nannies? Do they provide a nanny/family work agreement? Will they help you resolve any disputes between you and the nanny?

Also: Talk to other parents who have used the agency to gauge their reputation in the community. Check with the Better Business Bureau to see if there have been any complaints registered against the agency. And pay attention to whether or not you can easily communicate with the placement counselor – Do they return calls and emails promptly? Can they answer all your questions, and do you feel at ease with them?

Here are some of the most-recommended local and national nanny placement agencies:

4 Nannies.com
www.4nannies.com
The extensive questionnaire prospective nannies fill out and the ability to sift through them to determine who you like enough to interview are big pluses. You can also browse nanny resumes before you sign up for the service. They also provide standard contracts and evaluation forms you can use, resources for background checks, and discounts on a nanny tax service.

A Choice Nanny
www.achoicenanny.com
Jeff Miah at the Arlington office comes highly recommended – DC parents say they really appreciated his honesty, attitude, and professionalism: 703.685.BABY. They also have a Maryland office serving Columbia and Baltimore.

A Nanny on the Net
Paige Gaddy for Washington, DC, 202.536.4130
Amy Hardison for Bethesda, 301.760.7317
www.anannyonthenet.com/washingtondc.html
www.anannyonthenet.com/bethesda.html
This is a national nanny placement agency with offices serving DC and
NoVa through locally-based consultant. They help with placing full-time
nannies only (32 hours or more per week). You can fill out a family
application online, though an application fee is required before your
request will be processed.

DC Nanny
www.dcnanny.com
It doesn't cost a dime to register with DCNanny.com, but the downside is
that you must do your own screening, interviewing, management, etc.
Families post job announcements with specific requirements, and nannies
can post a detailed list of their qualifications and job preferences. In many
ways, DCNanny.com operates more like a specialized newspaper
classified section or Craig's List. It's not a nanny agency, but it does help
you find what you're looking for in a one-stop location.

eNannySource
www.enannysource.com
I heard from parents who used this service not to find a nanny, but for a
background check on a nanny they found on their own – Everyone said
they were happy with the service.

Metropolitan Nannies
703.481.3181
www.metronannies.com
Based in Herndon, VA, this agency places full-time, part-time, emergency,
and temporary nannies throughout NoVa, suburban Maryland, and the
District.

Monday Morning Moms, Montgomery County
301.528.4616
www.mondaymorningmomsmcmd.com
Monday Morning Moms is a family childcare management service helping
Montgomery County families find infant, toddler, or preschool childcare

81

in a home setting. They serve North Bethesda, North Potomac, Gaithersburg, Takoma Park, Germantown, Rockville, Montgomery Village, and Burtonsville.

Nannies, Inc.
703.255.5312 in NoVa
301.205.0100 in Bethesda
www.nanniesinc.net
Founded by a single dad and Johnson & Johnson executive, this agency has won a local "parents' choice" award. They specialize in full-time placements, both live-in and live-out. They offer a one-year replacement guarantee, as well as tax and payroll help.

Nanny Match
301.365.7078 or 703.273.7077
Though you end up doing extensive screening/interviewing yourself, I have heard from several DC parents who say they eventually found great matches here.

Potomac Nannies
7910 Woodmont Ave., Ste. 1120, Bethesda
301.986.0048
Potomac Nannies has been around since 1985, and they place both live-in and live-out nannies. Complete application materials, references, and background checks are provided.

Special Care Nannies
703.356.3118
www.specialcarenannies.com
This Mclean-based agency serves families throughout the area who have a child with autism, Asperger's Syndrome, ADHD, learning disabilities or other special needs. They have child care providers who do full- or part-time, live-in or live-out – as well as support care such as after-school, mentoring/big brother/big sister, school shadows/classroom support, etc. If you already have a nanny: They offer training and instruction to nannies who are currently working with families who have special needs children.

Teacher Care
888.TEACH.07, 703.204.0511

www.teachercare.com
A new alternative to the traditional agency, the small national chain
Teacher Care has a DC-area branch that places individuals who have been
specifically trained in early childhood, education, or child psychology.
They serve children from birth to school age. DC mamas recommend
Teacher Care for children with special needs and gifted/talented abilities,
as well as multiples and international adoptions.

The Nanny Agency of Greater Washington, Inc.

(formerly The Nanny Agency, LLC)
800.921.2340, ext. 1
Serves: DC, VA, & MD
Malika Holder, president and CEO of The Nanny Agency of Greater
Washington, is herself the mother of twin toddler boys, and she tells me,
"I know first-hand the importance of quality, reliable, and affordable
childcare." They offer nanny placement and payroll services to families
throughout the DC area.

The Nanny Placement Agency

703.218.1805 in NoVa
301.578.4488 in Maryland & DC
www.thenannyplacementagency.com
The best thing about The Nanny Placement agency is that they offer a
one-year replacement guarantee, which some agencies do not. They can
place both temporary and permanent, full- and part-time caregivers
throughout the DC area.

White House Nannies

7200 Wisconsin Ave, Suite 409, Bethesda
800.266.9024
332 Commerce St., Alexandria
703.838.2100
www.whitehousenannies.com
White House Nannies offers several nice perks and extras that you won't
find at other agencies – provided you're willing to pay a bit extra. They
place live-in, live-out, full-time, temporary, and emergency nannies to
households throughout the DC metro area. Former clients generally say
they were worth the extra expense and gave plenty of individual

attention to their clients. Parents also like that you can begin the process at any time, day or night, by using their online family application.

> **author's note:**
> Some of the most successful nanny matches are facilitated on neighborhood parents' listservs. Announcements can be posted by families who have a great nanny and are looking for a nanny-share situation, or by families who can recommend a trusted caregiver who is looking for work. Expectant and new parents looking for childcare can also post to the list, to let neighbors know they are in the market for a fabulous nanny.

Also check out these resources:

DC Childcare Listserv
http://groups.yahoo.com/group/dcchildcare
This is a free listserv through Yahoogroups whose members are DC-area parents and childcare providers. You can post if you are looking for a nanny or babysitter, and you will also receive notices of caregivers looking for work. Screening, interviewing, and paperwork are up to you. The list is huge and active, with over 1,200 members. Many DC mamas have found a perfect match on this list.

DC Urban Moms Nanny / Babysitter Job Board
www.dcurbanmom.com
This free, online job board has been a lifesaver for many a DC mama. Nannies and babysitters looking for work can post to the board, as can parents looking for help. You'll find it organized geographically, with DC, NoVa, and Maryland sections. If you find someone you like, you can exchange contact info for a phone interview and an in-person meeting. The downside is, you're on your own for screening, interviewing, and all paperwork and management, without the support of an agency. But you save a lot of money, and some parents prefer the do-it-yourself approach.

> **HAVE CHILDCARE, BUT NEED WHEELS?**
> Kidz on the Go
> 301.871.KIDZ
> http://gokidzgo.net/

> A local mama-owned business, Kidz on the Go provides transportation to children in Montgomery County, MD – to and from school, camps, field trips, and after-school activities.

FINDING AN AU PAIR

AuPairCare
800.4-AUPAIR
www.aupaircare.com
An international program matching au pairs with American families. They use a comprehensive online matching system, supported by in-home visits from a locally-based coordinator.

Au Pair in America
800.928.7247
www.aupairinamerica.com
One of the first and largest au pair agencies in the country, Au Pair in America has an extensive network and DC mamas say they recommend their home counselors, who are knowledgeable and professional about working with families. The agency is based out of Stamford, Connecticut. You can request a brochure at their website to learn more, and you can also apply to the program online.

Au Pair USA / InterExchange
800.AU.PAIRS
www.aupairusa.org
Another national au pair agency who will work with you via a local coordinator in the DC area.

CHI Au Pair USA
800.432.4643
www.chiaupairusa.org
National agency with local representatives to work with you through the process. Another cost-effective au pair option.

Cultural Care Au Pair
800.333.6056

www.culturalcare.com
Another large and very reputable national agency, Cultural Au Pairs has local counselors who will work with you as you go through the process. They get kudos for a strong one-on-one matching process. Their website has lots of information about how their program works and what you can expect. Many DC families have had positive experiences with CCAP.

Great AuPair.com
925.478.4100
www.greataupair.com
A national agency centered around a web network, Great AuPair.com allows families to register for free. You post information about your family and your au pair needs, and an electronic system generates a list of potential matches based on several criteria. You can then get in touch by email with any of the matches you are interested in interviewing. If you find candidates you like, you then join as a paid member, with 30-day or 90-day options. They help facilitate the process as you interview, screen, and hire a candidate. Great AuPair.com essentially works as a "try before you buy" online agency.

FINDING A DAYCARE CENTER

Info & Referrals:

o   NACCRRA's downloadable booklet, "Is this the Right Place for My Child? 38 Research-Based Indicators of High-Quality Childcare," www.naccrra.org
o   National Association for the Education of Young Children (NAEYC), www.naeyc.org
o   National Childcare Information Center, www.nccic.org
o   National Association for Family Childcare, www.nafcc.org
o   Zero to Three, www.zerotothree.org
o   Washington, DC Child Development Council, http://daycareindc.org
o   Virginia Child Care Resource & Referral Network, www.vaccrrn.org
o   Maryland Committee for Children, http://mdchildcare.org/mdcfc/mcc.html
o   DayCareVirginia.com, www.daycarevirginia.com
o   Fairfax County Office for Children, Childcare Referrals, www.fairfaxcounty.gov/childcare

- o Prince George's County Child Resource Center, www.childresource.org
- o Montgomery County Childcare Referrals, www.mongtomerycountymd.gov/earlychildhoodservices
- o Child Care Resource and Referral Agency (CCRRA), www.infanttoddler.com (free service for Alexandria, Arlington, Loudon, Manassas, Manassas Park, and Prince William)

A FEW OF DC'S FAVORITE DAYCARE CENTERS

Abracadabra Child Care
700 Commonwealth Ave., Alexandria, 703.548.7796

American University Child Development Center
4400 Massachusetts Ave. NW, DC, www.american.edu/hr/cdc.html

Bright Horizons (locations throughout DC and the metro area)
www.brighthorizons.com

> *"Bright Horizons has one of the best corporate programs I have seen, especially as they have a rigorous training program for teachers. I do prefer nonprofit to corporate childcare, but if you have to go corporate, Bright Horizons is a good choice."*
>
> - Mimi Carter, author of the now-out-of-print "Insider's Guide to Quality Childcare in Greater Washington"

Coast Guard Child Development Center
2100 2nd Street SW, 202.267.6075

Dept. of Commerce Kids
15th & Pennsylvania Ave. NW, 202.482.1587

Dept. of Energy Child Development Center
1000 Independence Ave. SW, 202.586.6736

Dept. of Transportation Child Development Center
800 Independence Ave. SW, 202.267.7672

Federal Children's Center of NoVa
530 Huntmar Park Dr., Herndon, 703.471.2821

Federal Trade Commission Child Care
600 Pennsylvania Ave. NW, 202.326.2088

FERC Child Development Center
888 First St. NE, 202.502.8610

Georgetown University Hoya Kids Learning Center
3624 P St. NW, 202.687.7667, www3.georgetown.edu/hr/hoya_kids

Infant/Toddler Family Daycare
10560 Main St., Fairfax, www.infanttoddler.com

Innovation Station Child Development Center
500 Dulaney St., Alexandria, 571.272.2880

IRS National Office Child Development Center
1111 Constitution Ave. NW, DC, 202.622.8672

Jewish Community Center of NoVa
8900 Little River Turnpike, Fairfax, 703.323.0880
www.jccnv.org

Little Explorers
1315 East-West Hwy., Silver Spring, 301.713.2657

NSF Child Development Center
4201 Wilson Blvd., Arlington, 703.292.4794

State Department Childcare & Diplotots Center
2401 E St. NW, 202.663.3555

> **author's note:**
> The State Department sponsors two on-site childcare centers for staff: Columbia Plaza or State Department Annex-1, across from the Truman Building between 21st and 23rd Sts. NW, and the Foreign Service Institute's Childcare Center on-campus in Arlington. Both provide curriculum-based programs for infants through preschool. The Diplotots Center at Annex-1 also offers kindergarten.

Senate Employees' Childcare
321 Massachusetts Ave. NE, 202.224.1461

Sheila Watkins Child Development Center
19901 Germantown Rd., Germantown, 301.903.8600

Sunny Days
4700 River Rd., Riverdale, 301.734.7705

Smithsonian Early Enrichment Center
National Museum of Natural History, www.seec.si.edu

> *"I am a big fan of the Department of Transportation, Senate, and Smithsonian childcare programs. They have EXCELLENT directors. What you're looking for in an infant program is a high quality provider who has a great track record and ideally a strong interest in professional development. Infant care should have a ratio of 1 to 3 or at most, 1 to 4. Make frequent site visits to the centers during all times of the day, especially at naptime, to determine their policies and make sure you like what you see."*
>
> - Mimi Carter, author of the now-out-of-print "Insider's Guide to Quality Childcare in Greater Washington"

Triangle Tots
1300 Pennsylvania Ave. NW, DC, 202.565.3018

USDA Children's Discovery Center
201 14th St. SW, 202.205.1133

U.S. Kids
1425 New York Ave. NW, DC, 202.233.4623

World Bank Children's Center
600 19th St. NW, 202.473.7081

FINDING A PRESCHOOL

As I once blogged... In Washington, admissions for the still-pooping-in-my-pants crowd can be competitive and crass, complete with long waiting lists, lotto-style admissions decisions, "letters of recommendation," and the feeling that you are endlessly writing blank checks. That said, there are many wonderful programs worth applying to. And here are some tips from those of us who learned the ropes the hard way:

o There are more interested families wanting quality preschools than there are spaces for children. Openings fill up quickly – many by late January or February prior to the fall start date.

o Getting into a two-year-old class seems to be the most competitive. That's because getting into the twos puts you on the fast track, guaranteeing your child a spot at the same school for years to come. Because of this policy ("once you're in, you're in"), new spaces open to the public become harder and harder to secure as children get older.

o Do the open house/application circuit the winter before you want to enroll your child. (For example, if you want to start preschool in fall 2009, you need to do your research on programs and get application packets in fall 2008, attend open houses at the preschools in late 2008/early 2009, and turn in your applications in January/February 2009. Most schools notify you of your child's admission status between late March and May. And most schools do have a waiting list that is valid for up to one year – You could get a spot if a registered family moves or has to withdraw from the school.

- When you apply, expect to pay a NON-refundable application fee of anywhere from $35 to $150. (Yes, I'm serious.) Applying to more than one school you're interested in is a good idea if you want the best odds.

- Once accepted to a program, expect to pay half a month's tuition or even a full month's tuition up-front. (Yes, I'm serious.)

- It may be easier to get into a cooperative preschool than a non-co-op. But it's not for everyone – You will be expected to work in your child's classroom 1-3x per month, plus additional time working on committees, special events, seasonal cleanings, or other projects around the school. The upside: You get to be involved first-hand in your child's classroom on a regular basis. The downside: You get to be involved first-hand in your child's classroom on a regular basis. And if you work full-time outside the home or have a younger child not yet in preschool who needs your care, co-oping may prove difficult to impossible.

- I recommend checking out this resource before you start preschool-shopping: NAEYC's new website just for parents, at www.rightchoiceforkids.org.

A FEW OF DC'S FAVORITE PRESCHOOLS

WASHINGTON, DC:

Aidan Montessori School
2700 27th St. NW
www.aidanschool.org, 202.387.2700

August Montessori
3600 Ellicott St. NW, 202.237.1788

Pre-K at The Beauvoir School
3500 Woodley Park Rd. NW
www.beauvoirschool.org, 202.537.6485

Capitol Hill Cooperative Playschool
222 E. Capitol St. NE, 202.543.7355

Caterpillar Co-Op (Spanish immersion)
3920 Alton Place NW, 202.244.6944

Chevy Chase Presbyterian Church Weekday Nursery School
1 Chevy Chase Circle, 202.363.2209

Capitol Hill Day School
210 South Carolina Ave., SE, 202.547.2244, www.chds.org

Chevy Chase Presbyterian Church Weekday Nursery School
1 Chevy Chase Circle, 202.363.2209

Community Preschool of the Palisades
5200 Cathedral Ave. NW, 202.364.8424

DC Jewish Community Center Preschool
1529 16th St. NW
www.dcjcc.org/kidsparents/preschool, 202.777.3278

DC Parks & Rec Department Preschool Co-Ops
locations throughout the District of Columbia
Office of Educational Services, 202.671.0372, http://dpr.dc.gov

El Jardin Infantil (Spanish immersion)
2108 48th St. NW, 202.486.0293

Episcopal Center for Children
5901 Utah Ave. NW, 202.363.1333, www.eccofdc.org

The French Maternal School
3115 P St. NW, 202.276.0465, www.frenchmaternalschool.com

Georgetown Montessori School
1041 Wisconsin Ave. NW, 202.337.8058,
http://georgetownmontessori.com

The Hill Cooperative Preschool
337 North Carolina Ave. SE
www.hillpreschool.org, 202.543.5372

Preschool & Pre-K at Tyler Elementary School (Spanish immersion)
1001 G St. SE, www.tylerschool.org

Montessori School of Washington
NEW location: 4380 MacArthur Blvd., 202.338.1557
www.montessoriwashington.org

National Child Research Center
3209 Highland Place NW, 202.363.8777, www.ncrcpreschool.org

Pre-K at the Owl School (Bilingual English/Spanish)
1920 G Street NW, 202.828.1001

Lab School of Washington
4759 Reservoir Road NW, 202.965.6600
www.labschool.org

Little Flower Montessori School
3029 16th St. NW, 202.667.6803
www.littleflowermontessori.com

Pre-K at the Lowell School
1640 Kalmia Rd., NW, 202.577.2000
www.lowellschool.org

Peaceful Preschool (Homeschool preschool group for parents in Columbia Heights, DC)
http://groups.yahoo.com/group/peacefulpreschool

Preparatory School for Early Learning
3220 17th St. NW, 202.462.6835

River Park Nursery School
212 E. Capitol St. NE, 202.546.7767
www.riverparknurseryschool.org

The River School
4880 Macarthur Blvd. NW, 202.337.3554, www.riverschool.net

School for Friends
2121 Decatur Place NW, 202.328.1789, www.schoolforfriends.org

Smithsonian Early Enrichment Center
1300 Constitution Ave. NW, 202.633.4079

Spanish Education Development Center
2630 Adams Mill Rd. NW, 202.462.6886

St. Columba's Nursery School
4201 Albemarle St. NW, 202.363.4121, www.columba.org

St. John's Episcopal Preschool
3240 Q St. NW, 202.338.2574
http://www.stjohnsgeorgetown.org/preschool

St. Patrick's Episcopal Day School
4700 Whitehaven Pkwy. NW, 202.342.2805,
www.stpatsdc.org/program/nurseryschoolnpk.asp

Takoma Children's School
6925 Willow St. NW, 202.726.9220, http://takomachildren.org

Washington Hebrew Congregation Early Childhood Center
3935 Macomb St. NW, 202.895.6334
www.whctemple.org

MARYLAND SUBURBS:

Abingdon Montessori School
5144 Massachusetts Ave., Bethesda, 301.320.3646
www.abingdonschool.org

Acorn Hill Waldorf School
9504 Brunett Ave., Silver Spring, 301.565.2282
www.acornhill.org

The Barrie School (Montessori)
13500 Layhill Rd., Silver Spring, 301.576.2800
www.barrie.org

Beth Ami
14330 Travila Rd., Rockville, 301.340.6818
www.bethami.org/education/nursery

Beth El Preschool
8215 Old Georgetown Rd., Bethesda, 301.652.8569, ext. 311
www.bethelpreschool.org

Bethesda-Chevy Chase Cooperative Nursery School
4700 Norwood Dr., Chevy Chase, 301.986.0677
www.bccnurseryschool.org

Bethesda Montessori School
7611 Clarendon Rd., Bethesda, 301.986.1260
www.bethesdamontessori.com

Bowie Montessori School
5004 Randonstone Ln., Bowie, 301.262.3566
www.bmch.net

Bradley Hills Presbyterian Nursery School
6601 Bradley Blvd., Bethesda, 301.365.2909
www.bradleyhillschurch.org/affiliatedgroups

Cedar Lane Nursery School
9601 Cedar Ln., Bethesda, 301.530.5443
http://clns.org

Chevy Chase United Methodist Church Preschool
7001 Connecticut Ave., Chevy Chase, 301.652.7660
www.ccumcpreschool.org

Covenant United Methodist Preschool & Kindergarten
20301 Pleasant Ridge Dr., Montgomery Village, 301.527.9300
www.covenant-umc.org

Epworth Preschool & Kindergarten
9008 Rosemont Dr., Gaithersburg, 301.977.3421
www.epworthsteeple.org

Franklin Schools (Montessori)
10500 Darnestown Rd., Rockville, 301.279.2799
www.montessori-mmi.com

Franklin Schools (Montessori)
10500 Darnestown Rd., Rockville, 301.279.2799
www.montessori-mmi.com

Ganon Gil Preschool, Jewish Community Center of Greater Washington
6125 Montrose Rd., Rockville, 301.881.0100
www.jccgw.org

Garrett Park Nursery School
4806 Oxford St., Garrett Park, 301.946.6192
www.garrettparknurseryschool.org

Geneva Day School
11931 Seven Locks Rd., Potomac, 301.340.7704
www.genevadayschool.org

Grace Episcopal Day School
9115 Georgia Ave., Silver Spring, 301.585.3513
9411 Connecticut Ave., Kensington, 301.949.5860
www.geds.org

Green Acres School
11701 Danville Dr., Rockville, 301.881.4100
www.greenacres.org

Har Tzeon-Agudath Achim Early Childhood Center
1840 University Blvd. W., Silver Spring, 301.649.3800
www.htaa.org

Harbor School
7701 Bradley Blvd., Bethesda, 703.560.4379
www.theharborschool.org

Preschool at Jewish Community Center of Greater Washington
6125 Montrose Rd., Rockville, 301.881.0100
www.jccgw.org

Katherine Maddux Early Learning Center
11614 Seven Locks Rd., Rockville, 301.469.0223
www.ivymount.org/maddux.html

Laura & Joel Greenzaid Early Childhood Center
10621 S. Glen Rd., Potomac, 301.299.1149
www.bnaitzedek.org

Lone Oak Montessori
Bethesda & Potomac, 301.469.4888 and 301.299.7400
www.loneoakmontessori.com

Manor Montessori School
Potomac, Rockville, & Bethesda, 301.299.7400
www.manormontessori.com

Oneness-Family School
6701 Wisconsin Ave., Bethesda, 301.652.7751
www.onenessfamilyschool.org

Paint Branch Montessori School
3215 Powder Mill Rd., Adelphi, 301.937.2244
http://pbmontessori.com

Patuxent Montessori School
14210 Old Stage Rd., Bowie, 301.464.4506
www.patuxent-montessori.org

Paint Branch Montessori School
3215 Powder Mill Rd., Adelphi, 301.937.2244
http://pbmontessori.com

Patuxent Montessori School
14210 Old Stage Rd., Bowie, 301.464.4506
www.patuxent-montessori.org

Potomac Glen Day School
9908 S. Glen Rd., Potomac, 301.299.9193
www.potomacglendayschool.com

Potomac Nursery School
12300 Falls Rd., Potomac, 301.340.0579

Rock Creek Montessori School
3701 Spruell Dr., Silver Spring, 301.942.9561
www.rockcreekmontessori.com

Rockville Nursery School & Kindergarten
301 Adclare Rd., Rockville, 301.762.2678
www.rnsandk.com

Rockville Presbyterian Co-Op Nursery School
215 W. Montgomery Ave., Rockville, 301.762.1293
www.rpcns.org

Silver Spring Cooperative Nursery School
10309 New Hampshire Ave., Silver Spring, 301.434.2313
www.silverspringnurseryschool.org

Silver Spring Learning Center (affiliated with the Silver Spring Jewish Center)
1401 Arcola Ave., Silver Spring, 301.649.1373
www.silverspringlearningcenter.org

Spring Bilingual Montessori School
3514 Plyers Mill Rd., Kensington, 301.587.3511
www.spring-bilingual.org

Spring Knolls Cooperative Early Learning Center
8900 Georgia Ave., Silver Spring, 301. 650.0086
www.springknolls.org

St. Francis Episcopal Day School
100333 River Rd., Potomac, 301.365.2642
www.sfeds.org

Har Shalom Early Childhood Education Center
11510 Falls Rd., Potomac, 301.299.7087
www.harshalomecec.org

The Primary Day School
7300 River Rd., Bethesda, 301.365.4355
www.theprimarydayschool.org
Takoma Park Child Development Center
310 Tulip Ave., Takoma Park, 301.270.6824
www.tpcdc.org

Walden Montessori Academy
7730 Bradley Blvd., Bethesda, 301.469.8123

Washington Hebrew Congregation Early Childhood Center / Primary School
11810 Falls Rd., Potomac, 301.279.7505
www.whctemple.org

Washington Waldorf School
4800 Sangamore Rd., Bethesda, 301.229.6107
www.washingtonwaldorf.org

Westmoreland Children's Center
5112 Allan Terrace, Bethesda, 301.229.7161
www.westmorelandchildrenscenter.com

NORTHERN VIRGINIA SUBURBS:

Annandale Cooperative Preschool
8410 Little River Turnpike, Annandale, 703.978.6127
www.annandalecoop.org

Arlington Unitarian Cooperative Preschool
4444 Arlington Blvd., Arlington, 703.892.3878
www.aucpva.org

Aquinas Montessori School
8334 Mt. Vernon Hwy., Alexandria, 703.780.8484
www.aquinasmontessorischool.com

Beverly Hills Church Co-Op Preschool
3512 Old Dominion Rd., Alexandria, 703.549.7441
www.bhcpnet.org

Burke United Methodist Church Preschool
6200 Burke Centre Pkwy., Burke, 703.250.3657
www.bumponline.org

Children's International School
Alexandria & Arlington, 703.751.7266
www.childrensinternationalschool.com

Christ the King Lutheran Mother's Day Out
10550 Georgetown Pike, Great Falls, 703.759.6935
www.christ-the-king-lutheran.org

Community Montessori School
1700 Reston Pkwy., Reston, 703.478.3656
www.communitymontessorischool.com

Congressional School
3229 Sleepy Hollow Rd., Falls Church, 703.533.9711
www.congressionalschools.org

Country Woodland School
7152 Woodland Dr., Springfield, 703.256.9400
www.countrywoodland.com

Creative Beginnings Preschool
Del Ray, Alexandria, 703.203.5121
www.creative-beginnings.net

Early Years Montessori School
3241 Brush Dr., Falls Church, 703.237.0264
www.earlyyearsschool.com

Fairfax Academy
820 S. Carlin Springs Rd., Arlington, 703.671.5555
www.ffxacademy.com

Fairfax Presbyterian Preschool
10723 Main St., Fairfax, 703.273.4333
www.fairfaxpresby.com/preschool

Faith Lutheran Preschool
3313 Arlington Blvd., Arlington, 703.525.9283
www.faithlutheranarlington.org

Falls Church Children's House (Montessori)
3335 Annandale Rd., Falls Church, 703.573.7599
www.vamontessori.com

Falls Church Episcopal Day School
115 E. Fairfax St., Falls Church, 703.534.8687

Ft. Hunt Cooperative Preschool
1909 Windmill Ln., Alexandria, 703.768.7584
www.forthuntpreschool.com

Good Shepherd Lutheran School
1516 Moorings Dr., Reston, 703.437.4511
www.goodshepherd-lutheran.org

Grace Episcopal School
3601 Russell Rd., Alexandria, 703.549.5067
www.gracealex.org

Grasshopper Green School
4955 Sunset Ln., Annandale, , 703.256.4711
www.grasshoppergreen.com

Green Hedges School (Montessori)
415 Windover Ave. NW, Vienna, 703.938.8323
www.greenhedgesschool.org

Hunters Woods Co-Op Preschool
11510 Running Cedar Rd., Reston, 703.860.2077
www.hunterswoodspreschool.org

Jewish Community Center of NoVa Preschool at Beth El Temple
3830 Seminary Rd., Alexandria, 703.537.3086
www.jccnv.org

> *"The Arlington public school system has a great program that few school districts offer: A preschool program for two-year-olds who have special needs or developmental delays. Children have to be evaluated in order to determine if they are eligible, but it is a great program to help kids who need a little help catching up, and it is part of the public school services, so it is free!"*
>
> *- Amanda*

Pre-K at The Key School / Escuela Key (Bilingual English/Spanish)
2300 Key Blvd., Arlington, 703.228.4210
www.arlington.k12.va.us/schools/key

Meeting House Cooperative Preschool
316 S. Royal St., Alexandria, 703.549.8037
www.opmh.org

Merritt Academy
9211 Arlington Blvd., Fairfax, 703.273.8001
www.merrittacademy.org

Montessori of Chantilly / Casa de Bambini
4212 Technology Ct., Chantilly, 703.961.0211
www.mcdbc.com

Montessori School, Holmes Run
3335 Annandale Rd., Falls Church, 703.573.7599
www.vamontessori.com
Montessori School of Cedar Lane
3035 Cedar Ln., Fairfax, 703.560.4379
www.preschoolmontessori.com

Montessori School of Fairfax
3411 Lee Corner Rd., Chantilly, 571.323.0222
www.montessori-fairfax.com

Montessori School of Mclean
1711 Kirby Rd., Mclean, 703.790.1049
www.mcleanmontessori.org

Mt. Olivet UMC Preschool
1500 N. Glebe Rd., Arlington, 703.527.3934
www.mtolivet-umc.org

Nysmith School for the Gifted
13625 EDS Dr., Herndon, www.nysmith.com

Old Town Montessori School
115 S. Washington St., Alexandria, 703.684.7323
www.aquinasmontessorischool.com

Potomac Crescent School (Waldorf)
923 S. 23rd St., Arlington, 703.624.1309
www.potomaccrescentschool.org

Providence Cooperative Nursery School
9019 Little River Turnpike, Fairfax, 703.250.6101
www.providencenurseryschool.com

Redeemer Lutheran Preschool
1545 Chain Bridge, Mclean, 703.356.3567
www.redeemermclean.org

Reston Montessori School
1928 Isaac Newton Sq. W., Reston, 703.481.2922
www.restonmontessori.com

Rock Spring Cooperative Preschool
Rock Spring Congregational UCC, Little Falls at Rock Spring Rd.
www.rockspringpreschool.org, 703.237.4991

Sleepy Hollow Cooperative Preschool
7610 Newcastle Rd., Annandale, 703.941.9791
www.sleepyhollowpreschool.com

Spring-Mar Cooperative Preschool
10125 Lakehaven Ct., Burke, 703.239.1213
www.spring-mar.org

St. Anthony's Day School
321 First St., Alexandria, 703.836.9123
www.stanthonysdayschool.org

St. Clement Episcopal Preschool
1701 N. Quaker Ln., Alexandria, 703.998.8795
www.saintclement.org

St. Luke's United Methodist Preschool
7628 Leesburg Pike, Falls Church, 703.893.9221
www.stlukesumccc.com

St. Paul's Episcopal Preschool & Day School
228 S. Pitt St., Alexandria, 703.549.3312
www.stpaulsepis.com/preschool.htm

Valleybrook School
3433 Rose Ln., Falls Church, 703.534.7463
www.valleybrookschool.com

Valley Drive Cooperative Preschool
1819 N. Quaker Ln., Alexandria, 703.379.6918
www.valleydrive.com

Virginia Hills Baptist Church Preschool
6507 Telegraph Rd., Alexandria, 703.971.4222, ext. 103
www.virginiahillsbaptistchurch.com

Washington St. United Methodist Preschool
115 S. Washington St., Alexandria, 703.836.8407
www.washingtonstreetchurch.com/preschool.html

Wesley Preschool
711 Spring St. SE, Vienna, 703.938.3970
http://wesleyumpreschool.com

Westminster Weekday Preschool
2701 Cameron Mills Rd., Alexandria, 703.549.5267
www.wpc-alex.org

CHAPTER 3
Children's Enrichment Programs

SELECTED SPOTLIGHTS

Jonah's Treehouse
2121 Wisconsin Ave. NW, C1 Level (Glover Park/Georgetown)
202.298.6805
info@jonahstreehouse.com
www.jonahstreehouse.com

Vicki Gersten founded Jonah's Treehouse after searching in vain for challenging movement opportunities in downtown DC for her then three-year-old son, Jonah. This lawyer and mother of two (Jonah and younger brother Gabriel) was already a veteran of enrichment classes ("I feel my sons and I attended, at one time or another, every play and movement class, music program, gymnastics program and story time under the sun!") and had a strong vision of what she wanted in the Jonah's Treehouse curriculum. Gersten, a literature major with a music background, believed that many children's movement programs out there lacked an element of artistry that she was determined to incorporate into her classes. Each Jonah's Treehouse class devotes a few minutes to children's literature and poetry, with the teacher reciting poems and encouraging the children to act out the literature in interesting ways.

The gross motor movement segment of the program is characterized by challenging obstacle courses of mat shapes and wooden climbing pieces (Gersten had custom climbing pieces designed by a local artist because she wanted pieces that could be reconfigured to create new internal "landscapes"). Never a big fan of waiting in line ("my son Jonah could not wait in line – lost interest when he had to sit and wait his turn – so I didn't want other parents to have to go through that... apologizing when the child's actions are actually age-appropriate"), Gersten enlisted the advice of movement consultants and instructors at her son's preschool to develop the idea of movement "stations." Classes often break into small groups, with one group concentrating on balance activities, for instance, and another group working on climbing or jumping.

Eurhythmics and co-movement activities with parents form the core of "circle time" at Jonah's Treehouse, because Gersten feels that "there is an inherent level of musicality in every child... a part of his/her inner self that is expressed through rhythm and melody. When the parent shares this experience with the child, the result is an integration of inner and external worlds that is deeply satisfying for the child." The program has become wildly popular among families throughout DC and the surrounding suburbs. Vicki tells me, "I feel truly fortunate that, as Jonah's Treehouse is an independent program rather than a franchise, the classes can really evolve organically from our experiences as a community and the needs of the children and parents."

We held the launch party for the first edition of this book at Jonah's Treehouse in fall 2005, and immediately fell for the space and the friendly, professional staff. Never have we been to an indoor play space like it – Beautiful, fun play equipment and soft playspaces, plenty of room to romp, colorful and bright. Jonah's Treehouse also offers space for custom playgroups and birthday party hosting. And since the first edition of this book in 2005, they've added loads of new programming – including summer and holiday day camp programs for preschoolers and more open play offerings. Get the details on their website!

¡Hola Baby!
Classes meet at Mt. Olivet United Methodist Church, 1500 N. Glebe Rd., Arlington
maria@holababy.net
www.holababy.net

Arlington mama Maria Elena Greene didn't find what she wanted for her child in her neighborhood, so she took the initiative to make it happen herself. Greene, who grew up in a bilingual household as a first-generation American with parents from Colombia and Puerto Rico, searched unsuccessfully for a Spanish immersion program for her toddler that was located near her home. She didn't find it, so she decided to do it herself, designing an early introduction to Spanish and test-driving it with her own child. Enter ¡Hola Baby!

Maria told me, "My motivation for starting the program is that I wanted my twelve-month-old daughter to grow up with Spanish AND English. And I thought the earlier she could do this, the better."

A five-week pilot program in the summer of 2005 included five children ranging in age from seven to 11 months. The kids had a blast, and Maria had the opportunity to fine-tune her vision. Classes started in fall 2005 and the program has grown by leaps and bounds since then – going strong with several sessions a year, and both weekday and weekend classes for several age groups.

¡Hola Baby! uses a developmentally-appropriate playgroup model, with Maria and her talented bilingual staff as the main facilitators, bolstered by plenty of parent involvement. Singing, dancing, movement, storytelling, and role-play are on the menu, shaped by a fun theme each time the group meets (e.g. animals, foods, parts of the body, colors, numbers). Given the developmental needs of very young children, the program is a quite basic intro to the Spanish language, with lots and lots of repetition. (The way babies learn best!) The older playgroup (two to four years) will enjoy many of the same activities, but will also have arts and crafts, and may cover more advanced themes. Maria's goal is for the kids to HAVE FUN with language, and the learning will naturally follow. Each class has a max enrollment of eight to 10 children, so there's no overcrowding and plenty of individual attention. Best of all, the fees for classes are among the most reasonable you'll find anywhere in the DC area.

Our family are ¡Hola Baby! devotees. Over the past few years we've done several sessions in the program with our daughter, and we know first-hand how much fun it is to meet new friends and practice our Spanish with "Tia Maria" and her team. We love Maria's boundless energy, the diversity of families in the classes, and the curriculum. While neither my husband nor myself is a native Spanish speaker (and certainly we are not fluent), one of the most important people in our lives is our children's Spanish-speaking caregiver. ¡Hola Baby! has been a great reinforcement of Spanish for our children and ourselves, bolstering what's being spoken in our home. Our daughter is now truly bilingual, fluent in both English and Spanish, and this enrichment program has played an important role.

Tiny Fingers
Classes meet throughout the DC metro area

classes@tinyfingers.com
www.tinyfingers.com

Research continues to show that teaching sign language to pre-verbal tots offers cognitive, linguistic, and social benefits. It seems that long before babies can verbalize words out loud, they are receiving, processing, and forming language that simple signs can help them express. Founded by NoVa mama Eileen Ladino, Tiny Fingers offers sign language classes for hearing babies and toddlers, parents, and caregivers who want to try this fun way of communicating.

Eileen and her group of experienced teachers are trained in American Sign Language and have specialized experience with very young children. Classes are offered at fixed locations throughout the DC area, as well as private or group instruction at the site of your choice. (Often a group of families organizes a workshop at a neighborhood home.) The options are flexible – one-time classes, a three-week session, or a six-week session – appropriate for ages six months to two-and-a-half years.

Here's what a Springfield mama, Katherine, told me about her family's experience with Tiny Fingers classes:

"Teaching Nicolas sign language has been the single most important thing we've ever done for him. First, teaching children of ALL abilities sign language is highly recommended—not just those with 'presumed' speech/language delays. Countless parents want their children to learn sign language because it is a great transition between 'uh, uh, uh!' and 'More milk please, Mommy.' In my opinion, the benefits for children with disabilities are that much greater because it's true, our little ones tend to speak later than other children without disabilities. Without sign language, we would have no idea how much our little guy really knew... As much as I would love for him to be talking, he is simply not developmentally ready for that now. The signs are a lifesaver until he is."

Moore Than Yoga
Classes meet at Bethel United Church of Christ, 4903 S. 30th St., Arlington
info@moorethanyoga.com, 703.671.2435
www.moorethanyoga.com

Jennifer Moore at Moore Than Yoga makes yoga and wellness fun and accessible for all ages and all fitness abilities. I had one of the most relaxing and pleasant afternoons ever in Jennifer's annual Mother's Day yoga and pampering sessions, and I immediately felt at home with her down-to-earth, easygoing style.

Jennifer specializes in working with prenatal and postpartum women, children, and families – offering classes and special workshops for pregnancy, moms and babies, children's classes and family classes, "pajama yoga," and more. She also teaches infant massage classes for babies one to eight months of age, with a parent or caregiver. Jennifer is certified to teach Hatha yoga, prenatal and postpartum yoga, children's yoga, and infant massage. She is also a trained practitioner of reflexology and Reiki.

Jennifer's classes are a great opportunity to practice relaxation and mindful breathing, to meet other pregnant women and moms, and to help your children learn to enjoy movement and body-awareness. One student from Jennifer's postpartum yoga class says it all: *"I truly enjoyed being able to take my first yoga class ever. And being able to bring my baby, too. It's something I'll tell him about when he's all grown up. I feel more at peace when I leave than when I arrive."*

Music Together
Classes meeting in DC, Mclean, Falls Church, Arlington, Alexandria, Burke, Ashburn, Fairfax, Stafford, Vienna, Hayfield, Kingstowne, Reston, Oakton, Woodbridge, Sterling, Gainesville, and throughout Montgomery County
www.musictogether.com

We did several sessions of Music Together with a beloved local instructor who later relocated away from the DC area – and we enjoyed not just our instructor but the songs, the research-based and developmentally-appropriate curriculum, and the Music Together materials (CDs, song books) for use outside of class.

Music Together classes are geared toward infants through age four, attending with a parent or caregiver. Each class incorporates singing (accompanied and not), movement, dancing, chants and rhymes, and exploring musical instruments. Our daughter's favorite part of each class was the freestyle "jam session" using a range of instruments and lively music from a wide range of styles and cultural traditions. The classes are fun for parents, too – and although you'll probably enjoy it most if you are musically inclined, no special skills or abilities are required.

Music Together offers free demonstration classes, so you can "try before you buy." Each session's registration comes with a new songbook,

CDs, and educational parent materials covering the program's philosophy and how children develop musically.

To look up the Music Together instructor nearest you, go to the national website and do a location search. Many of the local instructors have their own independent sites where you can get specific information on dates, times, and places.

Parent Child University
Classes held at Arlington County Rec Centers, Parenting Playgroups in Alexandria, and at preschools and Moms' groups throughout metro DC
571.643.1002
www.parentchildu.com

Parent Child University offers Signing Smart play classes and Signing Smart parent workshops, Kindermusik classes, ABC Music & Me preschool and childcare music classes, music/movement/ASL storytimes, parenting classes (including Happiest Baby on the Block), and a preschool conflict resolution class, "Playground Diplomacy." They also host a parenting book club, after-school programs, birthday party entertainment, and sales of award-winning musical toys and resources.

Parent Child University was founded by local mama and longtime child advocate and parent educator Tracey Kretzer, MS, LPSC, a.k.a. "Miss Tracey." She is licensed to teach Kindermusik and Signing Smart, and has certifications as an educator with the Happiest Baby, Guiding Good Choices, and Get Real About Violence programs - in addition to years of experience as an early childhood educator and with the National Effective Parenting Initiative (NEPI). She's also long been active locally as a volunteer for family-centered causes.

We first got to know Tracey shortly after the publication of the first edition of this book, and she struck us as a professional truly dedicated to the wellbeing of local children and parents. We've been impressed with her dedication to early childhood and parenting enrichment in the DC area, and have been pleased to watch Parent Child University grow and thrive. In addition to teaching and facilitating programs herself, Tracey has even added another talented instructor to her team in "Miss Lisa" Bartley, M.Ed., who has helped expand Parent Child University into North Carolina.

As one of Parent Child University's clients, Katherine, puts it, *"Miss Tracey's classes are fun and educational. She is a very energetic and flexible instructor, which is important in teaching little ones. She makes you and your child feel at ease, even if it's the first time you've been in an organized class together. She creates an environment that is great for learning, and also gives parents the time to talk and share their experiences."*

ONESIES DC
www.onesiesdc.com
Brilliant! Long overdue! That's ONESIES DC. This innovative program exposes both newbie and veteran moms to a wide variety of early childhood and parent ed opportunities available in the DC area, saving potentially expensive trial-and-error while making new friends. Here's how it works: You get to sample a different activity or program every week for six weeks with your young child, testing out a range of classes available on the local scene and learning from a variety of local experts along the way. No commitment needed to a single program or a long session that might or might not turn out to be the right fit. Recent offerings in the lineup have included mama-and-baby fitness and yoga, music, infant massage, photography services, keepsake services (such as baby footprint plaques), sleep coaching, CPR instruction, pediatrician and nutritionist advice, and lactation consulting. Founded and managed by Bethesda mama Robyn Cohen Churilla, ONESIES DC partners with local faves like PEP, Rock-n-Tot, and Hot Mama Fitness to offer you a smorgasbord of baby fun.

MORE OF DC'S FAVORITE PROGRAMS

Alexandria Academy of Fine Arts & Science
www.alexacademy.com
Classes in dance, music, art, drama, science, languages (French, Spanish, Latin, Chinese), and Kindermusik for early childhood to early school-age children.

Alexandria Ballet
www.thealexandriaballet.com
Alexandria Ballet offers pre-ballet/creative movement classes for ages three to seven. Classes combine ballet stretches, warm-ups, exercises, and take-home dance art projects. Classes are for children who are able to participate independently, with parents waiting in the school's lobby but not in view.

Alexandria Rec Centers
www.ci.alexandria.va.us/recreation
Offers early childhood classes including music, movement, play, pre-ballet, tumbling, art, and swimming. Schedules vary according to location and time of year.

Andy's Parties
Gaithersburg, Great Falls, Stafford, Bristow
www.andysparties.com
In addition to their fabulous children's party services, Andy's Parties hosts early childhood enrichment programs including Kaleidoscope Adventure Classes for ages three to four and five to six (incorporating imaginative crafts, costume dress-up time, music, movement, and storytime), Kaleidoscope Chronicles Programs for ages three to 10 (bringing books alive in an interactive way, with playacting, singing, dancing, and crafts), Kaleidoscope Mommy & Me Playgroups for babies and parents (for ages birth to 30 months), a storytime club, and open play sessions (for ages birth to five).

> "Andy's Parties isn't just parties. Their classes for young children are really good, too. A nice mix of different types of play and movement rolled into one. Definitely would recommend them to other parents."
>
> - Liz

Arlington Rec Centers
www.arlingtonva.us/departments/parksrecreation
Offers early childhood classes including music, movement, play, swimming, pre-ballet, tumbling, and art. Schedules vary by location and time of year.

Art at the Center
Alexandria
www.artatthecenter.org
Art at the Center offers enrichment classes in studio art – including drop-off classes and family classes – for ages 18 months+. Summers feature arts day camp programs for all ages.

Art in Hand
Old Town Alexandria, Herndon, Falls Church
www.artinhand.org
Taught by art therapist and educator Julie Liddle, Art in Hand classes are designed for toddlers and preschoolers. One of the program's guiding principles: "Art is the vehicle, but not necessarily the destination," with a focus on the process, on discovery, on imagination and exploration.

ArtsPlay at Wolf Trap
www.wolftrap.org/education/classes/artsplay.html
Wolf Trap's ArtsPlay program provides early childhood arts enrichment classes for ages six months to six years.

Baby Ballerina
Sterling, www.babyballerina.net
A ballet studio focusing on fun and developmentally appropriate classes for tots to school-age dancers, ages one to six. They also offer camp sessions, a cheer and tumble class, and "baby Nutcracker" at Christmas-time.

Baby Signs by Trish
Montgomery County, www.babysignsbytrish.com
trish.stone@yahoo.com
Baby sign language classes for little ones and their parents/caregivers are taught by Kensington mama, pediatric occupational therapist and certified Baby Signs instructor Trish Stone (along with "Beebo" the Baby Signs program bear). Classes are designed for infants and toddlers, birth to age three. Trish also teaches Baby Signs workshops and classes for expectant and new parents.

Ballet Petite
Bethesda, Potomac, Gaithersburg, and Mclean
www.balletpetite.com
Mommy & Me classes for ages two and three, movement classes for ages
three and four, pre-ballet for ages five and six, and ballet for ages seven
through nine (including an imaginative ballet/theater class).

The Ballet Studio
Del Ray, Alexandria
www.delraydance.com
Creative movement, pre-ballet, ballet, tap, and jazz for girls and boys ages
three+.

> *author's note:*
> The Ballet Studio's founder and lead instructor, "Ms. Mary,"
> is a local legend. Our daughter has enjoyed their creative
> movement/pre-ballet classes for preschoolers, complete
> with the joys of imaginary and dress-up play. A nice, no-
> pressure introduction to classical ballet for little ones, with
> the opportunity to move into more disciplined studies as
> they grow older. The unassuming studio is minimally
> marked, but you'll find it on the Mt. Vernon Ave. corridor,
> across from the 7-Eleven. Classes fill up quickly, so email
> your request via the website well in advance.

Beanstalk Montessori
Bethesda, www.beanstalkmontessori.com
Beanstalk Montessori offers a one-hour Mommy & Me / Daddy & Me
class based on the Montessori model of development and play. Focuses
on developing fine motor skills, concentration, and independence,
incorporating circle time, songs and finger plays, painting, and storytime.

Budding Yogis Program at Circle Yoga
Chevy Chase, www.buddingyogis.com
Tummy Time yoga for mothers and babies, Postpartum Pilates for
mothers and babies, Movers & Twisters yoga for ages two to four,
Storytime Yoga for ages three to five, Kids & Pre-Teen yoga, Teen yoga,
Family yoga for kids and adults together, and therapeutic yoga classes for
children with special needs.

Body in Balance Center
Alexandria/Slaters Ln. corridor, www.bodyinbalancecenter.com
Creative movement classes for preschool-age children, kids' yoga, and
Mommy & Me classes – in addition to many yoga class options for moms
and dads.

> *author's note:*
> We've loved the children's creative movement classes taught
> by Sara Lavan at Body in Balance. Such fun for both girls and
> boys in a relaxed, informal setting that encourages kids to
> enjoy dance and fitness, while building self-confidence. A
> very positive experience for our daughter. And did I
> mention? The yummy Buzz coffee shop and bakery is just
> around the corner from the Body in Balance Center, allowing
> mom or dad to get a little "me time" while the kids are in
> class.

Capitol Hill Arts Workshop
Capitol Hill, www.chaw.org
Toddler music class, tumbling, pre-ballet, kiddie art, visual arts class, Wee
Wonders group for ages two to five (which incorporates science
experiments, creative arts, drama, songs, and movement, a story, and a
snack). Also after-school program for older kids, summer camp programs,
and classes for adults.

Capitol Hill Yoga
Capitol Hill, www.capitolhillyoga.com
Capitol Hill Yoga offers a Baby & Me class incorporating yoga postures
with infant massage and baby movement. Also, Big & Little Yoga, a class
for ages three to four with a parent or caregiver, and Yin/Yang Yogini for
ages five to seven. They have many adult classes and prenatal yoga, as
well.

Center for Music, Movement, & Art
Bethesda, www.centerformusic.org
Classes for ages birth to teens, incorporating music and movement. Age-
appropriate classes for little ones involve parents or caregiver. Music
classes and individual lessons for older children.

Classic Tales 'n Tunes

Falls Church, Vienna, Reston, Great Falls, Alexandria, Arlington
www.classictnt.com
Founded by talented musician and children's arts educator Jody Katz,
Classic Tales 'n Tunes offers classes for infants through age four in
Northern Virginia. Classes incorporate songs, stories, gross motor
movement, puppets, and basic Spanish and American Sign Language
(ASL), woven together in age-appropriate fun. There are two program
options: Their signature class for ages 18 months to four years, and Tiny
Tunes, suited to newborn infants through 17 months. Free preview
classes are open to the public several times a year, so you can "try before
you buy."

> "My daughter participated in Jody's wonderful Classic Tales
> 'n Tunes classes for approximately a year before entering
> preschool. She loved the class. After all, what two-year-old
> would not love singing, dancing, stories and making new
> friends? There are a number of music classes, a number of
> movement classes, and many storytimes in the area, but
> Jody's class combines all of these activities into one! It is
> perfect to keep those active toddlers' attention.
>
> - Lori

Classika Studio

Arlington, www.classika.org
Classika offers theater classes for ages four and up. Also summer camps
for ages four and up. Specialized classes in the arts for all ages.

Creativity

Georgetown, www.creativitygeorgetown.com
Creativity at the Georgetown Mall offers drop-off play for children over
age five while you shop – with arts and crafts activities and free play.
Children under age five are also welcome in the store, accompanied by an
adult. Each week they host a lineup of special events, including a
children's yoga class, storytime, and movie screening. Also available for

birthday parties. A great destination for stir-crazy rainy days and wintertime.

Dance Place
Capitol Hill, www.danceplace.org
Creative movement classes for ages three to five, a Kids' Creative Combo class for ages five to seven, jazz classes for ages 10+, ballet for ages eight+, modern dance for ages 12 to 16, and hip-hop for ages 13 to 16.

DC Jewish Community Center
Dupont Circle, www.dcjcc.org
DCJCC's Parenting Center has many programs for new parents and young children, including Baby & Me and Motion Commotion classes, a PACE group for mothers, Yoga Tots, and breastfeeding support. Also a preschool program and an after-school program for older kids.

DC Rec Centers
http://dpr.dc.gov/dpr
DC Parks & Recreation centers offer a variety of classes for early childhood, including music, movement, and play. Each center offers a different lineup of offerings, so check the schedule for the location in your neighborhood.

Extracurricular, Etc.: Nature Hikes for Kids
National, state, and local parks in DC and suburbs
www.extracurricularetc.com
Nature/science hikes for preschoolers and older kids, led by a guide experienced in early education. Length/time of hikes varies according to age group. Parents hike with their child.

Fairfax County Rec Centers
www.fairfaxcounty.gov/parks/rec/classes/children.htm
Offers early childhood classes including music, movement, dance, and art. Schedules vary by location and time of year.

Falls Church City Rec Centers
www.ci.falls-church.va.us/community/recsandparks/recsandparks.html
Offers a number of classes and events for early childhood, including music, movement, and art. Schedules vary by location and time of year.

The Family Room
Capitol Hill, www.thefamilyroomdc.com
At last, a custom play space on Capitol Hill! This new-on-the scene indoor play area for children and families offers enrichment classes in languages (including baby sign language), Kindermusik, and crafts – as well as regularly scheduled activities such as storytimes and music sessions. Their space has a climbing structure, a variety of toys, art supplies, and children's books. They also host special events, such as Movie Night Fridays. And you can rent their space for occasions like birthday parties and baby showers.

Flow Yoga Center
Logan Circle, www.flowyogacenter.com
Flow Yoga Center offers Yoga Mama / Yoga Papa for a new parent and newborns up to the pre-crawling stage. Also kids' yoga in conjunction with the Budding Yogis program of Circle Yoga, prenatal yoga and prenatal massage classes, and many other offerings for adults. They also have a unique Child Care Co-Op program, which encourages parents to bring their young children along and take turns "sitting out" with the kiddos while the other parents take a class. Registration is required to take part.

Funfit
Rockville, Mclean, www.funfit.us
Play-oriented movement and fitness for ages eight months to eight years. Family classes. Special needs programs for ages two to 10. Ballet for ages three to five. Kindermusik for infants to age five. Combined movement and art class. Sport and games program for homeschooling families. Teen and adult tai chi classes. Programs are held both on-site in Rockville and Mclean, and at many participating Parks & Rec centers, preschools, and daycares in suburban Maryland and NoVa.

German School of Washington , DC
Potomac, www.dswashington.org
Classes and events for German-speaking children and adults, starting in early childhood.

Gymboree Play & Music Centers
Bethesda, Alexandria, Silver Spring, Rockville, Vienna, Fairfax, Chantilly
www.gymboree.com
Play and music classes for infants through preschoolers. Some locations
also offer art classes.

Gymbugs Children's Fitness
Rockville, www.gymbugs.com
Movement/gym classes for infants and toddlers, designed to enhance
social and motor development.

Imagination Stage
Bethesda, www.imaginationstage.com
Imagination Stage hosts classes for toddlers and their parents/caregivers
that incorporate songs, stories, puppets, and play. Also summer day camp
programs for all ages.

International School of Music
Bethesda, www.ismw.org
Early childhood music program, plus private instrument and vocal lessons
for older children.

Jabberu
Gaithersburg, Bethesda, Ashburn, Great Falls
www.jabberu.com
Jabberu offers foreign language learning for children ages birth to 10.
Classes are immersion-style, surrounding the child with the language
from the moment you enter the room. Native speakers teach the classes
in a dynamic, interactive, age-appropriate environment. Lively classes in
Spanish, French, Chinese, Arabic, and Italian.

Jewish Community Center of Greater Washington
Rockville, www.jccgw.org
Variety of parent/child classes available for toddlers through school-age,
including music, movement, and art.

Joy of Motion Dance Center
Dupont Circle, NE DC, Bethesda, Friendship Heights
www.joyofmotion.org

Joy of Motion offers over 50 classes for age three through teens. Early childhood creative movement and dance basics. For older kids: pre-ballet, ballet, prep for pointe, tap, jazz, street jazz, modern, belly dance, street jam, creative rhythms. Also classes for adults.

JW Tumbles
Rockville, Alexandria, Arlington, Ashburn, Herndon, Bristow
www.jwtumbles.com
JW Tumbles is a children's gym with classes for ages four months to nine years. In a non-competitive atmosphere, they focus on enhancing physical skills, fine and gross motor skills, spatial awareness, coordination, balance, agility, and flexibility.

Kids Moving Company
Bethesda, www.kidsmovingco.com
Team-taught movement classes for ages nine months to 10 years, incorporating music, dance, tumbling. Also, Mommy & Me yoga. Pom-pom, tumbling, and dance for older kids. Summer camps and in-school programs.

Kidville
Rockville, www.kidville.com
NYC-based Kidville recently opened its first DC-area location at Rockville's Congressional Plaza, offering early childhood music classes for infants to age five with a parent or caregiver. Each class features four live musicians who sing and play guitar, piano, and drums, incorporating songs from all genres, imaginative play, puppet shows, "babble music," language development activities, and musical storytimes.

Kids Sport League
Potomac, www.kidssportsleague.com
Nonprofit organization offering sports activities and groups for ages three to nine.

Kindermusik
Alexandria, Arlington, DC, Fairfax, Hyatsville, Burke, Takoma Park, McLean, Bethesda, College Park, Waldorf, Silver Spring, Bowie, Reston, Centreville, Crofton, Olney, Gaithersburg... and more!
www.kindermusik.com

Kindermusik offers a widely respected and developmentally appropriate music and movement classes for children with their parents or caregivers, infants to age seven. The program has been around for 30 years and incorporates musical learning into every aspect of a child's growth and development – from language to motor skills, social skills to cognitive development and emotional growth. The set of at-home materials you get at registration helps you incorporate the classroom experience into your daily family life.

> *"We highly recommend Kindermusik classes, and have incorporated them into the programming offered by Andy's Parties. Our daughter LOVES her Kindermusik instructor, Kathy."*
>
> *- Andrew, founder/owner of Andy's Parties*

Levine School of Music
NW & SE DC, Suburban Maryland, and NoVa
www.levineschool.org
The Levine School offers Music Time for Baby for ages six to 18 months, Singing Games for the Family for ages 18 to 36 months, Exploring Music for Preschoolers for ages three and four, Musical Morning for ages three and four, Music & Movement for ages three to 14, and Creative Dance for Boys & Girls for ages four to six. They also offer a summer music and arts camp for kids of all ages, as well as Suzuki, tradition, and group classes for voice and instruments.

Little Hands Kindermusik
Ashburn, Centreville, Fairfax, Manassas, Lake Ridge, Alexandria, Mclean, and Reston
www.littlehands.com
Music and movement classes for ages newborn to seven years. Also offers a "Sign and Sing" class combining sign language and music.

Little Sprouts
Gaithersburg, www.littlesproutsplay.com
Baby Music & Play for ages six to 15 months, Toddler Music & Play for ages 15 to 36 months, and Preschool Music & Play for ages 36 to 48

months. Also a Mom's Morning Out program for ages two+, and a Kids' Cooking class for older children.

Loudon County Rec Centers

www.loudoun.gov/prcs

Early childhood classes include music, movement, play, swimming, art, and more. Schedules vary according to location and time of year.

Marva Tots & Teens

Rockville, www.marvatotsnteens.com

Movement, tumbling, and gymnastics classes for toddlers through high schoolers. Also private lessons for older kids.

Mind the Mat

Del Ray, Alexandria

www.mindthemat.com

Mind the Mat offers children's yoga and creative movement classes for all ages – in addition to great offerings for mom and dad.

McLean Community Center

www.mcleancenter.org

Many types of classes, theater performances, and special events for young children and families, as well as summer camps for older kids.

Melody Kids

Centreville

www.melodykids.org

Music and movement classes for newborns to age five. Small group piano lessons for ages five to 10.

Monkey Business

Falls Church, www.monkeybiz4kids.com

New on the scene is this independently-owned and -operated music and movement enrichment center. A range of programs for all ages, in a bright and brand new play setting.

Montgomery County Rec Centers

www.co.mo.md.us/rec/calendar.html

Many programs for early childhood, including music, movement, and play. Schedule varies by location and time of year.

musiKids
Bethesda, Chevy Chase, Rockville, Kentlands, Alexandria
www.musikids.com
MusiKids offers a highly acclaimed, locally-owned and -operated music and movement program with a variety of cool programs and classes for infants to five years.

> *"Fun songs at musiKids. Fun people. Fun teacher. Structured, but loose enough for the age group!"*
>
> *- Wendy*

Music Play
Reston, Herndon
www.musicplayva.com
Music Play offers weekday music enrichment programs for infants to five-year-olds. Founded by Heather Smith, a master's-degreed former elementary music teacher for the Loudon County and Fairfax County Public Schools, who was one of six music educators featured in the PBS documentary "Music Play: Ba Ba, Be-Bop, Beethoven."

Music Tots
Alexandria, Arlington, Mclean, Herndon, Vienna
www.musictots.com
Music enrichment classes for newborns to age five. Both day and evening classes.

My Gym Children's Fitness Center
Potomac, Alexandria, Chantilly, Burke, and Leesburg
www.my-gym.com
Parent-child movement programs for ages three months to three years. Mommy & Me classes. Independent tumbling and fitness classes for ages three-and-a-half to nine years.

Noodles & Noggins Music Studio
www.noodlesandnoggins.com/musicstudio.html

This children's shop in NoVa's historic Clifton community has opened a new Music Studio offering age-appropriate and play-oriented lessons for kids of all ages in piano, guitar, woodwinds...plus "musical adventures" classes featuring an introduction to instruments from the brass, woodwinds, strings and percussion families.

Parenting Playgroups

Alexandria, www.parentingplaygroups.com

Parenting Playgroups offers a well-respected and unique early childhood play program for toddlers and preschoolers that incorporates parent education/parenting support, facilitated by developmental psychologist Dr. Rene Hackney in a relaxed setting. They also offer open play sessions, a range of parenting education programs, and resources for families.

> *"I considered myself to be a good and involved parent, and never expected the Parenting Playgroups classes to change my relationship with my daughter so much for the better. My attitude and perspective improved and I am a happier, calmer parent."*
>
> *- Carrie*

Parlez Vous

Old Town Alexandria, www.parlezvous.org

Saturday language and culture programs for ages three months to 10, offering German, Chinese, Spanish, and Italian. Various summer language camps for early walkers to age 15 in French, Spanish, and Italian. Various special events for the whole family, including Parlez Vous Café one Sunday each month. Also tutoring and classes for older kids and adults.

Potomac Horse Center

Potomac, www.potomachorse.com

Mini Mites introduction to riding class for ages five to eight. Also offers advanced riding classes for older children, teens, and adults.

Pure Prana Yoga

Old Town Alexandria, www.pureprana.com

Pure Prana offers a Mommy & Me class for newborns to six months, YogaKids, and Yoga for Teens. They also offer prenatal and many other adult classes.

Prince George's County Parks & Rec Centers
www.pgparks.com
Offers several early childhood enrichment programs, with schedules varying by location and time of year.

Radiant Child Yoga at Spiral Flight Yoga
Upper Georgetown / Glover Park, www.spiralflightyoga.com
Yoga classes for ages two years through teenagers at this partner of the Budding Yogis program of Circle Yoga. Also offers Tummy Time yoga for caregiver and baby (age six weeks to walking). And they do kids' yoga parties.

Reddemeade Farm
Silver Spring, www.reddemeade.com
Reddemeade Farm offers an introduction to riding for young children through adults, with an emphasis on safety and horsemanship. Also summer camps for kids.

Reston Community Center
www.restoncommunitycenter.com
Offers a Traveling Tots program for parents and kids age two to six for field trips around town, as well as parent/child activity classes for ages two and three. Also Tot Time, an unstructured play session twice weekly, and a Kids Night Out program on Friday evenings.

Rock Creek Park Horse Center
www.rockcreekhorsecenter.com
Among its many programs, RCPHC offers safe pony rides for preschoolers (weekends, by appointment), as well as a parent/child class that is hugely popular and has a waiting list. Also summer day camps for older kids.

Signing Family
www.signingfamily.com
Private and small-group instruction in American Sign Language (ASL) held at homes throughout metro DC, with day, evening, or weekend available.

Great for parents of infants and toddlers, as well as families with older children. Classes also offered at Holy Cross Hospital in Silver Spring.

Silver Stars Gymnastics
Silver Spring, Wheaton
www.gosilverstars.com
Silver Stars offers a Parent & Child class for ages 18 to 36 months, preschool classes for ages three through five, co-ed tumbling for ages five and six, boys' tumbling and gymnastics for ages five+, and tumbling/trampoline for ages six+. They also offer classes and coaching for tweens and teens, and a Special Stars tumbling/gymnastics program for children with special needs.

Sitar Center for the Arts
Kalorama, www.sitarcenter.org
The Sitar Center offers early childhood music classes for infants through age five, as well as collage art workshops for parents and kids.

Songcatchers
Falls Church, www.songcatchers.net
Songcatchers offers music classes for infants to age 16. Group classes, private lessons, summer camps, sibling classes, choral groups.

Spanish Amigos
Reston, www.spanish-amigos.com
Spanish Amigos offers playgroup-style Spanish immersion classes for ages two to six. Classes incorporate music, stories, crafts, worksheets, dialogue, and language videos, with an introduction to the culture of Spain and Latin America. Each lesson is theme-based.

> *"My daughter had an amazing experience with her Spanish Amigos playgroup. Having grown up in a bilingual family, I wanted to provide the same experience for my daughter, and Spanish Amigos helped nurture that environment."*
>
> *- Rhina*

Spanish for Children
Kensington, zifcamb@erols.com or 301.962.8795

Taught by Elizabeth Zifcak, this Spanish language program is geared toward ages two to six, with a parent or caregiver. Classes typically meet Saturday mornings. Contact Elizabeth for the current schedule.

Studio Serenity Yoga
Adams Morgan, www.studioserenity.com
Offers a four-week postpartum yoga class for mothers (or fathers!) and babies age five weeks to one year. They also offer a prenatal class and other events for women.

Takoma Park Rec Center
www.collabitat.com/tprecreation
The Rec Center in Takoma Park offers a variety of early childhood classes, including movement, music, and play for parent and child.

Tot Talk
Chevy Chase, tottalkpg@yahoo.com
Facilitated by Angela Harris (accompanied by "Beebo," the Baby Signs bear), this baby sign language playgroup meets at Chevy Chase Baptist Church. Classes are geared toward ages three months to three years, with a parent or caregiver.

The Little Gym
Potomac, Silver Spring, Germantown, Olney, Ashburn, Alexandria, Cascades, Sterling, Fairfax, and Springfield
www.thelittlegym.com
The Little Gym offers movement programs for ages four months to 12 years, designed to build motor skills and confidence. Classes incorporate movement, dance, gymnastics, sports, and games.

Tranquil Space Yoga
Dupont Circle, Bethesda
www.tranquilspace.com
Tranquil Space offers Baby & Me yoga for infants from birth to six months, as well as several children's yoga classes for preschoolers through tweens and teens. Classes offered at both Dupont and Bethesda studios.

> **author's note:**
> Between its Dupont and Bethesda studios, Tranquil Space
> offers one of the most comprehensive programs we've seen
> for children's yoga – starting at infancy with moms and
> continuing at developmentally appropriate stages through
> the tween and teen years.

Wee Play

Herndon, www.weeplayinfo.com
A hub for early childhood enrichment and just plain fun in Herndon.
Offers a range of classes for toddlers to age five, incorporating age-
appropriate activities including movement, music, puppets and
imaginative play, stories, fine motor manipulatives, and art/crafts
projects. They also host drop-in open play sessions, parent education
workshops, and special events.

WeeSpeak Spanish

Del Ray, Alexandria
www.weespeakspanish.com
Taught by founder Sharon Slatery, WeeSpeak brings Spanish to life
through play – including singing, dancing, games, and stories. Classes are
"Mommy (or Daddy) and Me"-style, so your participation is an important
part of the fun.
Brings Spanish to life for young children in a way they naturally learn and
enjoy themselves—through singing, dancing, games, and stories.

Willow Street Yoga

Takoma Park, Silver Spring, www.willowstreetyoga.com
Willow Street offers Parent/Baby yoga for infants not yet crawling, a kids'
class for ages five to eight and nine to 12, and a teen class for ages 13 to
16. Also many classes for adults and prenatal yoga.

YMCA of DC Metro Area

DC and suburbs
www.ymcawashdc.org
Offers a number of kids' classes, including pre-ballet for ages three to
five, creative movement and dance, tumbling, swimming, and art.
Schedules vary by location and time of year.

Yoga Tales
Bethesda, www.yogatales.com
Yoga tales offers classes and special events for children and families. Classes incorporate storytelling with yoga poses, as well as other age appropriate play activities such as music, props, and art. They offer a Moms & Babies Happy Hour (bring a brown bag lunch for a supportive chat session with your babies), a postpartum yoga class for mothers and infants four weeks old to crawling, a child/caregiver yoga class for ages two and three, a 45-minute independent class for potty-trained ages three to five, and additional classes divided by age groups for ages six to 18. In addition to family yoga for families with children age three and up, they also offer a mother/daughter yoga class, sports yoga for young athletes, and music yoga for budding music lovers. Hip-hop yoga for ages eight to 10 incorporates fun dance choreography.

CHAPTER 4
Support for Parents

Parenting is not for the faint of heart. But the DC area has a wealth of organizations, support groups, and resources to lighten the load. You are not alone!

DC'S FAVORITE SUPPORT GROUPS

Attachment Parenting International, DC Area Chapters

API-DC is the local chapter of Attachment Parenting International, a nonprofit network of parents and professionals who promote the principles of "attachment parenting." They hold support group meetings, referrals and speaker services, educational materials and research information, as well as playgroups. For more details, go to www.attachmentparentingdc.org.

DC Metro Dads

This is a nonprofit network of stay-at-home fathers who live in the DC metro area. The organization is open to stay-at-home fathers and those who are considering staying at home with their children, as well as single-parent dads who are their children's primary caregiver. In addition to its popular listserv discussion group, DC Metro Dads hosts playgroups, a monthly Dads Only night out, and an occasional luncheon for fathers and their kids. Activities also include field trips and formal playgroups that meet regularly in member homes. In addition to the umbrella group, chapters exist in Montgomery and Howard Counties and in the Bowie area. To learn more or to join, visit www.dcmetrodads.com.

DC Working Moms

DC Working Moms started as a listserv, but has evolved into a group that regularly meets for lunches, playgroups, and happy hours. The listserv itself is quite large, and recently moved from Yahoo! to Big Tent, where there are several active sub-groups for various interests and topics. For more info and to join the list, go to their website: www.dcworkingmoms.com.

ICAN of NoVa
ICAN of Northern Virginia "works to lower the rate of unnecessary cesareans, supports vaginal birth after cesarean (VBAC), and encourages positive birthing through education and advocacy." The group meets once a month and often features guest speakers. For information, call 703.237.6136 or go to www.icanofnova.org.

IFC
Interracial Family Circle (IFC) is a support group for interracial families, offering educational programs for members and the larger community. They also have a listserv and they sponsor social events and activities for young children and teenagers. For more info, visit www.interracialfamilycircle.org.

Mocha Moms of Southern DC
Mocha Moms is a local support group for stay-at-home mothers of color. Their platform includes "consciousness-raising, breastfeeding, attachment parenting, natural and holistic living, international sisterhood, nation-building, voluntary simplicity, community service, and education." For more info, go to www.southerndcmochamoms.com.

MOMS Club Chapters
MOMS Club has many, many active chapters throughout the DC metro area – For example, four chapters in the Silver Spring area alone! The International MOMS Club (Moms offering Moms Support) is a nonprofit organization providing support for mamas who chose to stay at home either full- or part-time to raise their children. Stated goals include "providing moral support to at-home mothers, providing a forum for topics of interest to women, giving mothers more of a voice in the community, and performing service projects, especially those benefiting children." Many MOMS chapters host playgroups, family activities, girls' night out, etc. To find the chapter in your neighborhood, visit the International MOMS Club website at www.momsclub.org.

Mothers & More of NoVa
This group of mamas who live in NoVa is for those who are juggling work and family, as an opportunity to network and share resources and support. They meet regularly and organize social events. Mothers & More

is a national organization, and this is their local chapter. Learn more about them at www.novamoms.org.

MONA

Mothers of North Arlington (MONA) is a support group for mamas who primarily stay at home with their children, including those who have home-based businesses or work part-time but are home with their children during the day. MONA holds regular meetings and social activities offering friendship and support. To find out more, go to www.monamoms.org.

MOPS

Mothers of Preschoolers (MOPS) is a faith-based Christian organization that "helps moms through relationships established in local groups, providing a caring atmosphere." They also share resources (including a website and radio program). To find out more, visit www.mops.org.

Mothers First

Mothers First is a nonprofit organization for mamas who are transitioning into stay-at-home motherhood. They hold bi-weekly support group meetings throughout the DC area, a lecture series, mom's night out, special interest groups, and children's/family activities. To find out more, visit www.mothersfirst.org or call 703.827.5922.

NINO Babywearing Group

This is the "Nine In Nine Out" (NINO) chapter for the DC metro area. They meet once a month (sometimes more). NINO is a nonprofit babywearing organization founded on the work of the anthropologist Ashley Montagu and his 1986 book, *Touching.* These mamas strive for "exterogestation" during the first nine months of a baby's life, which is facilitated by using a sling, wrap, or other soft carrier. To find out more or join their discussion online, visit http://groups.yahoo.com/group/nino_dc-md-va.

Northern Virginia Parents of Multiples (NVPOM)

This group has been around since 1969 and is made up of parents who have twins, triplets, or higher multiples. They hold regular monthly meetings, frequent social events, a "Big Sister" program, support activities for new mamas, playgroups, a monthly newsletter, and a

listserv. For more information, visit
http://groups.yahoo.com/group/nvpom.

Old Town Moms
This group of mamas who live in Old Town Alexandria and the
surrounding neighborhoods meets occasionally for lunch (little ones
welcome, but optional). Old Town Moms also have regular, weekly
playgroups organized by age, and an active listserv. The membership is
diverse, including both work-outside-the-home moms and full-time stay-
at-home moms. For more info, visit
http://groups.yahoo.com/group/oldtownmoms.

Outreach for Children with Gender-Variant Traits & Their Families
This is a monthly parenting support group sponsored by Children's
National Medical Center. It helps parents of children with gender-variant
behaviors "by affirming their uniqueness." For info, call 202.884.2504 or
send email to pgroup@cnmc.org.

Parents Without Partners
This group of single parents hosts picnics and outings, parent socials,
children's parties, and sports events in DC and Alexandria, as well as
sharing information, resources, and support. To find out more, call
703.354.6992 or visit www.parentswithoutpartners.org.

PG Parents Club
This is an organization for parents who live in and around Prince George's
County, Maryland. They share information through a listserv, organize
local activities and events, and host playgroups for infants through age
four. Their website also offers links and suggestions for kid-friendly places
to go. Open to all mamas and daddies, whether they work inside and/or
outside the home. To learn more, go to www.pgparents.com.

Postpartum Support International (PSI)
This national support network is made up of caring volunteers who are
knowledgeable about postpartum depression (PPD) and other mood
disorders that occur during pregnancy and after having a baby. PSI's
volunteers in the DC area are mothers who have personally faced – and
successfully overcome – PPD. There are several peer support groups
meeting regularly in the Washington metro area (NW DC, Arlington,

Fairfax). Volunteers can also share names and contact information for professionals throughout the metro area (including therapists and psychiatrists) who specialize in treating perinatal depression, anxiety, and other mood disorders. To visit the national PSI website, go to www.postpartum.net. For local support and information, contact DC Coordinator Lynne McIntyre at 202.744.3639 or lynne@lynnemcintyre.com; Virginia Coordinator Adrienne Griffen at 703.243.2904 or griffens@comcast.net; or Maryland coordinator Sara Evans at 301.869.6886 or sarajevans@gmail.com.

Postpartum Support Virginia

After many months of hard work and planning, our friend and longtime PPD advocate Adrienne Griffen launched a new not-for-profit organization serving women and families in NoVa and beyond. Postpartum Support Virginia offers one-on-one support and groups, resources and info for expectant and new mothers and their partners and families, and outreach to local communities. Adrienne, an Arlington mother of three, suffered from severe postpartum depression (PPD) after the birth of her second child. After struggling to find help and eventually getting her groove back, she vowed to improve resources and support for women in the DC area going through similar experiences. If you are suffering from symptoms of depression and/or anxiety during pregnancy or in the first year after having a baby, visit the website for more information and reach out for help – it's available: www.postpartumva.org, info@postpartumva.org.

See Mommy Run

This is a free-to-join network through a website, where you can locate or start your own running or walking group in the metro DC area. The DC-NoVa-suburban Maryland region has over 2,100 members, and the newest group in the fall of 2005 was the Ft. Washington "Moms on the Run." For details, go to www.seemommyrun.com.

Single Mothers By Choice

This group of single mamas – those who have made the decision to have a child or adopt a child as the primary caregiver – meets twice a month to network and share information and resources. To find out more, go to http://singlemothersbychoice.com.

SPAL (Subsequent Pregnancy After a Loss)
SPAL is a support group led by local mom Carolyn Mara, bringing together women who are pregnant again after experiencing the loss of a baby. They meet regularly in Falls Church, providing a safe, supportive environment in which to talk about concerns and fears, as well as to meet other women who understand what you've been through. For more info, contact Carolyn at 703.754.5836.

SPARK (Single Parents Raising Kids)
SPARK is an organization for single parents in Montgomery County and the surrounding Washington, DC suburbs. The group was founded by nine single parents in 1987. Their stated mission is "to build a community where single parents can share the knowledge and provide the mutual support needed to experience a rewarding life for ourselves while raising our children to be competent and well-adjusted people." SPARK hosts a full roster of family activities, education for parents, and social events. Among these are pot-luck dinners, outings to museums/concerts/theater, discussions and guest speakers on parenting issues, adult-only social gatherings, and lots of activities for families to attend together. They also have a members-only listserv. For more information or to join, visit www.corphome.com/spark.

DC'S FAVORITE LISTSERVS

A listserv group is a virtual community existing primarily through email and message board communication. Some groups also meet in person for playgroups or outings.

Each list has its own rules and protocol. Follow list etiquette and you'll find yourself among friends. When you sign up, take the time to read fully the guidelines for the list. It's always a nice gesture to introduce yourself to list members when you sign on, with a brief note about yourself and why you joined. One word of warning: Though over time you can build true friendships with list members, do take the precaution of guarding your child's personal information, your family's home address and phone number, etc. on the list at large. Then, if you join a related playgroup or meet up with another list member in real-time, you can share more about yourself at your discretion, one-on-one. While the vast majority of listserv members have only the best intentions, in rare cases an inappropriate individual signs up for a list under false pretenses. Even these folks are usually harmless – Typically looking to "spam" the group with unwanted advertising. Don't let this prevent you from getting involved – Just use common sense as your guide.

Listservs can be great sources of information, encouragement, and support. Whatever your interests, your needs, your belief system or your lifestyle, you'll probably find at least one listserv in the DC area where you feel at home. You might even make a friend for life.

AAPAC Montgomery County
AAPAC Montgomery County is the Asian American Parents Advocacy Council, with approximately 200 members. The group's stated mission is to "Support and speak on behalf of Asian American children and youth, assist Asian American parents in developing skills, encourage Asian American parent involvement in the schools, and foster linkages between the Asian American community and the larger community, inclusive of all groups with diverse backgrounds." To learn more or to join, visit http://groups.yahoo.com/group/AAPAC.

AU Park Parents
This steadily growing list keeps parents who live in (and around) the American University (AU) Park neighborhood of NW DC connected. For more details or to join, visit:
http://groups.yahoo.com/group/auparkparents.

Autism Maryland
This group has approximately 350 member families in Maryland who have a child with an Autism Spectrum Disorder (ASD). Members also include professionals who work with kids and adults who have ASDs. The list facilitates the sharing of information between parents and professionals and information about ASDs, as well as providing a forum for support and resources. Membership is free. To learn more or to join, visit http://health.groups.yahoo.com/group/Autism_Maryland.

Brookland Kids
This list is a virtual community with approximately 300 members, made up of parents to babies, toddlers, and preschoolers in the Brookland neighborhood of Washington, DC. For more details or to join, visit http://groups.yahoo.com/group/brookland_kids.

Culture at Home

Culture at Home is a group of approximately 200 African American homeschooling parents in the DC metro area. The group's stated mission is "to provide an educational outreach support program and to supplement the curriculum of homeschoolers with children ages 10 to 18, but we also provide some resources for homeschooled children ages six to 10. We emphasize excellence in literacy by offering a monthly reading group for ages six to 10, a children's Internet book club for ages 6 to 18, participation in the Annual African American Read-In, plus guided field trips, free books, study abroad programs, discounted performances in the arts, tutorial information, and museum outreach. Parental resources and information will also be provided to supplement and direct your homeschool experiences." To learn more or to join, visit http://groups.yahoo.com/group/cultureathome.

DC Expectant Moms

The DC Expectant Moms listserv has a membership of mamas-to-be from DC and throughout the metro area. The list is active but not overwhelming, and flame wars are virtually unheard of. These ladies are known to organize happy hour gatherings and other informal get-togethers, though none of these real-time events are required for membership on the list. The group is moderated by childbirth educator and mother-of-two Melody Kisor, who is a great help in answering pregnancy questions. Other members of the list include professionals from the local prenatal, birth, and pediatrics community who can share helpful information and resources with pregnant list members. Membership is free. To learn more or to join the group, visit http://health.groups.yahoo.com/group/dcexpectantmoms.

DC Extended Nursing

This listserv of approximately 125 members is a discussion and support forum for mamas in the DC area who are breastfeeding or plan to breastfeed their child past his or her first birthday. According to the listowner, "Topics may include benefits and challenges of nursing past one year, nursing through pregnancy, tandem nursing, handling criticism, nursing in public, when and how to wean, and more." Membership is free. To learn more or to join, visit http://groups.yahoo.com/group/dcextendednursing.

DC-Metro-China Playgroup
This group includes approximately 165 families from the DC metro area who have adopted children from China. The listserv is primarily a forum for posting info about play dates and social events. To learn more or to join, visit http://groups.yahoo.com/group/dc-metro-china-playgroup.

DC Metro Dads
This is the listserv for a network of stay-at-home fathers, the nonprofit organization known as DC Metro Dads. The list of about 300 members offers support and information to stay-at-home fathers, those who are considering staying at home with their children, and all primary-care fathers. In addition to the list, this organization has playgroups, a monthly Dads Only night out, and an occasional luncheon for fathers and their kids. Activities also include field trips and formal playgroups that meet regularly in member homes. In addition to the umbrella group, chapters exist in Montgomery and Howard Counties and in the Bowie area. To learn more or join the list, visit http://groups.yahoo.com/group/dcmetrodads. The organization's website is www.dcmetrodads.com.

DC Urban Moms
www.dcurbanmom.com
The DCUM list can be a lifesaver, no matter where in the metro area you live. One of Washington's best resources for pregnant women and parents of young children, DC Urban Moms was founded by a couple of local parents and has evolved into a busy, comprehensive support network for a diverse group of area residents. Not without its "flame wars," there's never a dull moment on the list – And for the most part members are respectful of each others' differences. If you can block out the occasional flame-fest where tempers ignite over a controversial topic, you'll find endless information that will make your life easier and a sense of cyberspace community that will surprise you with its warmth and generosity. There are many postings a day, but to help manage your in-box you can subscribe to the "digest" version, which consolidates posts into one email on a daily basis. Subscribe to the DCUM listserv group by visiting the website and following the instructions. As a list member you can also search the archives by keyword to find old posts on a particular subject – Most of which prove to be timeless! Another perk: Message

boards for mamas looking to form playgroups and a nanny job board at http://dcurbanmom.com/nannies. Membership is free.

Del Ray Parents
This list of about 350 members is for moms and dads who live in the Del Ray neighborhood of Alexandria (and surrounding neighborhoods). The list is active without being overwhelming in its volume of mail, and allows neighboring parents to share information, news, resources, and to meet for playdates. Membership is free. For more info or to join, go to http://groups.yahoo.com/group/delrayparents.

Dupont Circle Parents
This is a listserv of approximately 200 parents of babies and toddlers who live in the Dupont Circle neighborhood. Membership is free. To learn more or to join, visit http://groups.yahoo.com/group/dupontcircleparents.

Dupont-Logan Parents
This is a group of approximately 30 parents who live in Dupont Circle or Logan Circle. List messaging is light, but it's a good resource for socializing and sharing parenting advice and information. One of the group's stated goals is "to encourage community building and the development of Dupont Circle and Logan Circle as family-friendly neighborhoods. This is a restricted membership group, so after you apply you'll need to be approved by the moderator before you're "official." Membership is free. To apply for membership or to learn more, visit http://groups.yahoo.com/group/dupontloganparents.

Ft. Washington Moms
A relatively new, interactive group, Ft. Washington Moms invites mothers in the Ft. Washington/Accokeek/Temple Hills/Clinton/Waldorf area to join. Membership is free. Find out more or join the group by visiting http://groups.yahoo.com/group/fortwashingtonmoms.

Georgetown Moms
This list of about 200 Georgetown mamas is a nice source of information and support. Advertisers will be removed from this list, but recommendations for your favorite shops or services are fine!

Membership is free. To find out more or to join the group, visit
http://groups.yahoo.com/group/georgetownmoms.

Glover Park Families
This listserv with approximately 200 members is made up of families
living in the Glover Park neighborhood of DC. Members share advice,
recommendations, and connect with other interested parents.
Membership is free. To learn more or to join, visit
http://groups.yahoo.com/group/gloverparkfamilies.

The Joy Troupe
This laid-back and spunky group of Alexandria (and other NoVa) mamas
has no membership fees, but plenty of playgroups for children of all ages
– including groups for moms of kids with developmental delays, work-
away mamas, and expectant mothers. They also host a babysitting
exchange. To learn more, visit www.joytroupe.com.

Loudon Moms
Loudon Moms is an online forum and resource offering information on
Loudon County businesses and service providers relied upon by local
families. It's also a virtual networking space, allowing local mamas to
connect with each other, make new friends, form playgroups, etc. To
learn more, visit www.loudounmoms.com.

MD POBC
This group of about 60 members is made up of Maryland parents of blind
and visually impaired children. Their stated mission: "Sharing information,
offering support, and actively pursuing projects and programs in the best
interest of our children's lives." To learn more or to join, visit
http://groups.yahoo.com/group/mdpobc.

Metro DC Multiples Moms
This listserv of approximately 100 members links up mamas and mamas-
to-be of twins and other multiples. Members come from throughout the
DC metro area. Membership is free. To learn more or to join, visit
http://groups.yahoo.com/group/metrodcmultiplesmoms.

MOTH (Moms on the Hill)

MOTH welcomes all families living on Capitol Hill. Because they are both a virtual *and* real community, they have some concerns about privacy and ask that current members invite new members. Unlike some other parent groups, MOTH doesn't charge membership fees or require applications, but they reinforce their commitment to the neighborhood through the invitation process. To find out more, send email to momsonthehill-owner@yahoogroups.com.

NoVA Families for Natural Living

This list of approximately 400 members is a forum for families who want to explore natural alternatives. Their stated mission is to "offer support and education on topics such as nutrition, birth options, attachment parenting, vaccinations, alternative health choices, concern for the environment, and much more." In addition to the listserv, members have weekly gatherings (children welcome) at various NoVa locations, as well as family outings and monthly potlucks. Membership is free. To find out more or to join, visit http://groups.yahoo.com/group/nova-famnatliv.

NoVa Moms & Families (a.k.a. NoVaMoms)

The busy list of approximately 1,000 members draws mamas (and some daddies, too) from throughout the NoVa suburbs. The group's stated goal is "to help its busy members share information and make connections that support and enrich their parenting experiences." Members announce relevant upcoming events, share parenting tips and personal experiences, and do lots of networking that builds community. To learn more or to join the list, go to http://lists.topica.com/lists/novamoms.

Old Town Moms

Old Town Moms was founded by a group of mothers in Old Town Alexandria, but has since expanded to include those who live in the surrounding neighborhoods. All are welcome, including stay-at-home mamas and those who work outside the home. In addition to their active (but not overwhelming) list, Old Town Moms have other real-time activities, such as weekly playgroups divided by age and monthly lunch meet-ups. Membership is free.
To learn more or to join, visit
http://groups.yahoo.com/group/oldtownmoms.

Parents of Kids with Special Needs, DC

This brand-new and tiny listserv group has a lot of potential. It needs new and active members to grow! If you have a child with special needs and you live anywhere in the DC metro area, check it out. For details or to join, visit http://groups.yahoo.com/group/parentsofkidswithspecialneeds.

RF DC Dads

This group of approximately 200 members is for gay dads and dads-to-be. Members live in the DC metro area *only* – This is a requirement for membership. When joining the group, you need to include your neighborhood/city/town of residence, if it is not part of your Yahoo ID. In addition to the listserv, this group also gets together for socializing, playdates, and networking. To find out more, visit http://groups.yahoo.com/group/rfdcdads. To subscribe, send email to rfdcdads-subscribe@yahoogroups.com.

Silver Spring Mom's Swap

This group of about 60 mamas in Silver Spring is a support community that shares information and resources, parenting tips, outing ideas – and they also trade and sell items their kids have outgrown or no longer use. To learn more or to join, visit http://groups.yahoo.com/group/SS_Moms_Swap.

Southern Maryland Parents of Multiples

This listserv of about 50 members is made up of parents, expectant parents, grandparents, and guardians of multiples born in St. Mary's and Calvert Counties. Members share experience, advice, and information. To join, visit http://groups.yahoo.com/group/somdpom.

Students as Parents

This group is made up of approximately 125 parents of young children. Their commonality: All are students at the University of Maryland, College Park. Members share "social, informational, and political support." The group is diverse, including men and women, grad students and undergrads. For more information or to join, visit http://groups.yahoo.com/group/studentsasparents.

Takoma PAKK
Takoma PAKK is a group of about 900 parents who live in the Takoma Park community. They are actually an extension of the Takoma Park Family Resource Center, helping to connect and support local families. This is an active listserv that allows parents to find playgroups, field trips, local activities, coffee meet-ups, and support for themselves and their children. To find out more or to join, visit http://groups.yahoo.com/group/takomapakk.

Young Moms in Prince William County
A group of approximately 100 members, geared toward moms in their 20s and late teens who live in NoVa. Membership is free. To join, visit http://groups.yahoo.com/group/youngparentsnorthernva.

DC'S FAVORITE PARENTING CLASSES & CONSULTANTS

"Co-Parenting: Two Parents, Two Homes"
703.277.2666
This class is sponsored by the Fairfax County Parenting Education Center and features several sessions each month. It is designed for parents who are negotiating custody, visitation, and child support, with a focus on the responsibilities of parenting from separate households.

Francine Ronis, LPC
Francine Ronis is a therapist specializing in working with children, parents, and families. She also offers a popular parenting workshop, based on the principles of the bestseller "How to Talk So Kids Will Listen and Listen So Kids Will Talk." Francine is also a parent coach, with expertise in mindful parenting, attachment parenting, positive discipline, and meditation. Contact her at frgilbert@hotmail.com, or visit her website at www.francineronis.com.

Janna Sandmeyer, PhD
301.915.0995
Psychologist Dr. Janna Sandmeyer, whose office is located in downtown Bethesda, specializes in working with new mothers – both those who go back to work and those who stay home full-time. She offers an eight-week "Mommy Group" that focuses on newborn issues and encouraging mamas to connect with each other. Individual counseling is also available.

Maria Zimmitti, PhD & Associates
www.drzimmitti.com
Dr. Maria Zimmitti, also affectionately known inside the Beltway as "the potty lady," offers counseling/consulting for moms, children, and families. Her local renown comes from her particular skill in helping with the potty-training blues. Dr. Zimmitti and her team can help with everything from sleeping problems to shyness. And they now offer a series of nanny classes, as well as a group for emerging readers.

Momease
www.momease.com
Alexandria-based Momease offers a variety of parenting classes. Among them: A "Dadease Day," daddy's day to be with baby, meet other dads and their babies, and talk about fatherhood issues. The male facilitator can help the guys with basics like feeding and diaper changing, as well as more complex issues like the "baby blues" and relationship-maintenance. The two-hour course if offered monthly. Also offered: a "Momease Meeting" that combines an informal gathering of new mamas and their babies with CPR training and information on breastfeeding, childcare, family adjustments, and other topics the group decides on. Separate "Infant CPR" classes teach expecting and new parents, grandparents, and babysitters how to prevent, recognize, and provide care for an infant in an emergency, until medical personnel arrive. A "Breastfeeding Tips for Working Moms" class addresses the challenges and logistics of continuing to nurse after maternity leave is over. Finally, "Infant Massage" classes (for two months to crawling) teach mamas and daddies all you need to know to share soothing touch with your baby.

Parenting Playgroups
www.parentingplaygroups.com
Alexandria-based Parenting Playgroups, founded by developmental psychologist Dr. Rene Hackney, offers a one-of-a-kind toddler program. It combines a comprehensive parenting course with a well-managed and equipped playgroup program for children 15 to 36 months. They also offer a popular positive discipline course for the parents of children three to eight years old, and many other parenting workshops throughout the year. One-day intensive versions of some of these classes offer a condensed option for time-challenged parents.

PACE (Parent & Communication Education)
www.pacemoms.org
Parent and Community Education (PACE) is a support group for new mamas with infants up to six months. Originally known as Parents After Childbirth Education, the group has been around since 1973. They meet for eight sessions of two hours each, with locations in DC, Montgomery County, and NoVa. Topics include eating, sleeping, emotional attachment, safety, relationships, and parenting issues. Most groups continue as playgroups after the PACE sessions end. Groups are available for first-time mamas, second-time mamas, and for workplace settings.

"Parenting with Confidence" Coffeehouse
www.kayabrams.com
Dr. Kay Abrams leads a "Parenting with Confidence" coffeehouse one evening a month in Kensington, September through May. She offers her perspective on becoming a calm, confident parent and maximizing your relationship with your children. The sessions incorporate lots of time for Q&A. She also offers private consultations and sessions for parents.

PEP
www.parentencouragement.org
Parent Encouragement Program (PEP) offers education, skills training, and support for parents. Their classes and workshops cover everything from sibling relationships to positive discipline, from managing anger to holding a "family council." Parents of newborns through teenagers can take PEP classes in Alexandria, Chevy Chase/DC, Gaithersburg, Kensington, Reston, Rockville, and Silver Spring. Groups of 10-20 people (such as playgroups or PTAs) can also host PEP classes on-site. See the website for a full and updated calendar.

"Siblings Without Rivalry" Workshops
www.jenniferkogan.com
Professionally facilitated by Jennifer Kogan, LICSW, LCSW-C, this workshop is based on the well-respected book by Adele Faber and Elaine Mazlish. Groups meet in NW DC once a week for six sessions. For more info and the current schedule, visit the website or call 202.215.2790.

The Sleep Lady
www.sleeplady.com
DC mamas swear by Kim West, a.k.a. "The Sleep Lady." Based out of her
Annapolis office, West offers a phone class on newborn sleep, private
evaluations and phone coaching sessions for the parents of young
children. She's seen it all, she knows what she's doing, and she's fearless!
She can help you tackle the toughest sleeping issues with your babies and
young children.

The Women's Center of Northern Virginia
133 Park St. NE, Vienna
703.281.2657
1101 15th Street NW, Suite 202
202.293.4580
www.thewomenscenter.org
The nonprofit Women's Center provides counseling and education for
women and their families in both NoVa and DC, regardless of ability to
pay. Available counseling can include psychological, career, financial, and
legal. They offer many support groups centered on topics ranging from
"Eating Awareness" to "Healthy Relationships" to "Postpartum
Depression," filled with supportive people who have the same issues and
a professional therapist.

Trans-PARENTING:
703.219.2198
This class, offered at locations in Prince William County, Fairfax County,
and Springfield, offers parents "an opportunity to shift their attention
from the personal aspects of divorce or separation to the needs of their
children."

DC'S FAVORITE COUNSELING/THERAPY

Nancy Markoe, LCSW-C & Deborah Horan, LCSW-C
Counseling Associates of Metropolitan Washington
www.dccounseling.com
Nancy and Deborah offer individual and group counseling, as well as

professionally-facilitated support groups for both new moms and their babies and for moms-only (geared toward mothers of infants to preschoolers). They are based in Bethesda. For more info, contact Nancy at 202.494.6840 or Deborah at 301.325.3052.

The Counseling Center of Fairfax
www.ccf-web.com
The Counseling Center of Fairfax is a group of 15+ counselors and clinical psychologists with a range of specializations. On their staff, Terri Adams has been repeatedly recommended to us and has expertise in areas including: adoption and birth parent counseling, postpartum depression (PPD), women and couples facing fertility problems, women and couples dealing with miscarriage/stillbirth or the loss of a child, and couples therapy.

DCJCC New Parents Group
www.dcjcc.org
Professionally facilitated by Sarah Gershman, a Jewish Education Associate at the DC Jewish Community Center (DCJCC) and a social worker, this six-week group focuses on new parents. In a warm and informal discussion group setting, you get the opportunity to share the joys and struggles of being a new family, in the company of other new parents. For more info, send email to sarahg@dcjcc.org or call 202.77.3237.

Jennifer Grosman, PhD
Based in NW DC, clinical psychologist Dr. Jennifer Grosman specializes in women's issues and the challenges of mothering, and she is experienced in treating postpartum depression (PPD) and other perinatal mood disorders. To contact Dr. Grosman's office, call 202.363.8200.

Jennifer Kogan, LICSW, LCSW-C
www.jenniferkogan.com
Clinical social worker Jen Kogan provides individual and group therapy, as well as therapeutic support groups just for moms of babies and toddlers in Friendship Heights, NW DC. For more info, send email to jenniferkogan@verizon.net or call 202.215.2790.

The Adele Lebowitz Center for Youth & Families
www.wspdc.org/alc.htm
The Lebowitz Center in Friendship Heights, NW DC offers a therapeutic support group for both new and experienced mothers, as well as individual therapy, information and referrals, and a full spectrum of mental health care. Sliding scale fee options are available for those in financial need.

Francine Ronis, LPC
Francine Ronis is a therapist specializing in working with children, parents, and families. She also offers a popular parenting workshop based on the principles of the bestseller, "How to Talk So Kids Will Listen & Listen So Kids Will Talk." Francine is also a parent coach, with expertise in mindful parenting, attachment parenting, positive discipline, and meditation. Contact her at frgilbert@hotmail.com, or visit her website at www.francineronis.com.

Janna Sandmeyer, PhD
301.915.0995
Psychologist Dr. Janna Sandmeyer, whose office is located in downtown Bethesda, specializes in working with new mothers – both those who go back to work and those who stay home full-time. She offers both individual and group therapy.

The Women's Center of Northern Virginia
133 Park St. NE, Vienna
703.281.2657
1101 15th Street NW, Suite 202
202.293.4580
www.thewomenscenter.org
The nonprofit Women's Center provides counseling and education for women and their families in both NoVa and DC, regardless of ability to pay. Available counseling can include psychological, career, financial, and legal. They offer many support groups centered on topics ranging from "Eating Awareness" to "Healthy Relationships" to "Postpartum Depression," filled with supportive people who have the same issues and a professional therapist.

DC'S FAVORITE ON THE RADIO

"Parents' Perspective"
www.parentsperspective.org
"Parents' Perspective" features interviews with experts on a wide range
of parenting issues, produced and hosted by longtime DC residents Sandy
Burt and Linda Perlis. Its mission: "Giving parents the tools to help
themselves." Recent topics have included food safety, bullying at school,
happy babies and toddlers, parental guilt, sibling rivalry, and helping
children to manage their anger. If you're an early riser, you can catch it
Saturday and Sunday mornings at 5:30 a.m. on 1050 AM, Federal News
Radio, or at 6:30 a.m. on WRNR-FM (103.1) and WINX-FM (94.3). The
latest airing is on Sunday mornings at 7:30 a.m. on Z-104 (104.1).
Podcasts are also available on their website.

CHAPTER 5
Out & About

PLANNING AHEAD FOR SPONTANEITY

Thinking of leaving the house? Ironically, planning can promote spontaneity – especially when hitting the town with wee ones. If you're relatively prepared, you'll be free to enjoy your children without stressing over details and unpleasant surprises along the way.

A few tips:

- Nothing kills the spirit of family fun like packing up the goods, trekking all the way to your destination, and finding out it's closed. Call and/or visit the website before you go. Schedules, policies, and rates do change, so verify the details before you head out the door.
- Remember that hours can vary on holidays and during tourist seasons, so even if you've been to a destination before, it's still wise to call ahead.
- Don't forget to ask about discounts for families or "kids free" policies, even if such perks aren't advertised.
- If you take metro, remember that no public restroom facilities are available and that kids under age four ride FREE.
- In this security-conscious era, be prepared to have your bags checked and/or to go through metal detectors when you arrive at your destination.
- If they're old enough to understand, make a "just in case" plan with your kids. Designate a meeting spot in case you get separated, and be sure your children know how to recognize a security guard or museum docent so they can get help. It should go without saying that you never take your eyes off a small child, especially in a crowded place.

DC'S FAVORITE RESOURCE FOR OUTINGS & EVENTS

The Our Kids Newsletter
www.our-kids.com

The "Our Kids" e-mail newsletter, founded in 1999 and owned and managed by DC-area mama Amy Miller, is chock full of current events for the whole family. Over the years it has received rave reviews in *The Washington Post*, *The Observer*, WTOP Radio's "Mommy Track," and many others.

For a modest annual subscription fee, you get a weekly e-newsletter providing by far the best and most comprehensive calendar of events, activities, and entertainment for children and families. Our Kids covers the District, NoVa, and suburban Maryland – so no matter where you live in the DC metro area, you're going to find this an indispensible resource. From storytimes to live children's performances, from kids' movies to seasonal festivals and holiday happenings, it's all covered – complete with web links and contact info to help plan your outing. Our Kids also offers great promotions and discounts on area shows and events, a classified section for buying and selling children's items, information about area consignment sales, summer camp/preschool/private school coverage, first-hand reviews of area attractions from a parent's and kid's eye view, rainy-day destinations, and so much more. OurKids.com – the website affiliated with the newsletter – recently underwent a fabulous redesign. It offers an accessible database of area resources for pregnant women and parents with children of all ages.

We have been subscribers to Our Kids since moving to the DC area, and it's the one publication we consistently turn to for checking what's going on in our neighborhood and for planning our family fun. Refer a friend, and you can earn bonus time on your own subscription.

WE ALSO LIKE TO CONSULT:

***Washington Parent* magazine**
www.washingtonparent.com

***Washington Post*'s City Guide-Kids**
www.washingtonpost.com/wp-srv/cityguide/dc-kids-activities.html

Daily Candy – DC Kids Edition
http://www.dailycandy.com/kids

DC'S FAVORITE OUTINGS, TODDLERS TO KINDERGARTENERS

Rock Creek Park
5200 Glover Rd. NW
Stables at 5100 Glover Rd. NW, between 16th St. and Connecticut, south of Military Rd.
Nature Center: 202.895.6070
Stables: 202.362.0117
www.nps.gov/rocr
Metro-accessible: No

Rock Creek Park is DC's biggest stretch of natural beauty, and it has a lot to offer families. Pony rides (reservations required) are 15 minutes through the woods, ideal for ages four to seven. A teenage guide holds the reins, and kids are encouraged to pat their pony before and after the ride. On one-hour rides, guides take groups of riders age 12 and up along lovely wooded trails. The park's nature center houses all sorts of natural history from the mid-Atlantic area, and preschoolers can produce puppet shows in the Discovery Room. Computer setups for elementary-age children introduce the park's ecosystem, and a 75-seat planetarium is fun for stargazers, offering free Wednesday afternoon and weekend shows appropriate for ages four and up. Near the nature center are several trails for hiking. "Discovery Packs" are available at the center for kids, containing a field microscope, a magnifying lens, and binoculars. If you've got a stroller or a preschooler, we recommend the Edge of the Woods trail, which is a flat loop that makes for a 20-minute walk. Along the way your kids will get to see a small pond where tadpoles swim in the spring. Older children will probably prefer the Woodland Trail, which is more of a 60-minute trek. Rangers lead weekend hikes on this trail. *Heads Up:* Rock Creek Park is open from sunrise to sunset, but the nature center is only open Wednesday through Sunday, and pony rides are a weekend thing. Trail rides for older folks are typically scheduled on weekend afternoons (several times available) and one or two afternoons a week. Call or visit the website to confirm.

National Zoo
3001 Connecticut Ave. NW
202.673.4800 or 202.673.4717
www.si.edu/natzoo or www.fonz.org
Metro-accessible: Yes, Cleveland Park or Woodley Park / Zoo

Considerable renovation has been done – and is ongoing – at the National Zoo in DC, officially part of the Smithsonian Institution. In addition to the famous pandas, your kids might want to check out the Reptile Discovery Center, the Amazonian tropical rain forest, or the Great Flight Room where the birds fly free. In the Think Tank you can see orangutans who have learned to communicate with researchers using touch-screen computers. The sea lions and seals perform daily at approximately 11:30 a.m. All of the animals are most active in the coolest part of the day, when you'll also miss some of the crowds. Best times to visit the zoo are spring and fall, when there are fewer tourists in town and the weather is mild. There are several snack bars and two restaurants on the zoo premises. Lines at the snack bars and restaurants can be oh-so-long in summertime, so be forewarned. You can also bring a picnic – The best spot might be the grassy, hilly area at the back of the zoo, across from the farm exhibit where kids can see ducks, cows, goats, chickens, and other domesticated types. One of the best National Zoo offerings is their free summer concert series, "Sunset Serenades," which runs Thursday evenings from June through early August. Performances range from rock to jazz to folk and blues. Bring a picnic or purchase snacks. Strollers are available for rent on-site, if you don't want to lug your own. *Heads Up:* If you're taking the metro and are not in the mood to push a stroller uphill, get off at Cleveland Park instead of Woodley. Parking is available at the zoo for those who drive, but it fills up early in the morning during the summer and most weekends year-round. Parking in the neighborhood surrounding the zoo is a nightmare. Don't do it!

Saturday Mornings at the National
1321 Pennsylvania Ave. NW
202.783.3372
www.nationaltheatre.org/saturday/saturday.htm
Metro-accessible: Yes, Metro Center

"Saturday Mornings at the National" are just for families. Free shows run mid-September to early April, typically with two seatings at 9:30 and 11 a.m. On any given Saturday you might see juggling, magic, clowning, dance, music, or storytelling. These shows are incredibly popular, so you need to arrive early. Distribution happens 30 minutes before each showtime. Visit their website for the calendar.

Lake Accotink Park
7500 Accotink Park Rd., Springfield, VA
703.569.3464
Metro-accessible: No

This Springfield Park has lots to do, in a really pretty environment. In addition to walking trails around the lake, you can rent paddle boats, fish, play on the playground, and take a spin on the kiddie carousel. Plenty of parking is available at the entrance. Can get pretty busy during nice weather.

National Aquarium in DC
14th & Constitution Ave. NW
202.482.2825
www.nationalaquarium.com
Ages: One +
Metro-accessible: Yes, Federal Triangle

The National Aquarium, which has been around since the nineteenth century, is open year-round from 9 a.m. to 5 p.m. in the basement of the Department of Commerce. The museum is small and far more understated than Baltimore's aquarium, but this is a plus for young children. Wide aisles accommodate strollers, it's rarely crowded, and you can make the rounds in less than half an hour – Perfect for a toddler's attention span. There is a touch-pool where kids can get up close and personal with whelks, hermit crabs, and horseshoe crabs. The aquarium has more than 250 species, including alligators, clownfish, piranhas, and spiny lobsters. Shark feeding and piranha feeding happens at approximately 2 p.m., three days a week. Call for details. *Heads Up:* Though ticket prices are very affordable and kids under age two get in free, the National Aquarium could really use an extra donation on your way out the door. The site was saved by a group of citizens after the feds withdrew funding over 20 years ago. And as of early 2008, the aquarium's financial survival is said to be up in the air.

National Aquarium in Baltimore
501 E. Pratt St., Baltimore, MD
410.576.3800 or TYY/TDD 410.625.0720
Help with purchasing tickets online: 410.659.4278
www.aqua.org
Metro-accessible: No

If your kids adore fishtanks as much as our daughter does – or if the DC aquarium is too small and cozy for your liking – this day trip is a must. I especially love the atmosphere that comes along with its Inner Harbor location. We advise buying tickets in advance. To avoid the intense crowds, come first thing in the morning or on a weekday. Summer can be insane with tourists. Several dining areas of varying price ranges are on-site at the aquarium. Some are outdoors and only open seasonally. You can arrange to have box lunches prepared for your family before you arrive by calling catering services at 410.659.4299 or emailing your order to boxlunch@aqua.org. *Heads Up:* Because of the issues created by escalators and other people-movers inside, be prepared to check your stroller when you enter the aquarium. You may NOT bring it inside. The staff will store it for you and will provide a backpack child carrier. The upside is, a baby or young toddler can see better from this vantage point anyway, and you're not constantly playing bumper cars with other strollers as you try to navigate the aquarium. On the downside, your child might be "between" ideal ages to enjoy this outing – Too small to be able to walk independently without running off or getting exhausted, too big to happily ride in the backpack-carrier. Keep it in mind.

Good Hope Sprayground
14715 Good Hope Rd., Silver Spring, MD
301.989.1210
www.montgomerycountymd.gov
Ages: Toddlers +
Metro-accessible: No

Good Hope Sprayground isn't a swimming pool, but it's managed as such by Montgomery County Parks and Recreation. It's a splash area on a flat surface, with water spraying from six standing features. Toddlers and preschoolers LOVE this place, and it's perfect for a muggy summer day. As with most public pools, the kiddos need to be closely supervised. There's no running allowed, they can't bring toys (though some of the lifeguards are lenient on this point), and diaper-wearers must have on fitted plastic pants. Bring towels as you would at a traditional pool, and wear swimsuits. No street shoes or clothing allowed. Open strictly in summertime.

Boat Rides at the C&O Canal Historical Park
202.653.5190
www.nps.gov/choh
Metro-accessible: Yes, Foggy Bottom

Take a mule-drawn barge ride along the C&O Canal. Most kids love the mules – Ada, Frances, Katie, and Rhody – who pull the 12-ft.-wide barge along the towpath and under the bridge at Thomas Jefferson St. The trek is less than a mile, but the pace is, well, "leisurely." The guides are entertaining, with jokes and songs along the way. *Heads Up:* If you need to feed the family before or after the ride, Washington Harbour is at 3000 K St. NW, with several restaurants in the mixed-use complex. Best for kids might be Tony and Joe's (202.944.4545), where you can sit outside near the water.

National Capital Trolley Museum
1313 Bonifant Rd., Colesville, MD
301.384.6088
www.dctrolley.org
Metro-accessible: No

For the train-lover in all of us. The 20-minute trolley ride goes through a wooded area of just under two miles. Kids can look for animals like foxes, rabbits, and deer along the way. Luckily for squirmy toddlers, the trolley stops once during the ride, providing a break where kids can walk around. The museum itself has 17 trolley cars, which are all out for the springtime Calvalcade of Cars and the Fall Open House, both of which include music and craft activities. Santa goes along for the ride during the Holly Trolleyfest in December. *Heads Up*: Hours vary by season, so be sure to call ahead or check the website.

The Strathmore's Family Concerts
Tuckerman at Rockville Pike, North Bethesda, MD
301.581.5100
www.strathmore.org
Metro-accessible: Yes, Grosvenor

North Bethesda's swanky Strathmore hosts a couple of free outdoor family concerts on summer evenings. In 2005, DinoRock and SteveSongs made the kids go wild. These events are held at the center's Gudelsky Concert Pavilion, and no reservations are required. Food, ice cream, snacks, and drinks are for sale on-site during the concerts. You can also pre-order a picnic basket for your family – The delish menu has sandwiches, entrees, wine and cheese, and YES, a children's meal. *Heads Up*: Parking for the family series is located at the Grosvenor-Strathmore metro station and along Tuckerman Ln.

"The Pit" (a.k.a. the JetBlue Airways Toddler Play Center)
Dulles Town Center, Dulles, VA
703.404.7120
www.shopdullestowncenter.com

"The Pit" at Dulles Town Center isn't as ominous as it sounds. Think "cockpit." If you have an airplane-obsessed preschooler, it might be paradise. This free play area is a soft-sculpture mini airport terminal with its own baggage cart, control tower, slide, and cockpit for kids to crawl all over. Sound effects and lights make it feel almost high-tech, and there's bench-style padded seating surrounding the play area for parents to keep a watchful eye. Weekday mornings are best if you want to avoid crowds.

The Kennedy Center
2700 F St. NW (New Hampshire @ Rock Creek Pkwy.)
202.467.4600
www.kennedy-center.org
Metro-accessible: Yes, Foggy Bottom

Visiting the Kennedy Center is free, but children's performances range from free to approx. $15. Check the website for a current calendar and all the details of each production. The center hosts dozens of family events from September through May at their Imagination Celebration. These events incorporate storytelling, dancing, music, and puppet shows. Kinderkonzerts by the National Sympony Orchestra are fun, and if you arrive early your kids might get invited to clang around on some of the instruments. Also, non-reservation events held in the evenings on the Millennium Stage are intended to introduce kids to opera or classical music. In September the center hosts an open house, and a stage is devoted to children's performances. *Heads Up:* Crawlers and toddlers enjoy the wide, carpeted staircases at the Kennedy Center, where they zoom around safely before being corralled back into the stroller. Good, free fun for a rainy-day outing.

Claude Moore Colonial Farm at Turkey Run
6310 Georgetown Pike, McLean, VA
703.442.7557
www.1771.org
Metro-accessible: No

A charming colonial farm in suburban Virginia, dating to the 1770s. Guides dressed in period costume demonstrate many aspects of colonial life, and for most kids the farm animals are the highlight. A dirt path – walkable for most preschoolers who are in the mood and passable by a stroller if *you're* in the mood – skirts the barn, orchards, a pond, a small farmhouse, and a hog pen. Market fairs held on the third full weekends of May, July, and October feature Colonial craft-making for families, music, and puppet shows. Picnic tables are located at the entrance. *Heads Up*: Bathrooms are strictly "port-a-potty."

Children's Shows at Arlington Cinema & Drafthouse
2903 Columbia Pike, Arlington
703.486.2345
www.arlingtondrafthouse.com

The Arlington Cinema & Drafthouse offers many family-friendly, smoke-free events, including live entertainment for children of all ages. Several live music or magic show events are scheduled each month, featuring favorite kids' performers such as Rocknocerus, The Great Zucchini, Mr. Knick Knack, Uncle Pete, and The Magic of Joe Romano. Complete details and the current calendar are available on the website.

Imagination Stage
4908 Auburn Ave., Bethesda
www.imaginationstage.org
Metro-accessible: Yes, Bethesda

Imagination Stage produces shows year-round in the beautiful 400-seat Lerner Family Theatre. They do a range of productions – many appropriate for school-age children, but also a smattering of productions appropriate for preschoolers. From literary adaptations to innovative world premieres commissioned especially for their audience to classic plays, Imagination Stage is a class act with beautiful, professional productions. They also offer a nice lineup of early childhood enrichment classes and summer day camp programs for all ages. Subscribe to their free e-newsletter to keep up with the latest offerings and coming productions.

Way Off Broadway Children's Theater
5 Willowdale Dr., Frederick, MD
301.662.6600
www.wayoffbroadway.com
Metro-accessible: No

Children's plays are staged on Saturdays, with an admission price of approximately $10 per person (inclusive of lunch and drink). Shows do tend to book up early, so advance reservations are a must. Most productions last one hour and are appropriate for kids ages three to 12.

Discovery Creek Children's Museum
7300 MacArthur Blvd., Glen Echo, MD
202.337.5111
www.discoverycreek.org
Metro-accessible: No

Discovery Creek, located at Glen Echo Park and open on weekends, is an outdoor museum with a children's botanical garden, a wetlands area with an underground tunnel and bamboo trails, and a stable with a climbing wall. The space is small and the nature trails in the woods behind the site are lovely. Preschoolers will like Minnehaha Creek, where they can look for crayfish and navigate the stepping stones. *Heads Up:* Wear good walking shoes and be prepared to hold your child's hand on some segments of the trail.

Glen Echo Park
7300 MacArthur Blvd. @ Goldsboro Rd., Glen Echo, MD
301.492.6282
www.nps.gov/glec
www.thepuppetco.org
www.adventuretheatre.org
Metro-accessible: No

We love, love, love this place! It's like a step back in time. The Clara Barton National Historic Site (free), a carousel, puppet shows, and children's plays are all part of the fun at Glen Echo Park in suburban Maryland. There's lots of space for kids to romp freely, a playground, picnic benches, and plenty of shade. The Discovery Creek Children's Museum is located within this park. A snack bar is located on the grounds and picnic tables are available. *Heads Up:* Advance reservations are strongly recommended for the puppet shows and plays. And even with advance tix, arrive early to get a decent seat!

Discovery Theater at the Smithsonian
Ripley Center on the National Mall
202.633.8700
www.discoverytheater.org
Metro-accessible: Yes, Smithsonian

We think the Discovery Theater's new home is a delight. Tucked away in a not-so-easy-to-find but peaceful location underground in the Ripley Center (the copper-domed kiosk on Jefferson Dr., between the Castle and the Freer Gallery), the new space is well outfitted for kids' productions. The live performances staged at the Discovery are fabulous – ranging from kiddie rock groups to puppet shows to dance troupes from the DC area and around the world. Tickets are affordable and may be purchased in advance online (highly recommended). Sign up for their mailing list and you'll receive a performance calendar each season. Trying to park in the area is difficult to impossible, but the Smithsonian metro stop is a very short walk from the Ripley Center's domed entrance. More good news: There are elevators in the Ripley Center, and there is stroller parking inside Discovery Theater. *Heads Up:* When attending summertime shows, keep in mind that the theater will be well attended by day-camp groups. Be sure to get your tix online in advance, and show up early. The staff generally does a good job of shepherding families and small groups into the theater for priority seating, and dismissing them before turning the campers loose.

National Air & Space Museum
Jefferson or Independence @ Sixth St. SW
202.357.2700 or TDD 202.357.1729
Theater & Planetarium: 202.357.1686 or TDD 202.357.1505
www.nasm.edu
Metro-accessible: Yes, L'Enfant Plaza

The most popular of all Smithsonian museums, Air & Space is most beloved by kids. As a result, the place gets super-crowded. Try to visit on a weekday, or be there when the doors open in the morning. Historic planes hang from the vaulted ceilings, you can walk through the "backup" version of the Skylab and touch the moon rock, and you can sit in a Cessna cockpit. The "Explore the Universe" exhibit features telescopes, and the favorite IMAX film for children is "To Fly!" Also visit the Albert Einstein Planetarium and take the 20-minute tour. There's a good view of the Mall and the Capitol from upstairs, and a cafeteria is on-site. (Or your kids can eat like the astronauts do by purchasing freeze-dried space food at the gift shop!) Movies and planetarium shows have lines and sell out in the blink of an eye, so smart parents buy tickets in advance. *Heads Up:* Strollers are not allowed at the IMAX movies, which are intended for kids age four +.

Great Falls
11710 MacArthur Blvd., Potomac, MD
301.299.3613 or 301.767.3714
www.nps.gov/choh
Metro-accessible: No

You can visit the falls from either the Maryland side or the Virginia side, but the Maryland side is better for young kids. (The Virginia side is best for rock climbers). You can't swim or wade here, but you can fish, walk the trails, and enjoy the view of the beautiful waterfall. Info and a trail map are available at the tavern (a.k.a. visitor's center), where there is a display about the canal and its locks at kids-eye-view and protected by glass. Folks who have learned the hard way will tell you to avoid the Billy Goat Trail and the Gold Mine Loop with children, as they are too long and challenging. For the best waterfall view, take the stroller-friendly walkway to Olmsted Island. *Heads Up:* A snack bar is open spring through fall, just north of the "tavern." Picnics are fun, too. Cost for vehicle entrance at Great Falls is around $5, and is good for visiting both sides of the falls for up to three days.

National Gallery of Art
401 Constitution Ave. NW
Children's Film Program: 202.789.3030
Stories in Art Program: 202.789.3030
www.nga.gov/kids/kids.htm
Metro-accessible: Yes, Smithsonian or Archives

The National Gallery has a neat - and free - children's film series, held in the East Building's auditorium. They select great movies that your kiddos might not otherwise see. For example, they recently screened the classic "Babar: King of the Elephants," adapted from the Laurent de Brunhoff series of books. The schedule tends to include smart, beautiful, age-appropriate movies that provide a breath of fresh air – a nice break from the blockbuster Disneys at the major theaters. Check the website for a full film schedule, descriptions of the movies, and age recommendations. NGA also offers drop-in workshops for families with kids of different ages. These focus on the work of a single artist and are led by the museum educators with hands-on art activities, games, and films. Drop-in workshops are free for families with kids ages five +. Check the website for the current program dates, times, and topics. You can also sign up online for the family programs mailing list. Finally, NGA sponsors "Stories in Art," introducing kids to works of art using storytelling. Each program includes reading a children's book, a visit to the galleries, and a hands-on activity. This program is free for kids age four to eight accompanied by an adult. For all of these programs, no registration is required but space is limited. *Heads Up:* For a parent caring for an infant during the week, the NGA also provides a wonderful way to get out of the house but avoid steamy, frigid, or otherwise miserable weather. Strolling the galleries when they are relatively quiet and peaceful can make your day.

Sculpture Garden of the National Gallery of Art
Fourth St. & Constitution Ave. NW
202.737.4215 or TDD 202.842.6176
www.nga.gov/kids
Metro-accessible: Yes, Archives (or Smithsonian, or Judiciary Square)

A destination unto itself, the outdoor sculpture garden on the National Mall is fun for kids during nice weather. Spring through fall the big water fountain is a-flowin', and kids can toss pennies or splash their feet. (No actual wading or swimming, please!) In winter the fountain becomes an ice-skating rink. The oversized, contemporary sculpture in the garden are fun to look at, though you can't let kids climb on most of the art (check the signs near each piece). The one exception is "Six-Part Seating" by Scott Burton, whose granite chairs can be kid-tested. Children can also peek through the windows of Lichtenstein's "House I" (great photo opp).

Tip: The lovely Pavilion Café in the sculpture garden has sandwiches and other eats. *Heads Up:* The Sculpture Garden closes at 5 p.m. Monday through Saturday, and at 6 p.m. on Sunday – So don't plan a twilight stroll or you'll end up disappointed.

East Potomac Park
1100 Ohio Dr. SW @ Maine Ave.
202.485.9880
www.nps.gov/nacc
Metro-accessible: No

While some attractions have a charge (mini golf, tennis, golf, swimming), most of East Potomac Park is free and open to the public. There are picnic facilities and a golf course snack bar where you can purchase burgers or sandwiches. Maine Ave. is also dotted with seafood restaurants. Kids love playing on the much-larger-than-life sculptures on this 300+-acre stretch of park stretching from the Tidal Basin between the Washington Channel and the Potomac. Fishing along the Potomac is okay with a permit (202.727.4582). *Heads Up:* The swimming pool does not have a baby pool OR a diving board, and is open only between Memorial Day and Labor Day.

National Harbor
Potomac-front, Prince George's County, MD
www.nationalharbor.com
Metro-accessible: No, but there's plenty of parking, or you can take the water taxi from Old Town

Development of the National Harbor has come a long way since the first edition of this book was published in 2005. You can now take a water taxi from the Old Town Alexandria waterfront to the Harbor for a cost of about $14 round trip per person. The 20-minute ride across the river takes you to the burgeoning city-within-a-city, with the centerpiece Gaylord Convention Center. A nice respite from the heat on a summer day, with plenty of indoor fountains and abundant A/C! Little ones will love riding the glass elevators and walking the marina and piers. And the still-in-development National Children's Museum, which will eventually call the National Harbor home, sponsors Saturday family events at the Harbor's American Market (check their site at www.ccm.org for details). Also enjoyable for families: Seasonal events year-round, such as a summer concert series, Oktoberfest, and the Taste of Maryland foodie extravaganza. Casual restaurants and shopping abound, too. Sign up for their free e-newsletter at the website.

Leesburg Animal Park

19270 James Monroe Hwy. (U.S. 15) Leesburg, VA
703.433.0002
www.leesburganimalpark.com
Metro-accessible: No

Leesburg Animal Park has all the farm animals you might expect, plus exotics like llamas, antelope, and squirrel monkeys. Most animals are very friendly and will approach you for affection, though shy kids can keep their distance by looking at animals in stalls. Children can pet and feed the baby goats or ride the ponies. On weekends the park features live children's entertainment. A playground features sandboxes, a merry-go-round, slides, and a jungle gym. Admission cost is approx $8 for ages 13+, with a discount for ages two-12 and under-twos free. During October the park hosts Pumpkinville, which is best visited on a weekday to avoid the crowds. *Heads Up:* Hours vary according to the season, so be sure to call or visit the website.

Kenilworth National Aquatic Gardens

1550 Anacostia Ave. NE
202.426.6905
www.nps.gov/kepa
Metro-accessible: No

One of DC's secret treasures. Known to locals as "the lily ponds," the aquatic gardens in NE Washington are free and open to the public year-round. The site is a 12-acre national park alive with birds, water lilies and other plants, frogs, and turtles. Several trails intersect among the ponds. Morning is best for seeing the flowers at their prime, and water lilies flower through summer. Treasure-hunt lists are available for young kids, and they change every few months. Finding Kenilworth has baffled many a driver, so check the website, call ahead for directions, and bring a cell phone so you can call if you get lost en route. *Heads Up:* Keep a close eye on preschoolers at Kenilworth, as rocks can be slippery and you will be surrounded by water (albeit not deep). Have kids wear clothes that can get dirty, and wear comfortable walking shoes.

Bob Brown Puppet Productions
1415 S. Queen St., Arlington, VA
703.319.9102
www.bobbrownpuppets.com
Ages: Three +

Bob Brown and his puppets do shows at Fairfax County parks, theaters, schools, and often at the Wolf Trap summer theatre for children. Call or visit the website for a schedule of upcoming productions.

Long Branch Nature Center
625 S. Carlin Spring Rd., Arlington, VA
(703) 228-6535
www.co.arlington.va.us

Long Branch is a charming little nature center with a great "Children's Discovery Room," live animal displays, a viewing pond, gardens, and trails (some of which are stroller accessible). But their claim to fame among kids is the evening feeding of the center's flying squirrels. Yes, flying squirrels! Call to check the current feeding time (typically between 5:30 and 5 p.m.), and if you go during chilly weather seasons when it gets dark early, be sure to dress warmly and bring a flashlight. *Heads Up:* The nature center is closed on Mondays (but open Tuesday through Saturday from 10 a.m. to 5 p.m., and Sundays from 1 to 5 p.m.).

National Museum of Natural History
Constitution Ave. & Tenth St. NW
202.357.2700

www.nmnh.si.edu
Metro-accessible: Yes, Smithsonian

In the Discovery Room kids can get hands-on, which is, of course, their favorite way of learning. For some live action, visit the Orkin Insect Zoo, where your children will see all manner of creepy crawlies doing their thing. From the ants to the giant roaches, kids love this stuff. And of course there's Henry, the enormous stuffed elephant in Natural History's rotunda, and the impressive Dinosaur Hall. *Heads Up:* Though the museum is open daily from 10 a.m. to 5:30 p.m., the Discovery Room keeps more limited hours and is closed on Mondays. Be sure to visit their website or call ahead for times.

Wheaton Regional Park
2000 Shorefield Rd., Wheaton, MD
Nature Center: 1400 Glenallan Ave.
Gardens: 1800 Glenallan Ave.
301.680.3803
Nature Center: 301.946.9071
Gardens: 301.949.8230
www.mc-mncppc.org and www.brooksidegardens.org
Metro-accessible: No

Where to begin? This is one cool park. Young kids love the little red train and its 10-minute tours through the woods, the carousel, the huge sandbox complete with castle, the big playground with its wooden bridges and mazes, the slides of all sizes, the life-sized camel statue, or the wooden Jeeps with their big plastic steering wheels. The park also has basketball courts, an ice rink, tennis courts, trails, a baseball field, and the Brookside Nature Center, which has lots of free and discounted programs all year long. From April to June they offer a 45-minute nature-related storytime on Saturday mornings, with times arranged by age groups. A different story is featured each week, followed by a simple craft project. No registration is required, but call ahead to find out the current schedule. They also sponsor puppet shows and summer camps, and the kids love the nature center's live turtles, fish, and snakes. Brookside Gardens, next to the nature center, has seasonal displays of flowers and a gorgeous azalea garden. They hold an annual children's day on a Saturday in September with songs and games. In winter they do a strictly secular stroll (no Santa, crèche, or menorah), The Garden of Lights. Faux animals are aglow, as well as the trees and flowers.

Carousel on the National Mall
1000 Jefferson Dr. SW, on the Mall near the Smithsonian "castle"
202.357.2700
Metro-accessible: Yes, Smithsonian or Archives/Navy Memorial

The old-fashioned carousel on the National Mall is a memory-maker, and it's very affordable. The carousel runs 10 a.m. to 5:30 p.m. most days of the year. *Heads Up:* Occasionally the carousel is inexplicably shut down. The carousel works best as an outing combined with something else on the National Mall, so that you have something else on the agenda in case the horsies are "resting."

Union Station
50 Massachusetts Ave. NE
202.289.1908
www.unionstationdc.com
Metro-accessible: Yes, Union Station

Union Station is THE most visited tourist attraction in DC. Okay, so it helps that it has its own metro stop, is an Amtrak hub, and occupies prime real estate in Capitol Hill. But in truth, Union Station is worth a visit simply to bask in the Beaux-arts architecture and do some people watching. It just so happens that you can also shop and eat there (shops are open from 10 a.m. to 9 p.m. Monday through Saturday, and noon to 6 p.m. on Sunday). Also at Union Station: a nine-screen movie complex, three sightseeing companies (Gray Line, Old Town Trolley, and Tourmobile), plenty of parking, and beautiful décor (complete with a live tree and a Norwegian model train exhibit) during the Christmas holidays. Completed in 1908, Union Station has been a city within a city for 100 years. Over time it has housed Turkish baths, a police station, a YMCA, a butcher, a mortuary, a bowling alley, a hotel, and a liquor store. (Sorry, no longer.) Tours of the building are also available to groups of 15-20, by reservation only. *Heads Up:* As of fall 2008, the Union Station parking garage is still (yes, still) under renovation. At our last visit, there was no elevator for transporting a stroller from the mezzanine level of the garage into the station entrance itself. We happened to make this discovery as a tropical storm dumped torrential rain on the city! So if you drive to the station and bring a stroller, you'll need an extra set of hands to help you fold it and transport the kids down the escalator or stairs.

Alden Theatre
1234 Ingleside Av., McLean
703.790.9223
www.mcleancenter.org
Metro-accessible: No

Alden Theatre is housed at the McLean Community Center, and I love that it has plenty of parking. (A feature never underestimated with those who have multiple kids and/or strollers in tow.) Children's performances are appropriate for ages three +. Check their website for this season's calendar.

Wolf Trap National Park for the Performing Arts
1551 Wolf Trap Rd., off Rt. 7, Vienna
703.255.1860
Theater: 703.255.1827
Festival: 703.642.0862
www.wolftrap.org
Metro-accessible: No

Every summer Wolf Trap sponsors Theatre-in-the-Woods especially for children. The lineup changes every year but has featured children's musicians, puppeteers, storytellers, jugglers, dancers, and clowns. Some events affiliated with Theatre-in-the-Woods also offer workshops for kids ages five +. Before or after the Theatre-in-the-Woods performances, kids love to run through the park, picnic in the shade, and roll down the hills. Tickets are about $4 for kids age three+. In September, Wolf Trap also sponsors a week-long International Children's Festival with performances and music from cultures around the world. Three stages (including a covered amphitheater) feature puppet shows, clowns, and dancing. There is face-painting and an arts/technology pavilion for the older kids with computer and video setups. Tickets to the festival typically run $10 for ages 13+ and about $8 for ages three-12, with under-threes free. Heads-Up: Since food attracts bees and animals, it's not allowed at Theatre-in-the-Woods, with the exception of bottled water. If you bring picnic food, they ask that you keep it well wrapped until after the performance, when you are welcome to picnic (and fend off bees) on your own.

National Building Museum
401 F. St. NW
202.272.2448
www.nbm.org
Metro-accessible: Yes, Judiciary Square

Wanna escape the Smithsonian museum crowds? Is it freezing – or blistering – outside and your little one needs to crawl/walk/run/let off some steam? Get thee to the National Building Museum, pronto. For one thing, it's free. (Donations are appreciated, of course.) The Great Hall is an absolutely gorgeous, colossal space, often quiet and vacant, where toddlers can zoom around safely. The National Building Museum is open seven days a week, from mid- to late-morning (depending on the day) until 5 p.m., and is just across the street from a Red Line metro stop. Older preschoolers will enjoy touching models of the White House and the Capitol. The shop has nice gifts, and the museum's High Noon Café serves lunch. If you've got a sleepyhead in a stroller, you might enjoy taking one of the tours. After all, the museum has hosted 15 presidential inaugural balls and boasts some of the largest Corinthian columns in the world.

Free Summer Concerts at Pottery Barn Kids Stores
Locations at White Flint Mall in Bethesda, Fair Oaks Mall in Fairfax, Tysons Corner in McLean
Ages: Infants +
Metro-accessible: Feasible with bus connections
www.potterybarnkids.com

Pottery Barn Kids stores in the DC area host free summer children's concerts featuring well-known local acts that kids love. Recent performers have included Oh Susannah! and Bill Wellington. Show times are typically Tuesday or Thursday mornings, but call the store or visit the website for the current schedule.

Explore & Moore Children's Museum
12904 Occoquan Rd., Woodbridge, VA
703.492.2222
Ages: Two+
Metro-accessible: No
www.exploreandmoore.com

This small children's museum is hands-on, with an emphasis on exploration. There are more than 20 exhibits – among them a dance studio, shadow freeze room, climbing wall, toddler room, bubble room, sandbox, dress-up closet, puppet theater, fossil find, magnet play, beauty parlor, and space room. Photos of some of the exhibits are viewable on their website. *Heads Up:* The museum has not only a diaper changing station, but a nursing area. (High-five!)

Classika Theatre
4041 S. 28th St., Arlington, VA
703.824.6200
www.classika.org

Classika's Green Puppet Theatre will rivet the youngest audiences and makes for a fun introduction to the stage. They also host summer camps and workshops for kids, as well as outreach programs with local schools and community groups. Check their website for this season's calendar, where you can also order tickets online.

South Germantown Splash Playground
18056 Central Park Circle, Boyds, MD
www.mc-mncppc.org/parks
Metro-accessible: No

It costs a coupla bucks to get in, but when the weather is hot and sticky in Washington, the joy your little ones (and you) will get from this water playground is well worth it. Gazillions of jets and stationary toys spray the place with cool water. The restrooms won't make you run screaming, and there's even a snack bar.

Port Discovery
35 Market Place, Baltimore, MD
410.727.8120
www.portdiscovery.org
Metro-accessible: You can reach it via Baltimore's light rail system, or by MTA subway service at the Market Place / Shot Tower stop

Worth a day trip to Baltimore! *Child* magazine named Port Discovery one of the top five children's museums in the country in 2002. It's a big, contemporary place with three floors of interactive joy for toddlers through age 12. (Though don't rule out bringing a toddler, since there are mini-versions of some features, such as the "urban treehouse," and they recently added more exhibits for the two- to five-year-old crowd.) Check out their calendar of children's performances, including music, storytelling, theater, puppet shows, and even karaoke. The museum also features an art workshop, a construction/building area, a fun '50s-style diner where kids can serve their parents in linoleum booths, a play gas station and garage, an indoor soccer field, a mystery game, and various traveling/rotating exhibits. If you want to avoid crowds, go first thing in the morning or on a weekday. Summers are extra crowded with tourists. *Heads Up:* Port Discovery is closed on Mondays, except on select Maryland school holidays. On the weekends, museum guests can park for reduced rates at Central Parking's Harbor Park Garage, adjacent to the museum at the corner of Lombard St. and Market Place. Bring your parking ticket to the Port Discovery box office to get it validated.

Burke Lake Park
7315 Ox Rd., Fairfax Station, VA
703-323-6601
www.co.fairfax.va.us/parks/lakefront.htm
Metro-accessible: No

Burke Lake Park makes a fun family outing, with a shady playground, a train, carousel, a new mini golf course, an ice cream parlor, and plenty of space to have a picnic – complete with grills. The train and carousel cost approximately $1.50, with under-twos riding for free. The park has a 218-acre lake where you can rent rowboats, fish, take a tourboat ride, or camp. Non-residents may need to pay an entrance fee on the weekends, so call ahead or check their website for details.

Huntley Meadows Park
3701 Lockheed Blvd., Alexandria, VA
703.768.2525
www.fairfaxcounty.gov
Metro-accessible: No

A beautiful and fun place to introduce your baby or toddler to nature. Trails are wide enough for strollers and there's plenty of shade, making for lovely walks. Older preschoolers can watch for turtles, birds, frogs, and other critters. Can't metro, but there's plenty of parking.

Arlington Schools Planetarium
1426 N. Quincy St. Arlington, VA
703.228.6070
www.arlington.k12.va.us/instruct/science/planetarium

Smaller than the Air and Space Museum's planetarium – and thus cozier, with an intimate feel – the Arlington Schools Planetarium is a little-known gem. Unlike many school planetariums, this one is open to the public. They have several low-key programs that are folksy in a charming sort of way, and the cost is low – approximately $1.50 for kids under age 12 and seniors, $2.50 for the rest of us. Shows typically run Friday through Sunday and the first Monday of each month. Call for current times.

Jeepers
700 Hungerford Dr., Rockville, MD
301.982.2444
www.jeepers.com
Metro-accessible: No

Jeepers is an indoor amusement park and arcade for kids age two to 12, part of a national chain. They have rides and games, a softplay area, food, and they offer birthday party packages. Admission is free, though the activities and food are not. Discount coupons may be printed from their website. On the rides, adults get on board free with their child. Personally, the noise and overstimulation make me want to pull my hair out by the roots – But that in no way means your young one won't ADORE it. In fact, this is kid heaven.

Biking the Capital Crescent Trail
Access from several locations, including downtown Bethesda and Georgetown
Recorded info. about the trail: 202.234.4874
www.cctrail.org
Metro-accessible: Yes, Bethesda

The Capital Crescent Trail may well be the safest and best place in DC to bike with a young child in tow. Its southern-most seven-mile stretch links Georgetown and Bethesda with a nine-foot-wide asphalt surface that's in great condition. (A crushed gravel surface links Bethesda to Silver Spring via a new-ish tunnel.) Weekends are the most crowded on the trail, and on weekdays the trail is mostly populated by bike commuters going to work. If you want to get on the trail at its head in Georgetown, go to the western end of Water St. NW (underneath the Whitehurst Freeway and Key Bridge). The first few miles will give you beautiful views along the Potomac and the C&O Canal. Next, you'll cross Canal Rd. heading north, where the sightseeing is mostly high-rent real estate. Overpasses are located at the most-traveled crossings (including at River Rd.), and you'll go through a tunnel under MacArthur Blvd. The trail ends at Bethesda Ave., a couple of blocks west of Wisconsin Ave. Visit the website for maps, photos, history, safety updates, and more details. *Heads Up:* Walkers and runners should always stay to the right on the trail, and leave the headphones at home so you can hear what's happening around you. Bikers are urged to keep their speed reasonable, yield when approaching slower-moving trail users, and give audible signals if you're approaching to pass.

Biking the Mt. Vernon Trail
Access from several locations, including the GW Parkway and Old Town
Alexandria
www.nps.gov/gwmp/mvtmap.html
Metro-accessible: Yes, Reagan National Airport or King St.

Over 17 miles long, the Mt. Vernon Trail stretches along the Potomac
from Roosevelt Island to George's lovely old estate. If you get a thrill out
of watching airplanes land over your head (and who doesn't, really?),
stop at Gravelly Point at the north end of National's main runway. There's
no better view of the monuments and the river, in my opinion, and the
segment between Old Town Alexandria and Mt. Vernon is really pretty –
Winding through the woods along the shore, and with several nice picnic
spots to boot. (Just be aware that passing through Alexandria can get
tricky, because there are two route choices, and both are "on street." The
best of the two routes does not follow Pitt St. through town, but follows
Union St., with better access to waterfront parks and Old Town's
restaurants. This preferred route is easy to miss, so check out the online
map before you get rolling.) This is one of the area's oldest trails, and in
some spots it's narrow and winding – Consider getting off the bike and
walking it across narrow bridges, for example, when you have a child
attached! The surface is paved and several improvements (including
widening and resurfacing) have been tackled recently. Expect lots of
traffic on the trail on weekends and when the weather is nice.

Imagination Stage
4908 Auburn Ave., Bethesda, MD
301.280.1660 or TTY 301.718.8813
www.imaginationstage.org
Metro-accessible: Yes, Bethesda

Tickets range between $9 and $15 for productions at Imagination Stage,
which has done some lovely renditions of world classics. Recently
produced were Charlotte's Web, Perfectly Persephone, and James and
the Giant Peach, as well as a thriller for kids ages nine +, Callisto 5. Shows
run an hour and a half and typically are best for ages four+. They also

offer kids' classes in drama, music, dance, filmmaking, and the visual arts. *Heads Up:* Season tickets are available, and you can purchase online.

"Mom & Baby" Matinee Movies
www.consolidatedmovies.com/movie_mom.asp
www.nationalamusements.com/programs/baby_pictures.asp
http://loews.bipnet.com/reelmoms
www.arlingtondrafthouse.com
Ages: Newborns and pre-crawling older infants who are likely to be content in a sling, stroller, or your lap
Metro-accessible: Yes, for some of the participating theaters

Several area theaters – such as some owned by Loews, National and Consolidated, plus the Arlington Cinema & Drafthouse, host "moms with babies" movies once a week or once a month, usually mid-day. This is a chance for caregivers of small infants to get out of the house and relax in the presence of other parents who also have babies in tow. Lights are low, sound is slightly reduced, and no one will give it a second thought if your little darling wails in the middle of the film or if you need to nurse. Parents are free to get up and walk the aisle or lobby with baby.

College Park Aviation Museum
1985 Corporal Frank Scott Dr., College Park, MD
301.864.6029
Metro-accessible: Yes, College Park
www.pgparks.com/places/historic/cpam

Part of the Smithsonian Institution's affiliate program, the College Park Aviation Museum is located on the site of the College Park Airport, listed on the National Register of Historic Places. This is the world's oldest continuously-operating airport. It features a 1919 airmail hangar on the grounds, and your kids can watch the runway through the glass as pilots take off and land. The gallery has historic and reproduction aircraft on display. *Heads Up:* Although this is a Smithsonian affiliate, the Aviation Museum DOES charge admission. Check their website or call for current rates.

Maryland Science Center
601 Light St., Baltimore, MD
410.685.5225
www.mdsci.org
Metro-accessible: MARC trains and light rail stop at Camden Yards, four
blocks from the Science Center

Maryland Science Center is a well-kept secret among DC parents, many of
whom are more than happy to make the occasional day trip to Baltimore
in exchange for a good time. The Kids Room is a bright play space
designed for toddlers and preschoolers. A special area for the under-two
set, "Room to Grow," has squishy waterbeds and big, soft blocks to play
on. For all ages there's water play, Lego towers, dress-up costumes, and a
pretend fishing pier, deep sea covers, and Baltimore streetscape.
Consider scheduling your visit to coincide with one of the Maryland
Science Center's storytimes. Infant story time for ages birth to 18 months
is typically held on Thursday mornings and includes music and movement.
Preschool storytimes are usually on Tuesday mornings and Friday
afternoons, and include music, movement, and science activities. (As
always, call or check the website to confirm.) *Heads Up:* If you've already
exhausted the Inner Harbour stroll or your toddler is a restless hair-puller
who won't tolerate riding around in the Baltimore Aquarium's backpack-
carriers, Maryland Science Center is a dream come true. You can even
bring your stroller inside.

U.S. Botanic Garden
First St. SW, on the National Mall between Maryland Ave. and C St.
www.usbg.gov
Metro-accessible: Yes, Federal Center SW or Capital South

On a dreary cold day, or if you've got an infant in a stroller or sling and
just need to get out of the house, the U.S. Botanic Garden might be good
for your soul. You'll be surrounded by lush, warm, green and beautiful
blooming things, no matter what the season. Toddlers will love the sights
and sounds of crickets and frogs, and most young kids will really enjoy the
overall sensory experience of the gardens. There's also a neato model
train set. Admission is free, and the indoor conservatory (newly

remodeled) is open from 10 a.m. to 5 p.m. daily. The outdoor Bartholdi Park welcomes visitors from early morning until dusk.

Planet Play, Springfield Mall
6500 Springfield Mall, Springfield, VA
703.313.6770
www.planetplayspringfield.com
Metro-accessible: No

Planet Play has a two-story spiral slide, a moon bounce, a ball pit, bumper cars, and a carousel. When it gets crowded, this place can be overwhelming for a young toddler, so shy children and the newest walkers might do best to visit during off-peak hours, preferably on a weekday. Admission costs range from $2 to $11, depending on the activities you child is interested in. Call ahead for current times. There are additional locations in Burke (703.425.0007) and Centerville (703.502.7888), but they don't have as many features as the Springfield Planet Play.

Reston Zoo
1228 Hunter Mill Rd., Vienna, VA
703.757.6222
www.restonzoo.com
Metro-accessible: No

In the Main Barn of Reston's 30-acre zoo you'll find bottle-fed baby lambs, giraffes, ostrich, monkeys, camels, zebras, bison, and antelope. The Reston Zoo is also home to African lion cubs, and they offer safari wagon rides and pony rides for the kids. The best thing about this zoo is that it allows children to get up close and personal with many of the animals, incorporating a traditional petting zoo alongside exhibits featuring wild and exotics. Season passes are available, but be aware that they shut down from late November through mid-March. Toddlers under age two get in free.

Rollingcrest Chillum Splash Pool

6122 Sargent Rd., Chillum, MD
301.853.9115 or TTY 301.445.4512
www.pgparks.com

Perfect, perfect, perfect for young kids, especially in the dead of winter.
The Chillum Splash Pool, in the Hyattsville area just north of DC, is an
indoor playground in the middle of a wading pool, in addition to a child-
sized training pool, a heated 20-yard lap pool with a drop slide and lily
pad walk, a heated family pool with beach grade entry, a tube slide, an
otter slide, locker rooms with coin-operated lockers, and a family
changing room. Best of all, it's open YEAR-ROUND. They also host
swimming lessons, water aerobics classes, and deep water exercise
classes. Check the PG Parks website or call the Chillum Splash Pool for
current hours.

Eastern Market

7th St. & North Carolina Ave. SE
www.easternmarket.net
Metro-accessible: Yes, Eastern Market

We adore Eastern Market in the Capitol Hill neighborhood, one of the last
remaining public markets in the city. Especially on weekends when the
weather is mild, little ones will enjoy the being strolled around while
people-watching and taking in the bustle. The perk for parents is the
opportunity to shop local vendors for fresh foods, flowers, art, and
jewelry. Though recently damaged in a massive fire, Eastern Market is
being rebuilt AND is open with vendors in the meantime.

Children's Shows at Jammin' Java

227 Maple Ave. E., Vienna
703.255.1556
www.jamminjava.com

Jammin' Java is widely regarded as one of the best places to see live
music in the DC area. In addition to featuring national and regional
touring acts for the grownups, they also offer a full calendar of the best

children's bands and singer-songwriters – both local and touring acts. While the kiddie shows were once free admission (sorry, no more), and now require paid admission, these events are well worth the ticket price. The lineup includes both weekday and weekend shows, with performers such as Mr. Don, the Banjo Man, Rocknocerus, Jammin' Mamas, Mr. Knick Knack, Justin Roberts, Oh Susannah!, Buck Howdy, Cat's Pajamas, Thaddeus Rex, and many more. Go to the website to sign up for their kids' entertainment mailing list.

BOOGIE FEVER COMES TO DC:
Baby Loves Disco
Since the first edition of this book was published in 2005, national phenom Baby Loves Disco has taken DC's youngest movers and groovers by storm. This unique, hot-ticket family dance party is held monthly at the scrappy Rock & Roll Hotel, near Capitol Hill. Professional DJs spin classic 70s disco tunes for the dance floor, amid juice-boxes and snacks and bubbles and balloons and hoola-hoops and percussion instruments galore. They've tricked out the scene for all ages, with quieter spaces upstairs. Also upstairs: A balloon artist, face-painting, and more. Did we mention the adult drinks available at the cash bar? Like we said, fun for all ages. www.babylovesdisco.com

---

DC'S FAVORITE PLAYGROUPS

Below is just a smattering of the most well-known playgroups in and around DC. By nature, playgroups are informally organized, so this list couldn't possibly be comprehensive. If you don't find something appropriate in your neck of the woods, ask neighbors and friends about a group near you, or start your own!

Most playgroups are free or have a low-cost membership. Many of them are informal neighborhood groups or based on a shared special interest. A few combine parenting education with a more structured children's activity, or are closer to a co-op preschool model, and these come with fees. Ask up front about membership requirements – including any materials, membership costs, or volunteer commitment on the part of parents – to avoid surprises.

Playgroups can be a great way to meet other parents with similar interests, help your child make new friends, and get out of the house for some fun. Here are a few of the best-known:

Amigas Vecinas Spanish Playgroup
http://www.geocities.com/amigas_y_vecinas

Attachment Parenting Playgroup
www.attachmentparentingdc.org

Benning Stoddert Co-Op Playgroup, SE DC
Benning Stoddert Rec Center: 202.645.3956

Blue Igloo Playgroup
Georgetown, DC, 202.965.2488

Chevy Chase Community Center Co-Op Playgroup
Chevy Chase Community Center: 202.282.2204

DC International Families (Bicultural) Playgroup
Dc & metro area
http://groups.yahoo.com/group/DCinternationalfamilies

DC Parks & Rec Co-Op Playgroups
http://dpr.dc.gov/dpr

DC Working Moms Playgroups
DC & metro area
http://groups.yahoo.com/group/dcworkingmoms

Emery Rec Center Co-Op Playgroup
NW DC
Emery Rec Center: 202.576.3210

Friendship Rec Center Co-Op Playgroup
Friendship Rec Center: 202.282.2198

Intown Playgroup
Georgetown, DC, 202.337.2720

Japanese Playgroup
DC & metro area
Naoko Masaya, coordinator: naokomasaya@hotmail.com

The Joy Troupe
Alexandria & greater NoVa
www.joytruope.com

Langdon Park Co-Op Playgroup, NE DC
Langdon Park Community Center: 202.576.6596

Lee Center Co-Op Playgroup, Arlington County
Membership Coordinator: 703.34.060

Madison Center Co-Op Playgroup, Arlington County
Madison Center: 703.351.6238

Maryland Mommies Playgroup
http://groups.yahoo.com/group/MarylandMommies

MOMS Clubs Playgroups
Throughout DC metro area
www.momsclub.com

Mothers First Weekly Playgroups
NoVa & suburban Maryland
703.827.5922

Northern Virginia Parents of Multiples Playgroup
http://groups.yahoo.com/group/nvpom

Old Town Moms Playgroups
Old Town Alexandria & surrounding neighborhoods
http://groups.yahoo.com/group/oldtownmoms

Playgroup Moms of Maryland
Montgomery County
http://groups.yahoo.com/group/playgroupmomsofmd

PG Parents Playgroup
Prince George's County, Maryland
www.pgparents.org
http://groups.yahoo.com/group/pgparents

Stoddert Rec Center Co-Op Playgroup, Upper NW DC
Stoddert Rec Center: 202.282.2193

Swedish-Speaking Playgroup
DC & metro area
http://groups.yahoo.com/group/lekgruppDC

Tot Lot Playgroups, Suburban Maryland
www.thetotlot.org

Turtle Park Co-Op Playgroup
AU Park/Tenley, NW DC
Janet Smith, 202.282.0710 or http://turtlepark.org

Upper Montgomery County Playgroup
http://groups.yahoo.com/group/uppermontgomerycountyplaygroup

Volta Park Co-Op Playgroup
Georgetown, DC
Friends of Volta Park: 202.342.7424

SPEAKING OF PLAYGROUNDS
We were quoted in a June 24, 2007 story in the Washington Post spotlighting the crème de la crème of DC-area playgrounds:

Sarah Masterson, author of DC BABY...says she favors playgrounds that are sheltered from sun and traffic while still being open and welcoming.

"Since play is really the work of childhood, my favorite playgrounds offer many different types of challenges," she says. *"They may have a space for getting your hands in the sand or dirt to dig and build; wider open spaces for running and jumping and kicking a ball; climbing, swinging, and sliding; and transitional spaces for imaginative play."*

Post reporter Rina Rapuano reviewed and recommended several of our favorites – a mix of longtime neighborhood favorites and new-on-the-scene spots:

Clemyjontri Park in Mclean (www.clemypark.com)
Discovery Park in Sterling (www.sullypto.com)
Friendship/Turtle Park in NW DC (www.turtlepark.org)
Hadley's Playground in Potomac
(www.montgomeryparks.org)
Watkins Regional Park in Upper Marlboro
(www.pgparks.com/places/parks/watkins.html)

OUR FAVORITE PLAYGROUND: DC

Friendship Park (a.k.a. Turtle Park)
AU Park / Tenleytown, DC, Van Ness St. NW at 45th St.
Info: 202.282.2198
www.turtlepark.org

Turtle Park is our nostalgic favorite in the District. Great for infants to early school-age children, this beautifully landscaped and recently updated playground in NW DC's AU Park neighborhood is a joy to visit – and has been for several generations. Playscapes and slides for all ages abound (tall, short, and several in-between), as well as pint-sized climb-on turtles, a huge sandbox area with digging toys, swings for babies and big kids alike, push-toys and ride-on toys, a shady (and always clean) picnic area, a clean bathroom facility just steps away, and a "sprayground" splash play area where water shoots up out of the ground in summertime. The playscape and swing area is well padded with plenty of wood chips, and a safety fence surrounds the entire area. For parents and older kids, it's handy that a nice tennis court and basketball court are next door – the playground is a DC Parks & Rec site, and is part of the Friendship Rec Center.

Structured activities held here are many and varied. In the dead of winter, Saturday morning storytimes can be a lifesaver for parent sanity. They often include dancing, songs, finger plays, and snack time. The "host of the week" organizes each storytime gathering. "Turtle Time" play periods two afternoons a week give little ones a chance for open romping in the clubhouse. For a suggested donation of $5 per family, kids (with an adult supervisor in tow) can play, paint, read, and unwind with their peers. A different parent takes a turn organizing each playtime, and volunteers are always welcome. Parks & Rec Director Vince Cain also helps to oversee the fun. The annual ice cream social features a local children's performer, and Halloween is a big celebration each year. Friendship Park is also hosts the Northwest Little League and the Home Run Baseball Camp.

Plenty of street parking is available. During the week Turtle Park is frequented by nannies and stay-at-home parents, and on the weekends you'll see families, grandparents, and birthday parties. It can get crowded during nice weather, but the space is so well laid-out that it's usually not a problem. It's the centerpiece of a close-knit community of neighborhood families. Many of the parents (and nannies) who visit Turtle Park know each other by name.

To inquire about reserving the park, call 202.671.4135 or visit www.dpr.dc.gov.

Regulars take great pride in this play space and have formed Friends of Turtle Park, dedicated to keeping it a charming place to visit. New volunteers and charitable, tax-deductible donations are always appreciated. Check the website and find out how to get involved.

OUR FAVORITE PLAYGROUND: NoVa

Clemyjontri Park (a.k.a. Clemy Park)
6317 Georgetown Pike, Mclean
Info: 703.388.2807
www.clemypark.com

In June 2007, not long after the grand opening of Clemy Park, the *DC Baby* blog reviewed this new jewel:

"On my day off, [my daughter and I] headed to the brand-new and much-praised Clemyjontri Park in Mclean. We were not disappointed! As playgrounds go, this is holy ground. And...I have to recommend a visit. The two-acre Clemy Park, made up of four large playspace "rooms" encircling a central carousel, is accessible to all ages and abilities, beautifully and thoughtfully designed. We love the carousel, and really appreciate the covered picnic pavilion (as well as several additional picnic benches under shade trees) and the large, clean restrooms just steps away from the play equipment.

Some of my daughter's favorite features at the huge, sprawling Clemy space: The maze for chasing and hiding in, the low-to-the-ground monkey bars, plastic rock-climbing wall with oversized handles for even the littlest climbers, the big rainbow-hued arches, the balance beams and big yellow swings, and the mock fire truck. Clemy's soft surface is ideal for crawlers and early walkers, and is easy to navigate for children in wheelchairs or using special walkers. A soft-surface track circles the entire playground, so you can bring your favorite ride-on toy. And if you want a spin on the (lovely) carousel, be sure to have quarters or $1 bills on hand.

Even though we're not Mclean residents, we've found getting to Clemy a breeze. It's a quick jump off the GW Parkway, and well worth the trip! "

OUR FAVORITE PLAYGROUND: SUBURBAN MARYLAND

Hadley's Playground (a.k.a. Falls Road Park)
12600 Falls Rd., Potomac
Info: 301.299.0024
http://mcparkandplanning.org/parks

We first took our daughter to Hadley's Playground in Potomac when she was a barely-walking toddler and I was doing my research for the first edition of this book. It was such a hit with our toddler, and we were immediately impressed with how accessible and progressive the playground's design is. A few years later, that hasn't changed. Hadley's Playground is now seen as a ground-breaking model for what a community playground really can and should be, and helped set a standard for some of the best new spaces in the DC area, such as Clemy Park in Mclean.

At Hadley's Playground, children of all ages and abilities play together, side by side – all thanks to a proactive mother who wanted equality for her disabled young daughter. We love the easy-to-navigate soft surfacing, which happens to be great for babies and earlier walkers, and the play structures that encourage imaginative play. Pirate-lovers will have a blast on the ship, and young knights and princesses will enjoy the castle, while the frontier village brings out the pioneer in all ages. There are also plenty of swings (of varying types and sizes) and slides. Plus multi-sensory stationary toys (Including a cool mega-globe), signs in Braille, and a creatively colorful atmosphere. We also love the painted-on roadway snaking throughout the playground – perfect for bringing your own ride-on trike.

We wish the 34,000-square-foot playground had more shade, but that will improve with time, as the existing planter trees mature. We really like that the space is offset and protected from the busy traffic lanes nearby. Even if you don't live in Potomac, well worth a visit.

CHAPTER 6
'Tis The Season: Family Fun, All Year Long

SPRING

National Cherry Blossom Festival
Late March / Early April
Tidal Basin, DC
www.nationalcherryblossomfestival.org
There's nothing like 3,000 pink and white Japanese cherry trees in bloom to usher in springtime. The traditional festival marks the beginning of the busy tourist season in DC, so it can get crowded. But there's no family photo opp like this beautiful setting, and it's an annual ritual for many local families longing for warmth after a gray East Coast winter. Check the Post for its thorough coverage of the many festival events scheduled for the Mall and the monuments. And consider avoiding the traffic and parking hassles by taking metro. Get off at the Smithsonian stop on the blue or orange line, and walk west on Independence Ave. to 15th St. Turn left and head south along 15th St. You're there!

Annual White House Easter Egg Roll
White House Lawn
www.whitehouse.gov/easter
The White House Easter Egg Roll is an annual tradition dating to 1878. It's a free morning of chasing eggs, running races, visiting with the Easter Bunny, and storytelling on the best-groomed lawn in town. The all-ages family event is free and open to the public. Tickets are typically available at the Ellipse Visitors Pavilion starting around 7 or 7:30 a.m. on the morning of the event (usually the Monday after Easter). Only two adults are allowed per group, and each group must have at least one child under age seven to be admitted.

St. Patrick's Day Parades

Downtown DC

www.dcstpatsparade.com

Old Town Alexandria

www.ballyshaners.org

The DC parade takes place on the Sunday closest to St. Patrick's Day and moves down Constitution Ave. from Seventh to 17th Sts NW. Floats, marching bands, pipe bands, fire departments, military, and police take part. Local Irish pubs also sponsor parade parties with Irish musicians, dancers, and singers – some of which, believe it or not, are actually family-friendly. Old Town Alexandria also has an annual St. Pat's parade, starting on N. Pitt St. with an annual Invitational Classic Car Show and a Dog Show on the Market Square. The parade starts noonish and runs approximately two hours, moving from West and King Sts. to Fairfax and King Sts., with the reviewing stand at N. Royal and King Sts.

Flower Mart at the National Cathedral

Wisconsin Ave. at Massachusetts Ave. NW

www.cathedral.org

This annual event at the National Cathedral has lots of activities for kids, and is the ONLY time of year you can ride the Cathedral's antique carousel. Flower Mart takes place the first Friday and Saturday in May, features food, flowers, plants, and arts and crafts for purchase.

SUMMER

Taste of DC

Memorial Day weekend, days and times vary

Pennsylvania Ave NW (between Seventh and 14th Sts. NW)

www.tasteofdc.org

Dozens of DC's best restaurants share their creations during Taste of DC, in addition to concerts, booths, and exhibitions along Pennsylvania Ave. NW.

DC Memorial Day Parade

Memorial Day proper, late May

This parade features marching bands and veterans' units from all 50 states. It starts at Third St. and Madison, moving south to Independence Ave. From there it goes west down Independence to 12th St.

DC Caribbean Carnival
Weekend in June

This annual event draws some 500,000 visitors. The highlight is a parade featuring 25 bands of masqueraders, moving down George Ave. from Missouri Ave. NW to Banneker Park NW, across from Howard University. The parade and other Carnival events are free.

Alexandria Waterfront Festival
www.waterfrontfestival.org

A big annual fundraiser for the Red Cross, this festival is held on a Saturday and Sunday each June beside the Potomac River in Old Town. It includes carnival rides and games for the kids, loads of food vendors, local artisans and nonprofit groups, and live music.

Friday Evening Parades
Friday evenings throughout the summer, 8:30 p.m.
8th and I Sts. SE, US Marine Corps Barracks, DC
202.433.6060
www.mbw.usmc.mil

The Marine Corps Barracks downtown hosts 75-minute Friday night performances during the summer, featuring the U.S. Marine Drum and Bugle Corps, the U.S. Marine Band, and the Marine Corps Silent Drill Platoon. You must make a reservation to attend. Written requests are accepted for groups of 11 or more people, and an online reservation can be made for smaller groups. No phone reservations are accepted. Last-minute unclaimed seats are given away to those who want them, but there are no guarantees any will be available.

Smithsonian Folklife Festival
Late June – July Fourth weekend, National Mall, DC
www.folklife.si.edu

This annual festival runs the length of the Mall and celebrates national and international cultures. Lots of live performance, music, dance, storytelling, food and drink, and exhibitions. Each year features several different cultural traditions, with visiting artisans and performers from all over the nation – and all over the world.

National Independence Day Parade
Morning of July 4
Downtown DC
www.july4thparade.com
The parade begins in the morning and runs along Constitution Ave. from Seventh to 17th Sts. NW. It features bands, military units, floats, and famous faces.

Independence Day Fireworks
After dark on July 4
National Mall
Seeing fireworks in the nation's capital, against the background of the Washington Monument and the Lincoln Memorial, is something you must do at least once. It will be crowded, and it will be hot and sticky. But once your child is old enough or tolerant enough to brave it, you'll find it worthwhile. Many families make it an annual tradition. Metro is your best bet, but check the *Post* for any special routes or station closures. Come extra early if you can – Bring a blanket, plenty of cool drinks, and your sunscreen. The National Symphony Orchestra provides a patriotic soundtrack.

County Fairs:

Fairfax County 4-H Fair & Farm Show
Frying Pan Park (Reston-Herndon)
www.fairfaxcounty.gov
Montgomery County Agricultural Fair
Montgomery County Fairgrounds (Gaithersburg)
www.mcagfair.com
Arlington County Fair
Thomas Jefferson Community Center & Park Grounds (S. Arlington)
www.arlingtoncountyfair.org
Prince George's County Fair
Prince George's County Equestrian Center
www.countyfair.org

National Barbecue Battle
June, Downtown DC
www.barbecuebattle.com
This weekend event takes place along Pennsylvania Ave., from Ninth St. to 14th St., and draws about 100,000 people. It includes – as you might imagine – lots of barbecue making, competing, sampling, and demonstrating from local restaurants and barbecue experts from around the country. There are also children's activities at the event.

"Pick Your Own" Farms:

Becraft's Farm
14722 New Hampshire Ave., Silver Spring
301.236.4545
Strawberries, blueberries and vegetables in season

Brossman's Orchard
43975 Spinks Ferry Rd., Leesburg
703.777.1127
www.loudounfarms.org
Peaches, nectarines

Butler's Orchard
22200 Davis Mill Rd., Germantown
301.972.3299
http://butlersorchard.com
Cherries, blueberries, blackberries, red raspberries, strawberries, and vegetables

Homestead Farm
15600 Sugarland Rd., Poolesville
301.977.3761
www.homestead-farm.net
Strawberries, rhubarb, tart cherries, blackberries, assorted vegetables (picked and pick-your-own), peaches, nectarines, red raspberries, apples

Potomac Vegetable Farms
9627 Leesburg Pike (just west of Tysons Corner)

703.759.2119
www.potomacvegetablefarms.com
Combo of fresh-picked and pick-your-own blackberries, eggs, cut flowers, corn, tomatoes, peppers, green beans, summer and winter squash, carrots, onions, sweet potatoes, cucumbers, celery, bunched greens and lettuce

FALL

Annual Adams Morgan Day Festival
18th St. NW
www.adamsmorgandayfestival.com
This September street festival in the Adams Morgan neighborhood is big, fun, and very child-friendly. The Kid's Fair features balloon artists, face painting, a moonbounce, a trackless train, jugglers and juggling lessons, clowns, children's musicians, tennis lessons, martial arts performances, and lots more.

Blessing of the Animals at the National Cathedral
Wisconsin Ave. at Massachusetts Ave. NW
www.cathedral.org
On a weekday in early October, the National Cathedral hosts this festival day, during which animals and pets of all shapes and sizes are blessed on the Cathedral grounds, in the tradition of St. Francis of Assisi. Lots of fun for kids!

Takoma Park Folk Festival
Takoma Park Middle School, 7611 Piney Branch Rd.
www.tpff.org
This September event for the whole family has lots for the kids to enjoy, and it's free and open to the public. There's a children's stage with music and performances they'll love, designed for plenty of audience participation. Games, face painting, participatory crafts, and plenty of food and drink are on hand.

Open House Arts Festival at the Kennedy Center
2700 F St. NW

202.467.4600

www.kennedy-center.org

This September festival is free and open to the public. It features 300+ performances and workshops for all ages. Many of them are family-oriented and kid-friendly. A full schedule can be found on the website.

Boo at the Zoo

3001 Connecticut Ave. NW

202.633.3034

http://nationalzoo.si.edu

This children's event at the National Zoo is an annual Halloween tradition for families. It runs three consecutive evenings from 5:30 to 8:30 p.m., typically the weekend before Halloween proper. Costumed volunteers hand out treats and free giveaways at more than 40 stations, and the animals are often active because of the later hour and cool temperatures. Boo at the Zoo also features holiday decorations, keeper talks, and haunted trails. It's safe – and fun for ages two to 12, who should come in costume. Ticket prices vary, but there are discounts for FONZ members. Limited paid parking is available to FONZ members only. Tix sell out quickly, so watch the website!

Annual Pumpkin Festival at Butler's Orchard

22200 Davis Mill Rd., Germantown

301.972.3299

www.butlers-orchard.com

Pick-your own pumpkins at this farm, which holds its annual Pumpkin Festival weekends in October. Tickets run approx. $7 and are free for children under age two. They have wooden play structures, a small corn maze, a hayloft for jumping, hayrides, a pedal-tractor track, farm animals, a straw maze, cut-outs for photos, a Cinderella's Pumpkin Coach, and Pumpkinland, made up of 20+ familiar children's characters made from pumpkins, gourds, and squash. Pony rides are available for a fee, as well as face painting and kids' crafts. Live music is also a highlight. Pumpkin Harvest Days run some weekdays in October for approx. $5 per person. This includes a hayride, a small pumpkin, two apples, and several of the play areas. You can also book evening hayrides for groups.

Fall Festival at Burke Nursery

9401 Burke Rd., Burke

703.323.1188
www.pumpkinplayground.com
The fall festival and pumpkin playground takes place daily from late September through early November, with special weekend events. Admission runs approx. $7 to $10, free for under-twos. Hayrides (wheelchair accessible), a fort, pirate- and Western-themed activities, storytellers, inflatables, slides, tumbling tubes, farm animals, and a sand hill with buried "treasure" are among the offerings. Weekend performers include musicians, dancers, clowns, and musicians, as well as face painting, pony rides, balloon animals, a moon bounce, and temporary tattoos for additional fees. Food and drinks are for sale.

Fall Festival at Homestead Gardens
743 W. Central Ave. (Routes 424 and 214), Davidsonville
301.261.4550
www.homesteadgardens.com
They host an annual fall festival Saturdays and Sundays in October, featuring hayrides, free and inexpensive kids' activities like pumpkin painting, pumpkin bowling, storytelling, and pony rides. There's also a lineup of live entertainment and demonstrations, and scarecrow-building workshops for kids. A straw maze is open daily and a llama barn during the mid-day hours.

Family Festival at the Farm
Frederick County Office of Economic Development
5340 Spectrum Dr., Frederick
301.694.1058 or 800.248.2296
www.discoverfrederickmd.com/funfarm/ffhome.html
The Frederick County Office of Economic Development sponsors this annual free, self-guided tour of working farms, a vineyard, an orchard and a museum, usually during a weekend in mid-October. Animals, hayrides, pony rides, horse shows, scarecrow making, ice-cream making, and storytelling are aimed kids.

Fall Festival Weekend at Cox Farms
15621 Braddock Rd. (Pleasant Valley at Braddock), just west of Centreville
703.830.4121
www.coxfarms.com

Set on 50 acres of this huge farm, the Fall Festival Weekend includes hayrides, mountain slides, rope swings, farm animals (including petable bunnies and calves), goats to feed, face painting, entertainment, cider and apples, and a small pumpkin. There's also a smoking "Volcano Rumble Slide" and a walk-through replica of the Candyland board game. A special weekend features a "Pumpkin Madness Festival," where you can bring pumpkins to smash. Entry fees range from $7 to $10, depending on the date and the age, so call ahead or check the website. Kids under age two get in free. Lunch items and picnic tables are available.

Fantastic Fall Festival at Stadler Nursery
5504 Mount Zion Rd., Frederick
301.473.9042
www.stadlergardencenters.com
The one-day festival features hayrides, a straw toss, face painting, live music, and corn mazes. Admission is free and kids receive a treat bag. Food is sold by local Girl Scouts.

Fall Harvest Family Days at Mt. Vernon
George Washington Memorial Pkwy. (southern end, past Old Town)
703.780.2000
www.mountvernon.org
Fall Harvest Family Days are typically held consecutively on a weekend at George Washington's home, Mt. Vernon. Admission runs between $25 and $30 for a family of four (two adults and two kids ages six to 11), with wagon trains, an appearance by "George Washington" a straw bale maze designed by Adrian Fisher, colonial demonstrations, farm animals, and eighteenth-century games. Baked goods, sandwiches, and drinks are available for purchase.

Krop's Crops
11110 Georgetown Pike, Great Falls
703.430.8955.
During October you can take a free tractor-pulled hayride to the produce market's pick-your-own pumpkin patch. They also have farm animals, a Pumpkin Patch play area for tots, and picnic tables.

Mazes & Pumpkin Patch at North Run Farm
1701 Green Spring Valley Rd., Stevenson

410.241.3392
www.northrunfarm.com
Large corn maze (over one mile of pathways and six stations). Admission
runs between $5 and $7, depending on age, with children under age four
free and military discounts. Younger kids (under-six) can also go through
the mini-maze constructed of straw bales and look at farm animals like
piglets, lambs, miniature horses, and calves. They also have a pick-your-
own pumpkin patch and a produce stand that sells yummy baked goods
and cider.

Marine Corps Marathon & 5K

US Hwy 50, Arlington National Cemetery, Iwo Jima, Arlington
703.784.2225
www.marinemarathon.com
This late October, Sunday-morning event draws lots of spectators and
many celebrity participants. The weather is usually mild and beautiful,
and you can even take metro to watch the fun! Exit at Rosslyn or
Arlington Cemetery. If you have tweens or teens, consider the Youth Fun
Run, which typically begins around 9:30 a.m., an hour after the marathon
start.

Pumpkin Patch & Hayrides at Roha Farms

6009 Church Ln., Hydes
410.592.8040
www.rohafarms.com
Opens Saturdays and Sundays in October. Free hayrides to a pick-your-
own pumpkin patch – both are wheelchair accessible! Some other
activities have a small fee – horse and pony rides, pumpkin painting, face
painting, scarecrow making, a concession market, picnic tables, and
animals for petting.

Pumpkinville at Leesburg Gardens & Animal Park

19270 James Monroe Hwy. (Route 15 S.), just outside Leesburg
703.779.2332
www.leesburganimalpark.com
Open daily September and October. Pumpkinville includes entry into the
Leesburg Animal Park, hayrides along a path with cut-out characters, a
tot-sized hay maze, moon bounces, a small gift pumpkin, and apples and
cider. Their three-acre play space has big slides and tunnels, a rope swing,

straw mountains, mini-tractor rides, and a teepee. There's also a big inflatable slide shaped like a fire truck, with firefighter cut-outs. On weekends there's also live entertainment and pumpkin- and face painting. The final weekend of the event has pumpkin-smashing events for visitors. Admission runs approximately $5.50 to $10, depending on the day and age. Children under age two are free. Pony rides are about $3 and take place in the animal park every day. There's also a country store, picnic tables, and concession sales on weekends.

Montgomery County Annual Thanksgiving Parade
www.montgomerycountymd.gov
The Montgomery County Thanksgiving Parade takes place in Silver Spring, typically on the Saturday morning just before or after the holiday. It runs along Sligo and George Ave. and includes huge balloons, floats, marching bands and string bands, Shriners, antique cars, fire engines, dancers, and trained pets.

Thanksgiving Day Trot for Hunger
Thanksgiving Day, morning, DC
www.some.org/inv_eve_trot.html

Alexandria Turkey Trot Five-Miler
Thanksgiving Day, morning
www.pwba.org/turkeytrot

Bethesda Turkey Chase 10K & Two-Mile
Thanksgiving Day, morning
Sponsored by Bethesda-Chevy Chase YMCA, 301.530.3725

Thanksgiving with the Turkeys
301.428.8128
www.animalsanctuary.org
Poplar Spring Animal Sanctuary in Poolesville rescues abused or neglected farm animals. Their collection of more than 20 includes cows, pigs, goats, sheep, chickens, horses, mules, rabbits – and turkeys. At their annual bring-a-dish vegan event, you can have Thanksgiving dinner WITH the turkeys, who are the guests of honor. A $10 donation is suggested per family.

Reston Town Center Holiday Parade

www.restontowncenter.com

The annual Holiday Parade begins late morning at Market St. and
Freedom Dr. in Reston, kicking off the holiday season. Visits with Santa
follow the parade.

WINTER

Scottish Christmas Walk

First Saturday in December, Old Town Alexandria

www.campagnacenter.org

703.549.0111

If you love bagpipes, kilts, and dogs (especially Scotties, Irish Wolfhounds,
and Scottish Deerhounds), you'll have fun at Old Town's annual Scottish
Christmas Walk. Over 100 Scottish clans dressed in their tartans walk in
the parade. There are also dog clubs, antique cars, living history
reenactments, and Santa at the end of the parade, riding atop a fire truck.
From Thursday through Saturday of that week, the Campagna Center, 418
S. Washington St., sells heather and greens. The parade itself is free and
open to the public.

Old Town Holiday Parade of Boats

First Saturday in December, Old Town Alexandria

703.838.5005

http://visitalexandriava.com

Alexandria's harbor hosts more than 50 brightly lit sailing and powered
boats for the annual Holiday Parade of Boats at the city's historic
waterfront, typically held on the same weekend s the Scottish Christmas
Walk. The event begins at 3 p.m., with Santa and other special guests on
the dock. The boat parade begins at 5:30 p.m. at the Alexandria Marina,
at the foot of Cameron St., behind the Torpedo Factory. It's free and open
to the public.

Georgetown Holiday Parade of Lighted Boats

Washington Harbour, 3000 K St. NW

Typically held in the early evening during the first weekend of December
(check the *Post* for date), this parade along the Potomac features college
crew teams and beautifully lit boats. Depending on the weather, there's

often a beautiful view – You might even get one of those gorgeous Harbour sunsets.

Holiday Sing-Along at Wolf Trap
Filene Center at Wolf Trap, Vienna
www.wolf-trap.org
Usually held late afternoon on a weekend in early December (check the website), this hugely popular sing-along event is a Wolf Trap tradition featuring Christmas carols and Hanukkah songs by the U.S. Marine Band and other local choral groups. You can bring your own picnic, a candle, and a bell so you can take part in the candlelight procession during "Silent Night" and jingle along with "Jingle Bells." Admission is free.

Lighting of the National Menorah
The Ellipse, Connecticut Ave. NW
The Lighting of the National Menorah in December marks the eight-day Jewish festival of Hanukkah. It is attended by national and local notables – Among them have been the president, Cabinet members, members of Congress, Jewish community leaders, and ambassadors. The first lighting was in 1979 with President Carter. There are latkes, donuts, and mini menorahs for participants after the lighting. This event is free, but requires advance tickets.

Pathway of Peace & the National Christmas Tree
The Ellipse, Connecticut Ave. NW
The U.S. has an 80+ year-old tradition of lighting a National Christmas Tree. The 40-ft. live Colorado blue spruce is lit at the Ellipse, the grassy area just south of the White House. In 1954, a "Pathway of Peace" was constructed of 56 smaller, decorated trees representing the states, the territories, and the District of Columbia. These encircle the main tree. The tree and the Pathway of Peace are lit from dusk to 11 p.m. during December. Vendors sell cider and hot cocoa nearby, and there are live musical performances nightly.

Garden of Lights at Brookside Gardens
1800 Glenallan Ave., Wheaton
Garden of Lights Hotline: 301.962.1453
www.mc-mncppc.org and www.brooksidegardens.org

In December, Brookside Gardens hosts a strictly secular holiday stroll (no Santa, nativity scenes, or menorah) called the Garden of Lights. Faux animals are aglow, as well as the many trees and flowers, along this half-mile walk. You'll also find an animated moonvine bursting into bloom, flying and swimming birds, and a kaleidoscope caterpillar you can walk through. Cost is approximately $15 per car, cash only.

Holly Trolleyfest at the National Capitol Trolley Museum
1313 Bonifant Rd., Colesville
301.384.6088
www.dctrolley.org
Kids can take a ride with Santa on a streetcar and check out the toy trains on display. Closed Christmas Day. Admission runs approx. $3 per person.

Symphony of Lights
Merriweather Post Pavilion, Columbia
410.740.7666
This drive-through display has more than 70 huge, animated and stationary lighted figures marking the holiday season. Drive-through takes approximately 20 minutes and is usually open until 10 p.m.

Ice Skating at the National Gallery
Smithsonian National Gallery of Art Sculpture Garden
www.nga.gov/ginfo/skating.htm
The NGA's Sculpture Garden fountain is transformed into a traditional outdoor skating rink in winter – open through mid-March. Open until 11 p.m. Monday through Saturday, and until 9 p.m. on Sunday. Holiday music from a nice sound system makes it more fun, and concessions with cocoa and cider keep you warm.

Festival of Lights, Washington Temple of the Church of Jesus Christ of Latter-Day Saints
9900 Stoneybrook Dr., Kensington
301.587.0144
The Mormon temple, located just north of the Beltway in Kensington, has a live outdoor nativity scene, decorated trees, and over 400,000 lights during the month of December, from dusk to 10 p.m. each evening. They also host many musical programs during the Christmas season.

"Spirit of Kwanzaa" at the Kennedy Center
2700 F St. NW
202.467.4600
www.kennedy-center.org
The Kennedy Center's Concert Hall features "The Spirit of Kwanzaa" in late December, with the Dance Institute of Washington and the Washington Reflections Dance Company. The show, which includes dance, poetry, and song in honor of this African American holiday, features many guest artists and has received high praise from reviewers at the *Washington Post*. Tickets range from $12 to $20.

Winter Lights at Seneca Creek State Park
11950 Clopper Rd., Gaithersburg
301.258.6350
www.gaithersburgmd.gov
Seneca Creek State Park hosts a drive-through light show with more than 300 exhibits in an "enchanted forest" setting. The drive-through is approximately three and one-half miles, and cost is about $10 per car. Proceeds go to local charities. There are also open-air trolley rides on selected evenings, for about $5 per person.

Holiday Model Train at Union Station
www.unionstationdc.com
Union Station dusts off its 32x16-ft. train set for the winter holidays. It features a Norwegian setting with its own toboggan sled ramp and ice skating rink. The exhibit is open through early January from 10 a.m. to 7 p.m. daily.

Annual Jolly Fat Man's Run
Capital Crescent Trail, downtown Bethesda
This annual tradition, now a decade old, starts on a weekend morning in early December in Bethesda. It moves along the Capital Crescent Trail to Georgetown, with 700+ runners and walkers in support of the U.S. Marine Corps Toys for Tots campaign. Live entertainment is part of the fun.

Miracle of Lights at Bull Run Regional Park
Old Post Office Rd., Centreville
www.miracleoflights.com

Miracle of Lights runs daily from 5:30 to 10:30 p.m. from late November through early January. (Closed New Year's Eve.) The drive-through display has one million lights and animated scenes. Cost is approximately $12 per car, $25 per commercial van, or $50 per bus. A portion of proceeds is donated to children's charities.

Water-Skiing Santa
www.waterskiingsanta.com
The water-skiing Santa takes to the Potomac each year with his kneeboarding reindeer, flying elves, and a jet-skiing Grinch. This tradition is now 20+ years old – believe it or not – and has a loyal following. It's usually scheduled for Christmas Eve, early afternoon (check the website) and is free and open to the public. Best viewing is from Lady Bird Johnson Park on the GW Pkwy. in Virginia. There's free parking at the Columbia Island Marina nearby, and the marina's concession building will e the site of meet-and-greets with Santa, Mrs. Claus, special helpers, and the Grinch, both before and after the show. Get your picture made!

> **MAKING MEANING**
> *Looking for a way to have some fun while teaching your toddler or preschooler the true meaning of the holiday season? A DC organization called SOME (So Others Might Eat) runs a shoebox project for kids in need. Children can decorate a shoebox for a child their own age and help fill the box with treats like new mittens, hats, and socks, as well as a new toothbrush, toothpaste, and fun soaps. Shop together with your child to fill the box. SOME is located at 71 O St. NW, 20001 and may be reached by calling 202.797.8806 or 202.797.7562. Or visit them online at www.some.org.*

Christmas Tree Farms

Butler's Orchard
22200 Davis Mill Rd., Germantown, 301.972.3299
www.butlersorchard.com

Homestead Farm
15600 Sugarland Rd., Poolesville, 301.977.3761
www.homestead-farm.net

Clifton Christmas Tree Plantation
12360 Henderson Rd., Clifton, Virginia, 703.830.2863
www.blackacrefarms.com

Middleburg Christmas Tree Farm
Rt. 630 (Unison Rd.) at Christmas Tree Ln., Middleburg, 540.554.8625
www.middleburgxmastrees.com

Ticonderoga Farms
Rt. 613 (Ticonderoga Rd.), Chantilly, 703.327.4424
www.ticonderoga.com

Productions of *The Nutcracker*

The Nutcracker Puppet Production
Puppet Co. Playhouse, Glen Echo Park
www.thepuppetco.org

For young children and the adults who love them, you can't beat the elaborately beautiful production at the Puppet Co. Theatre in Glen Echo Park. It's wildly popular, so reserving advance tickets is a must! We love this larger-than-life puppetry rendition – Christmas wouldn't be Christmas without it.

The Nutcracker Ballet
www.thealexandriaballet.com
The Alexandria Ballet & the Alliance Dance Institute

We also love the young-child-oriented adaptation of the ballet, produced each year in an intimate space at Landmark Mall in Alexandria. Staged by the Alliance Dance Institute and the Alexandria Ballet, this "condensed" version of the classic ballet runs just one hour and is perfect for shorter attention spans. Lovely costuming and a mix of young dancers and adult professionals make this show enjoyable for adults, too. Kids have the opportunity to sit on the edge of the stage for an up-close-and-personal view, and the dancers come out into the audience after the show to hand out sweets to the children, shake hands, and pose for photo opps.

Cookies and cocoa are available for purchase outside the theater. We had a great time!

Kennedy Center
2700 F St. NW, 202.467.4600
www.kennedy-center.org

Olney Children's Ballet Theatre
Clarice Smith Performing Arts Center, University of Maryland, 301.405.ARTS
http://berrenddancecentre.com/OlneyBalletTheater.html

Momentum Dance Theatre at The Historic Takoma Theatre
6833 Fourth St. NW, 202.785.0035
http://momentumdancetheatre.com

The Washington Ballet at The Warner Theatre
1299 Pennsylvania Ave. NW, 202.397.7328
www.washingtonballet.org

Metropolitan Ballet Theatre at the Parilla Performing Arts Center, Montgomery College
51 Mannakee St., Rockville, 301.279.5301
www.mbtdance.org

Center for Ballet Arts at NoVa Community College, Alexandria Campus
3001 N. Beauregard St., 703.273.5344

Reston Conservatory Ballet at the Reston Community Center
2310 Colts Neck Rd., Reston, 703.715.8366

Kid-Friendly New Year's Eve:

First Night Alexandria
www.firstnightalexandria.org
This alcohol-free New Year's Eve family festival includes musical performances and other live entertainment inside Old Town's historic buildings, plus events at the Masonic Temple on Callahan Dr. The kids can

get their faces painted, see clowns, and hear music at the Jefferson Houston School on Cameron St. For those who can stay up 'til 12, there's the midnight fireworks display over the George Washington Masonic Temple.

First Night Annapolis
www.firstnightannapolis.org
A New Year's Eve celebration geared toward the whole family, featuring performances of music, dance, theater, and comedy at more than 40 venues throughout historic downtown Annapolis. Fireworks go off at midnight at the city dock. This is a non-alcoholic event.

George Washington's Birthday Parade
President's Day, Old Town Alexandria
www.washingtonbirthday.org
This annual parade on President's Day Monday is hit or miss when it comes to the weather. But on a mild winter day, it's a great outing with little ones. Touted as "the largest parade celebrating Washington's birthday in the USA!"

CHAPTER 7
Getting Around

METRO WITH BABY

Metro's official fare policy: "Up to two children, four years and younger, ride free with each adult paying full fare. Children five and older pay adult fares. Special discounted student farecards and passes are available for District of Columbia residents." This means all kids ride free until their fifth birthday, BUT at a ratio of two children max per adult.

Many of the metro escalators in DC are steep and/or crowded – definitely *not* stroller-safe. In fact, official metro rules state that strollers are not allowed on the escalators – period. If you have a small child who needs to be held on the escalator, use the elevator instead. Only kids who are old enough, confident enough, and are holding your hand should use the escalator.

Street-level elevator locations and directions are on the brown street pylons. Be aware that at several stops, the access elevator is located across the street from the metro entrance. Sometimes you have to hunt for it at an unfamiliar stop. Metro elevators have intercom systems you can use to communicate with the station attendant in case you have a problem.

If you have a stroller, use the extra-wide, wheelchair-accessible turnstile to enter the platform. Every station has at least one.

Inside the station, look for the electronic sign directing you to the elevator on the mezzanine level. Official policy is that if an elevator is out of service at a stop, shuttle service is available to take you to the nearest station with an operable elevator. (How this happens in practice is another matter entirely, though. If you get off a train with a stroller and find that the elevator is out of service, see the attendant for help.)

Before setting out on metro with a stroller, you can check the website to find out where elevators are located at the stops you're using, and if they are currently in service:
www.wmata.com/accessibility/elevator_escalator_report/systemmap.cfm

Rubber gap-reducers decrease the gap between the platform and the train, which is a big help in boarding with a stroller. Be sure you and your stroller have completely cleared the door of the train by the time you hear the chime – It's not worth a hasty dash with a little one. Unlike elevator doors, metro doors do *not* bounce back automatically when they sense an obstruction!

Designate a family member to collect the tickets of children five and older after passing through the entry turnstile. You'll need them again to exit, and paying twice is a bummer.

With older children on foot: Teach them to stay behind the bumpy domes while standing on the platform waiting for a train, and show them that the blinking lights along the ground indicate a train is coming into the station.

With children old enough to understand, tell them what to do if they become separated from you in the crowd. Show them how to recognize the station attendant and a transit police officer.

Metro begins running at 5 a.m. on weekdays and 7 a.m. on weekends. It closes at midnight Sunday through Thursday, and at 3 a.m. on Friday and Saturday nights. Holiday hours vary, but you can check the holiday schedule at www.wmata.com/riding/holiday_schedule.cfm.

You can sign up for customized e-mail alerts at the website, which will notify you when there is scheduled maintenance, a problem on your route, or other important changes: www.wmata.com/riding/system_alert.cfm.

Another e-mail alert sends you messages about elevator disruptions. Sign up at www.wmata.com/riding/ellen/ellen.cfm.

METRO BUS WITH BABY

Make yourself as compact as possible. (As impossible as that may be.)

Use only a very easy-to-fold, lightweight umbrella stroller on the bus. You will have to fold it down yourself, before you get on board, so it helps if you have a sling or soft carrier to attach the baby to your body before the bus arrives. This will also keep the baby secure on board and free your hands to deal with stroller and diaper bag.

If you need to use the bus regularly with a baby or toddler, and you must take a stroller along, buy the Maclaren Volo stroller. It's a stripped-down, lightweight model with no frills. It has a shoulder strap and folds up and out easy. The downside: Not as comfortable for your child and no accessory pack.

Consider using a backpack-style diaper bag. Just be sure to keep zippers and snaps closed, to help ward off pickpocketing.

Don't block the aisles with your stroller or impede people from getting on and off. (Thus, the recommendation of a very simple stroller, or no stroller at all.)

Bus schedules are online: www.wmata.com/timetables/bus_timetables.cfm.

Bus fare policy for children is exactly the same as the metro. Kids ride free until their fifth birthday, but no more than two children under age five per adult.

AMTRAK WITH BABY

Children ride free until their second birthday. If you wait to purchase your tickets until you're on board, you'll pay an extra, nonrefundable service fee. Buy in advance!

You can't really use a car seat on the train, because there are no seatbelts to secure it in place. Your car seat will also probably be counted as one of your pieces of luggage. Only bring the seat if you have to use it at your destination.

If your baby is young enough to ride in a sling or soft carrier, be sure to bring it. This gives you a hands-free way to negotiate the station and the crowds. Also makes babies feel more secure in the chaos.

People with babies and children of all ages can pre-board. Take advantage of it! Arrive 45 minutes before departure time.

Use the Red Cap porter service, if you can. The porter boards you early, carries your stuff, and gets you a good spot. Plus, it's free. You just need to tip. Be aware that Red Cap isn't available at all stations, but you can check the website to find out about yours: www.amtrak.com.

Look for seats at the end of the train, where you can be close to the oversized luggage/bike storage.

Choose one of the seat setups with four facing each other. It's easiest and most comfortable, and other people may avoid sitting in one of the four seats when they spot your little one.

Avoiding sitting in business class or near those who are obviously business travelers. They usually don't appreciate having small kids nearby, and it may make your trip less pleasant to deal with that.

There are no changing tables on Amtrak trains, except on the Acela Express. You'll have to bring a portable changing pad and do it at your seat.

Official Amtrak policy for carry-on items: "Each passenger may bring aboard two pieces of carry-on baggage. Not included in this limit are personal items such as infant paraphernalia such as strollers, diaper bags, and car seats, and personal items like briefcases, purses, and laptops." A visible tag with name and address is required for each piece.

Official checked baggage policy: "Each ticketed passenger may check up to three pieces of luggage at no charge. You may also check up to three additional pieces upon payment of $10 per piece."

The official policy babies and toddlers: "Children under two years of age traveling free may occupy a vacant seat only if it is not yet needed for a paying passenger. If a child under two years of age does occupy a seat without paying a fare, the conductor has the right to request the child be removed for a fare- paying passenger, or the passenger has the option of purchasing a ticket to allow the child to continue to occupy the seat."

There may be a "special handling charge" for baby items like strollers when you travel on Amtrak.

You can bring your own food and drinks on board, but federal health regulations stipulate that Amtrak staff can't heat your food in their ovens or store it in their refrigerators. This goes for bottles and baby food!

Meal service is provided on long-distance trains. Some have dining cars with sit-down meal service. Other trains have lounge, dinette, and café cars that are more informal.

On long-distance routes there's a family bedroom / sleeper available. It has space for up to two adults and two children. Details, including a virtual tour of the space, are online at www.amtrak.com.

TRAVEL TO & FROM AIRPORTS WITH BABY

Red Top Cab Service
703.522.3333
www.redtopcab.com

Red Top has been recommended by a number of DC parents. They'll pick you up at your home and take you to the airport, AND they can provide a child safety seat if you let them know in advance. (Plan on installing it yourself – This is a liability issue.) You can request a station wagon or SUV-type vehicle if you're loaded down with luggage and baby gear. Their fleet also has a lot of Crown Victorias, which are easy to get car seats into if you're brining your own. If you really want to travel in comfort, they have an executive sedan service. Red Top has been around since 1964 and they've been named "Best Taxi Service" by the readers of *Washingtonian*. They take credit cards and advance bookings, and operate 24/7.

Boston Coach
800.672.7676
www.bostoncoach.com

Boston Coach has also been recommended by several DC parents who've had good experiences. This car service, which offers executive sedans to and from the airport, also has car seats available. You do need to book in advance and let them know what you need. You will probably have to install the seat yourself, once the car arrives at your house. (This is standard procedure among all car services, it turns out…) Their fleet is mostly made up of late-model Cadillacs and Lincoln Towncars.

CHAPTER 8
Shopping for Baby & Child

DC'S FAVORITES:
CLOTHING & SHOES, FURNISHINGS, GEAR, & TOYS

Apple Seed
Old Town Alexandria
www.appleseedboutique.com
A newcomer on the scene since the first edition of this book, Apple Seed is a lovely, modern-upscale boutique featuring maternity clothing (including cute swimsuits, outerwear, and lingerie); gifts; and baby clothing and accessories – as well as Bugaboo strollers and New Native baby carriers. Apple Seed is unique in offering personal styling services for expectant and nursing mamas, as well as hosting special events. Their dressing rooms are lovely, designed with pregnant gals in mind. And we really appreciate the friendly, unpretentious attention given to customers by owners Dina Katsev Igoe and Elleni Vorvis and their staff. We have personally received outstanding customer service from Apple Seed's managers and associates – worth its weight in gold! Perhaps best of all for busy shoppers, Apple Seed now offers online shopping.

The Baby Hammock.com
www.thebabyhammock.com
Owned by entrepreneurial DC mama Trish Thackston, The Baby Hammock offers quality, parent-tested products for pregnancy through the toddler years. Thackston says, "I founded my business out of frustration over accumulating a closet full of useless products that didn't live up to the marketing hype when my firstborn was young. I thought I could create a company that would take the guesswork out of finding good baby products that are worth spending money on. If I don't love using a product with my family and would not feel good about giving it to a close friend as a gift, then I won't sell it." Among The Baby Hammock's most popular inventory: Maya sling wraps, ERGO baby carriers, Ella Roo baby carriers, "The Clean Shopper" for cute and germ-free grocery cart rides, natural morning sickness relief, pregnancy gift sets, natural skin care and massage products for baby and mama, Baby Sherpa and Breyla

217

backpacks, the Kiddopotamus line of baby gear, jewelry, and lots of breastfeeding products. It's a nice one-stop shop with carefully selected items, and they are known to offer specials such as flat-rate shipping at various times during the year.

Barstons Child's Play

Chevy Chase, 5536 Connecticut Ave. NW
Rockville, Congressional Plaza
www.barstonschildsplay.com

If you like knowledgeable salespeople who offer to help you AND really know their inventory, if you value educational and imaginative toys, and if you prefer to shop with your kids without the overstimulation of a big warehouse, you'll appreciate Barstons Child's Play. Ask for what you're looking for here and you're bound to have what you need in a flash. This small, independently owned toy store in the District (with a newer location in Rockville) has a great stock of moderately-priced toys, games, puzzles, trains, dress-up clothes and party costumes, arts and crafts, books, and music. They also happen to feature many of the most affordable toys you'd find at a big warehouse store, made by the well-known manufacturers, though their offerings in the "blaring electronic" niche are few. The Chevy Chase location is long, narrow, and cozy – No overwhelming rows of merchandise or fluorescent floodlights here. There's free parking in the lot behind Barstons, or you can walk from the Friendship Heights metro stop in about 10 minutes. The newer location at Congressional Plaza has plenty of space and easy parking.

Bellini Baby & Teen Furniture

Rockville, Rockville Pike Shopping Center
www.bellini.com

Bellini specializes in high-quality hardwood cribs and furniture, bedding and accessories for babies to teens. Think hand-finished Beechwood cribs that convert to beds, and Birchwood bedroom suites that can last a lifetime. Their Rockville boutique is the national Bellini chain's only DC-area location. The website doesn't represent all items Bellini makes, but it does give you a good idea of the range, finishes, and pricing of their furniture.

Beyda's Lads & Lassie Shop
Bethesda, 5444 Westbard Ave.
Tucked away in a tricky-to-find location, longtime boutique Beyda's leans toward the overpriced. But they carry high-quality lines and it's a convenient place for Bethesda's parents to find elusive items like children's dress coats and dressier attire for babies and older kids.

Boodleby's Posh Frocks & Lollipops
Leesburg, 107 S. King St.
Located in a lovely 18th century townhouse in historic downtown Leesburg, Boodleby's specializes in elegant, upscale and special-occasion baby and children's clothing, hand-painted furnishings, gifts, and old-fashioned toys. What makes Boodleby's unique is owner Jean Keeler, who has been a custom children's seamstress for over 20 years. It was the popularity of her hand-crafted clothing that led her to open her own bougique in 1990, expanding from original storefronts in Mclean and Middleburg to the current, larger boutique setting in Leesburg.

Bradshaw's Children's Shoes
Arlington, 4532 Lee Hwy.
703.527.1546
We've heard that the service can be unpredictable, but otherwise this children's shoe shop is an Arlington institution with many loyal customers and an inviting neighborhood feel. They stock everything from soft shoes for pre-walking babies through school-aged kids, with a wide range of brands to choose from and a high standard of quality. You'll also find socks and slippers for toddlers and older children. Not the bargain bin, for sure, but worth it if you have a difficult-to-fit child or have grown weary of the short-lived quality of bargain basement shoe purchases.

Bratt Décor
Mclean, Tysons Corner
www.brattdecor.com
The place to decorate and accessorize your little one like a rock star, Bratt Décor is an upscale destination for the well-heeled. Designer furnishing, bedding, décor, gear, and clothing lines include names like Kate Spade and Reed & Barton – with the price tags to match. High quality, but a bit of a world unto itself, Bratt Décor is a joyful splurge for some – and a fun fantasy for the rest of us.

Buy Buy Baby
Rockville, Congressional Plaza
Springfield, 6398 Springfield Plaza
www.buybuybaby.com
Buy Buy Baby was new to us, when we moved here from Texas in 2005. It quickly stole our heart for convenient, well-stocked, service-oriented baby and toddler shopping. The stores have a look-and-feel similar to Babies R Us, but with a slightly more compact sensibility (and less of the shopping-in-a-warehouse feeling). Buy Buy Baby stocks an extensive collection of nursery furnishings, bedding, and décor, with tons of options on matching sets, as well as individual pieces such as upholstered rockers, gliders, and bassinettes. They carry a nice selection of clothing for newborns to 24 months, Robeez shoes and booties, and seasonal must-haves (such as sun hats, swim diapers, swim shoes, and sun shades). Soft-soled shoes, hard-to-find items like Baby Bjorn trainer potties, loads of toys for babies and toddlers, and an astounding selection of strollers, swings, and car seats. We loved their complete stock of Medela breast pumps, accessories, bottles, etc. – and even the line of Medela nursing bras and maternity "lingerie" for mamas. Plus, gift wrap and a computerized registry that can ship gifts anywhere in the U.S.!

Cradle & Crayon
Reston Town Center
www.cradleandcrayon.com
This Reston, VA boutique offers upscale baby and children's furnishings, clothing (including maternity), gifts and unique toys – in a hip but relaxed atmosphere. Be sure to check the sales rack for bargains! They offer a convenient gift registry and host events for expectant and new parents, on topics like successful breastfeeding and infant/child CPR. And to sweeten the deal, Cradle & Crayon has established a strong reputation for friendly, attentive customer service.

Creativity
Georgetown, www.creativitygeorgetown.com
Creativity at the Georgetown Mall is an arts/crafts/toy store offering drop-off play for children over age five while you shop. Children under age five are also welcome in the store, accompanied by an adult. Each week they host a lineup of special events, including a children's yoga class, storytime, and movie screening. Also available for birthday parties.

Daisy Baby & Mommies Too
Downtown Bethesda
www.shopdaisybaby.com
Daisy Baby & Mommies Too, the retail offspring of the former Daisy boutique in Adams Morgan and Daisy Too in Bethesda, was founded by fashion-guru mamas Andrea Paro Sandler and Fabiana Zelaya. They specialize in upscale baby furnishings, bedding, décor and accessories, as well as gifts and clothing, carrying upscale lines with a modern sensibility. Among the many cool product lines they carry are Cariboo and Bratt Décor furnishings, Bloom and Bugaboo gear, and Dwell and Bananafish nursery linens, plus designer clothing lines for layette through toddler. Plus more from lines we love such as Skip Hop, Caden Lane, and Bravado.

Dawn Price Baby
Capitol Hill, 325 Seventh St. SE, DC
Georgetown, 3112 M St. NW, DC
www.dawnpricebaby.com
Down the block from Eastern Market on Capitol Hill, tucked away next to the dee-licious Montmatre restaurant, we happily discovered one of DC's retail treasures. The shops's founder, Dawn Price, former executive/attorney turned entrepreneur and mother, has created an upscale oasis for babies and children. Price has poured heart and soul into this boutique – as well as its new Georgetown location (in the former K Baby location) – and it shows. Dawn Price Baby has earned its local popularity and success one mama at a time, providing service you just won't find at Baby Gap. Many days you'll find Dawn herself in one of the stores, working with a client on a custom nursery design, helping an expectant mother select a baby registry, crafting a new display, or hosting a special after-hours shopping party. As for the inventory: Upscale and unique. Clothes, gifts, furniture and nursery couture, old-fashioned toys, hip strollers. Dawn hand-picks her inventory from lines like Bebe & Bacups, Petunia Pickle, Sam & Bellie, Icky Products, Bugaboo, and Bla Bla. Specialty items backed by service that really *is* special. And online shopping, to boot.

Doodlehopper 4 Kids
Springfield, Huntsman Square on Huntsman Blvd.
Falls Church, downtown on W. Broad St.
www.huntsmandoodlehopper.com

Doodlehopper's specialty is toys, toys, and more toys - ranging from educational and puzzles to craft-oriented and dress-up clothes. But they also stock books, baby gifts, and baby and children's clothing. At the Springfield location you'll find clothing sizes up to 4T, while the Falls Church shop carries sizes for school-age kids. Great stores with a local, small-town feel.

Full of Beans
Chevy Chase, 5502 Connecticut Ave. NW, DC
Potomac, 10144 River Rd.
High-end baby and children's clothing, shoes, accessories, and specialty books and toys. We particularly like their stock of girls' clothing and accessories, which leans toward the funky and fun. Full of Beans carries upscale lines including Baby Lulu, London Britches, and Charlie Rocket, and it's a great place to shop for a special occasion or gift. They have good sales... So if you're on a budget, hold out!

Great Beginnings Baby & Children's Design Center
Gaithersburg, 18501 N. Frederick Ave.
www.greatbeginnings.net
Great Beginnings is housed in a ginormous 80,000-square-foot warehouse space in Gaithersburg, and also has an online baby store and gift registry. They specialize in nursery and children's furniture, bedding, and décor - plus a huge inventory of gear (strollers, car seats, booster seats, and high chairs), with hundreds of makes and models on the storeroom floor. Most of Great Beginnings' inventory, with the exception of beds and dressers, can be shipped throughout the U.S.

IKEA Children's Department
Woodbridge, Potomac Mills
College Park, 10100 Baltimore Ave.
www.ikea.com
Thank goodness for the Swedes! IKEA has great prices, straightforward design, and strong customer service on nursery and children's furniture, bedding, toys, and accessories. Love the selection, the contemporary sensibility and the colorful palette of their kids' stuff. You can also sleep a bit better, knowing that they guarantee that their products are free from toxic substances - and the wood they use doesn't come from devastated forests. We have been pleased with various purchases for our children's

rooms, including beds, linens, rugs, step stools, tables and chairs, high chairs, lighting, wall art, and toys. A cafeteria-style restaurant is on site, with a (cheap) children's menu. Highchairs are available, as are bottle-warming stations and clean changing rooms. There are small playstations for toddlers throughout the store, and kids of all ages are free to enjoy the "ball pit" (around the corner from the kids' furnishings) and to test-drive the ride-on toys. Slightly older children can even stay in the supervised playroom while you shop in peace! Tips: Take measurements of the space you're filling. Make a list of what you need before you hit the store. Make sure there's room in the car. You can even check online to see if your item is currently in stock before you leave home. Try to shop on a weekday to avoid crowds.

Keedo Clothing
Alexandria, 1600 Belle View Blvd.
Arlington, 2491A N. Harrison
www.alexandriachildrensstore.com
What makes Keedo special is its 100 percent cotton, hand-printed, hand-dyed clothing and their matching mom-and-daughter outfits. So colorful and easy to care for. We've also heard rave reviews for the uniquely Keedo "Art Box," which holds up to 60 pages children's artwork in a hand-painted wooden frame. And they have cute children's linens, accessories, and gifts.

The Kid's Closet
Downtown DC, on Connecticut Ave. NW
www.kidsclosetdc.com
Washingtonians have been shopping at Kid's Closet for well over 20 years now. In part their success is about location, which is ideal for busy parents who work downtown. Specializing in baby and children's clothing, shoes, accessories, and both classic and contemporary toys, Kid's Closet stays open until 6 p.m. weekdays and hosts excellent seasonal sales events.

Kinder Haus
Arlington, Clarendon on N. Fillmore Ave.
www.kinderhaus.com
Kinder Haus is primarily a toy/books/hobby store, but they also stock a nice little selection of baby and children's clothing and accessories.

Several times we've popped in to pick up a pair of girls' tights or hair clips, and at Halloween they've had the last-minute costume accessories we need but couldn't find elsewhere. Their new-ish location in the hub of Clarendon is big and beautiful, making it a pleasure to shop. Little ones will enjoy the play area and the train set while you browse. And we really appreciated their attentiveness to toy safety during 2007's seemingly countless recalls. Kinder Haus staff went the extra mile to not only remove recalled items from their shelves, but to label toy shelves with country-of-origin information. And they stocked up on many of the harder-to-find American-made and European toys that are safe, long-lasting, and unique.

Lilly's Pad

Alexandria, 703.960.9254
www.shoplillyspad.com
Local mama, artist, and entrepreneur Susanne Seidman's baby and children's gifts and accessories have a personal touch that's all too rare these days. Her Lilly's Pad products are beautiful, whimsical, fun – and handmade. We love our tried-and-true toddler bibs and Susanne's unique smocks, which can be used for sand/water table play, art projects, kitchen play, or dressup. Lilly's Pad has booths at many DC-area events, where you can see Susanne's handiwork up close and personal. An events calendar is posted on the Lilly's Pad website. To check what's currently in stock or be added to the mailing list, send email to: shop@shoplillyspad.com. Or, you can just pick up the phone and make an appointment with Susanne. A human voice, the artist herself, will greet you on the other end of the line.

Livie & Luca

www.livieandluca.com
Contact DC-based mama and Livie & Luca co-founder Amie Garcia at amie@livieandluca.com, or shop online at www.livieandluca.com. These are adorable Euro-style leather shoes with soft, flexible soles for babies and toddlers – and we are repeat customers. Love the range of colors and styles! Reasonable, competitive prices. And the shoes are both comfy and durable, holding up remarkably well through all types of weather. We love them!

Lullaby Baby
Columbia, on Red Branch Rd.
www.lullaby-baby.com
This is a beautiful boutique carrying upscale nursery and children's furniture and décor, bedding, accessories, and silver gifts. They also stock select hand-made baby and toddler clothing, sizes newborn to 3T, as well as layette items, designer diaper bags, and wooden toys. Sign up for their free monthly e-newsletter at the website, which covers decorating tips and trends, new product updates, child safety articles, and exclusive specials and sale previews.

One Two Kangaroo Toys
Shirlington/Arlington, 4022 28th St. S.
We really like this relatively new toy store serving Arlington and Alexandria. And we've heard not one but several reports from moms who said the One Two Kangaroo staff went out of their way to help locate a hard-to-find or to special order an out-of-stock item, with truly attentive service and bend-over-backwards customer care. We love their impeccably selected stock, and especially the Euro toys they carry, from Germany, Sweden, and France. Their puppets and fantasy toys are beautiful, and they carry a wide range of educational games for all ages. One Two Kangaroo is a class act!

Piccolo Piggies
Georgetown, 1533 Wisconsin Ave. NW
Bethesda, Wildwood Shopping Center on Old Georgetown Rd.
www.piccolo-piggies.com
They've been voted DC's "hip boutique" in Washington Families magazine, but the suburban Bethesda location is no ugly stepsister (and it comes with parking!). Piccolo Piggies' stock of clothing, accessories, shoes, and gifts for children is stylish and upscale, with a loyal customer base that speaks volumes. Their clothing stock goes up to age 14 and includes specialty lines like Burberry, Lilly Pullitzer, Lili Gaufrette, and Cakewalk. Plus specialty bedding, layette, prams and strollers for baby. A recent addition: Online shopping for select clothing and accessories.

Pink & Brown
Old Town Alexandria, 1212 King St.
http://pinkandbrownboutique.com

Another super-cool shopping spot for babies and children in Old Town! Entering the scene in summer 2008, Pink & Brown is a hip and inviting boutique carrying a nice selection of organic infant and kids clothing, plus nursery décor, accessories and baby gear, and stylish gifts. Take advantage of the new – free! – Old Town trolley to shop this and other King St. children's boutiques. It runs from the King St. metro station to the Potomac waterfront, with numerous stops along the way.

The Purple Goose

Del Ray/Alexandria, 2005 Mt. Vernon Ave.
www.thepurplegoose.com
Since we published the first edition of this book in 2005, The Purple Goose has become even more stylish and appealing. Formerly a mix of consignment and new products, they have mostly phased out the second-hand offerings to make space for a full stock of new baby and children's clothing, shoes, décor, gear, and accessories. After a makeover in 2007, the boutique is even more inviting, and we have been impressed with their selection of moderately priced to upscale inventory. If you find the perfect gift at The Purple Goose, they can ship it anywhere in the world, taking one more task off your never-ending "to do" list.

Monday's Child

Old Town Alexandria, 218 N. Lee St.
www.mondayschildofalexandria.com
Monday's Child in Old Town, recently under new ownership, specializes in classic baby and children's clothing, shoes, accessories, and gifts. We think they're just about the best place around to shop for special occasion wear (think christening gowns, flower girl dresses, and first communion attire). If you love traditional touches like smocking, embroidery, and elegant fabrics this is the place to shop! They also offer personal shopping services and private appointments.

Petite Dekor

Old Town Leesburg, 22 W. Market St.
www.petitedekor.com
Petite Dekor's setting couldn't be more charming, in the heart of historic Leesburg. This upscale boutique, under new ownership since 2006, specializes in high-end nursery and children's clothing, custom bedding and décor, gifts, stationary, books, and specialty toys (such as Melissa &

Doug, Manhattan Toy, and Gund). They also offer a gift registry and occasionally host in-store events for parents and young children.

Noodles & Noggins
Historic Clifton, 12644 Chapel Rd.
www.noodlesandnoggins.com
Historic Clifton, VA is a destination unto itself, but for families with young children, Noodles and Noggins is the highlight. Named by Families magazine as the 2007 readers' choice favorite toy store in the Washington, DC area – along with "finalist" status for its storytimes and birthday parties – this toy store is well worth the drive. We appreciate their diverse and carefully selected stock, and particularly their "imaginative play" items and games. They also stock plenty of great children's music and books, and often host kid-friendly events and performances in the store. Their website offers online shopping.

The Pajama Squid
Takoma Park, 7320 Carroll Ave.
www.thepajamasquid.com
This adorable addition to the boutique shopping scene is such a breath of fresh air for Takoma Park. Owner Tiffany King has created a happy place with beautiful things for babies, children, and moms, located near the Takoma metro station on the red line. They also have an online storefront, for those of us who aren't in the neighborhood. The Pajama Squid was recently featured by CoolMomPicks.com for their impeccably-selected gifts and gear. And they host weekly storytimes for little ones.

Olly Shoes
Mt. Vernon Plaza, Alexandria
www.ollyshoes.com
Shortly after Olly Shoes opened in Alexandria, a friend of ours shopped there for her difficult-to-fit son. And after a first attempt with purchasing a pair of shoes that turned out to cause blisters, our friend reported excellent customer service and follow-up from the store manager. A return trip to the store for another measurement and consultation, and they went home happy with two (really cute and durable) pairs of shoes for their preschooler. We also love that Olly carries UGG boots for girls!

The Right Start
Gaithersburg, Washingtonian Waterfront

Reston, Plaza America
Dulles, Dulles Retail Plaza
www.rightstart.com
This national chain has recently expanded, now with three DC-area
locations, plus another in nearby Annapolis. They specialize in furniture,
bedding, gear, and toys for babies through preschoolers. We especially
like their line of organics (clothing, feeding gear, cookbooks, skin care
products, and bedding). They also stock a wide range of seasonal
products, such as baby pools, outdoor toys, and swim gear for warm
weather. And they offer a nice sampling of their inventory for online
shopping.

Ramer's Children's Shoes
Chevy Chase, DC (3810 Northampton St. NW)
202.244.2288
Alas, those pitter-pattering little feet grow fast. We recommend Ramer's
Children's Shoes for all-around quality, service, and selection. This ain't
the bargain bin, but at Ramer's you have peace of mind and perks you
won't receive anywhere else, saving your sanity and pocketbook in the
long run. The staff at Ramer's are exceptionally friendly and helpful,
patient with little ones, and they provide top-notch service while
educating you about your child's changing needs. They measure your
child's feet at each visit (who does THAT anymore?) and can give good
advice on the type and style of shoe appropriate for developmental level
and time of year. The "house brand" is the classic and hardy Stride Rite,
but they also stock others, including Kids, Capezio, and soft-soled Robeez.
You can sign up for their mailing list to be notified of sales, which they
have on a regular basis. Just like in the old days, Ramer's will keep your
child's measurements and information on file for future visits, and they
send out a reminder when it's probably time to check the fit of your
child's shoe again. Ramer's has old-fashioned integrity worthy of the
highest praise – If by some chance they don't have the right shoe for your
child, they won't hesitate to send you elsewhere. Since they specialize in
kids' shoes, Ramer's really knows their customer and their product lines.
Special needs are usually a breeze here, too. A child with extra-wide or
double-extra-wide feet can be properly measured and fitted, and they
even carry soccer cleats. Toys and books keep the kids occupied while you
shop.

Robcyn's

Fairlington/Alexandria, Bradlee Shopping Center on King St.
What Robcyn's storefront lacks in curb appeal, it makes up for with eclectic selection of baby and children's clothing, toys and books, and accessories. Plus plenty of good for grownups. We've had good luck purchasing ballet clothing and shoes for toddler and preschool girls at Robcyn's, and have always received helpful, friendly service.

Shoe Train

Potomac, Cabin John Mall
This small children's shoe store tucked away in Cabin John Mall takes the time to measure and properly fit what they sell. A nice selection of quality shoes for toddlers through school-age children, with a friendly staff who knows their stock well. Some families have been coming here for generations to outfit their feet! We love that they keep old-fashioned card files with your child's details, which can be very helpful on subsequent visits.

The Silken Thread

Alexandria/web-based boutique
www.thesilkenthread.com
We looove The Silken Thread's custom clothing, gifts, and accessories. (And not just because we like to support locally-owned small businesses founded by smart, talented entrepreneurial mamas.) While not exclusive to baby and children's offerings – they also specialize in weddings and other special occasions – The Silken Thread offers a nice selection of items that are perfect for gift-giving and keepsake wearables. We especially like their monogrammed, embroidered "welcome baby gift sets," hats, diaper covers, burp pads, and A-line jumpers for girls. Laura Swanstrom Reece and her staff have hand-picked quality items and made them into keepsakes with personal finishes. Shopping is easy online, with readily accessible, friendly customer service by phone or email if you need assistance.

Tree Top Kids

Arlington, Lee Heights on Lee Hwy.
Bethesda, Wildwood Center on Old Georgetown Rd.
NW DC, Foxhall Square on New Mexico Ave.
Mclean, Langley Shopping Center on Chain Bridge Rd.

Fairfax, Fairfax Corner on Grand Commons Ave.
Potomac, Cabin John Mall on Seven Locks Rd.
Falls Church, Idylwood Plaza on Leesburg Pike
www.treetopkids.com
This fabulous shop, with several locations throughout the DC area, carries
not only loads of the best toys and books, but also clothes for infants and
kids. We love that they stock the ever-so-soft and cuddly Little Giraffe
blankets, Lilly Pulitzer, Tea, and Robeez - plus harder-to-find children's
clothing lines, including many imports. Tree Top Kids boutiques also host
great children's events throughout the year, free or low-cost. And the
Arlington shop now has a great new bookstore!

Urban Chic
Bethesda, 7126 Bethesda Ln.
www.urbanchiconline.com
Urban Chic's Bethesda location carries the most extensive line of
children's clothing of their DC-area stores (other locations are in
Georgetown, National Harbor, Baltimore, and coming soon to Annapolis).
Think high-end designer fashions with a trendy edge. Think mini-sized
Juicy track suits and pacifiers. Seriously.

Whirligigs & Whimsies
Bethesda, Wildwood Shopping Plaza
301.897.4940
This small but special independent toy store carries a good selection of
unique toys – many old-fashioned and high-quality options. They're also
known to host a generously-discounted annual sale, and they offer free
gift wrap. The staff is helpful and truly kid-friendly!

Why Not?
Old Town Alexandria, 200 King St.
Long before I became a mother, my inner child and I loved to visit Why
Not? in Old Town. Both floors of the store are packed to the hilt with
upscale, imported infant and children's clothes, old-fashioned and
handcrafted toys, books, gifts and random delights. Since 1962, the shop
has been quietly succeeding, an institution for Alexandria families and a
hub for tourists as well. For shopping with a young child in tow, we love
the small "gated" play area on the first floor, complete with a train table
and kitchen. We also frequent the shop's window displays that change

with the seasons, the retro toys and hobby items, the Gotz dolls and dress-up clothes.

Wren & Divine
Mclean, at the Balducci's Shopping Center on Old Dominion Dr.
www.wrenanddivine.com
Divine is right! It's boutique shopping in a warehouse-size space. Wren & Divine carries a huge selection of specialty and custom furniture, bedding, high-end strollers, and accessories for babies and children, as well as lovely gifts. And you'll find no particle-board here – They only carry 100 percent hardwood furniture made in the US, Canada, and Chile. Their prices are competitive and the customer service is reputed to be among the best in the DC area. For expectant parents and easy gift-giving/baby shower planning, Wren & Divine also offers a registry. They even host live weekend performances by local kiddie rock stars such as Mr. Knick Knack.

Yiro
Georgetown, P St. NW
www.yirostores.com
For organic baby and children's clothing and accessories in the DC area, this is the spot! Yiro is a trendy and upscale boutique in the heart of Georgetown's shopping corridor that meets the growing market for organic shopping in our area. In addition to their large stock of soft and cuddly clothing for infants through school-age children, Yiro also sells modern and eco-friendly nursery furniture, Bugaboo strollers, and organic and natural pampering products for expectant and new mothers, baby carriers and slings, hip diaper bags, baby books, and custom gifts. What's more, Yiro provides services that take the cake. Their specialized concierge offerings include delivery of fresh, organic meals to new parents at home (or even in the hospital), preparation and delivery of an expectant mother's hospital bag, consulting artists who can help develop a custom nursery theme, sourcing and delivering baby items that could otherwise require multiple shopping trips, car seat fitting demonstrations, and even research on the best school programs in your neighborhood.

Zara Kids
Downtown DC, The Woodward & Lothrop ("Woodie's") Bldg. on F St.
www.zara.com
The new Zara store at the historic Woodie's building downtown brings

their fabulous European children's clothing line to the city – a one-of-a-kind spot in the DC area! The clothing is cool and stylish, without being pretentiously overpriced. Same goes for their women's and men's clothing, shoes, and accessories. To date, the DC Zara is one of only 29 locations in the US, though there are plans for major expansion throughout the country in 2008 and beyond.

ALSO CHECK OUT. . .

Hiccups
Rockville, 1616 Rockville Pike
www.hiccupsbaby.com

Les Enfants Children's Store
Bethesda, 5110 Ridgefield Rd.

Lemon Drop
Chevy Chase, 8534 Connecticut Ave.
301.986.0044

Osh Kosh B'Gosh
Rockville, 1661 Rockville Pike
www.oshkoshbgosh.com

Proper Topper
Georgetown/Glover Park, DC, 3213 P St. NW
Dupont Circle, DC, 1350 Connecticut Ave. NW
www.propertopper.com

Sullivan's Toys & Art Supplies
3412 Wisconsin Ave. NW, DC
202.362.1343

Toys, Etc.
Potomac, Cabin John Mall
301. 299.8300

Whistle Stop
Old Town Alexandria, 130 S. Royal St.
www.whistlestophobbies.com

SHOPPING, SIMPLIFIED & INSPIRED

CoolMomPicks.com is one of the best online discoveries we've made since publishing the first edition of this book in 2005. Visit the site to subscribe to their free mailing list for honest scoop and discerning taste on products for kids of all ages. Plus the chance to win many free giveaways and take advantage of special promotions. We love their style. And we're so glad they don't take compensation for their (100 percent independent) reviews. Advertising on the website is clearly marked as such – but the editorial can't be bought. It's the same approach we've taken with DC Baby publications, and as readers we SO appreciate the integrity of their content.

DC'S FAVORITE CONSIGNMENT

Classy Kids Consignment
Manassas
www.classykidsconsignment.com
These huge seasonal consignment blowouts in Manassas feature everything imaginable for babies and kids. Clothing, accessories, gear, toys, books...you name it. As a nice perk, they offer a limited number of first-come, first-served presale passes for expectant and new mamas. If you're pregnant or have a child 18 months or younger, you can shop early! Check the website for upcoming sale dates and presale passes.

Emma's Closet
Germantown, Fox Chapel Shopping Center
www.emmasclosetllc.com
From maternity through pre-teen, Emma's Closet in Germantown has a

constantly updated selection of seasonal clothing, shoes, accessories, baby gear, furnishings, and toys to choose from. You'll find brands ranging from Ralph Lauren, Baby Lulu, and Hanna Andersson to Baby Gap and Carter's. We appreciate their in-store play area for little ones! Consignments are accepted Tuesday through Saturday from 10 a.m. to 1 p.m., and they ask that you call ahead before bringing in any large items to consign. Print a coupon for 10 percent off from their website before you shop!

The Growing Years
Kensington, 10303 Kensington Pkwy.
www.growing-years.net
For some 15 years this consignment boutique in Kensington, MD has offered gently-loved clothing and shoes for babies to preteens, as well as maternity clothing, nursery and children's furniture and gear, books for kids (plus pregnancy and parenting titles), and a nice selection of popular new items, such as girls' hair accessories, select clothes and toys, and American Girl doll outfits. The store's environment makes shopping a bit easier on the weary mother's soul, with Disney movies and play areas.

Kensington Caboose
Kensington, 10508 Connecticut Ave.
www.kensingtoncaboose.com
Since 1989, this upscale consignment shop in Kensington has been a hub for shopping and consigning gently used maternity clothing, baby and kids' clothing, shoes, furnishings, gear, toys, and books. You'll even find the fabulous Melissa & Doug line of wooden toys, and Jack & Lily baby shoes. Consignment days are Monday through Saturday, by appointment only. Sign up for their free e-newsletter at the website.

Once Upon a Child
Manassas, 7692 Stream Walk Ln.
www.ouac.com
Once Upon a Child in Manassas is part of the nation's largest chain of kids' resale stores, buying and selling both gently used and new clothing, furnishings, gear, and toys. They are open seven days a week. No appointment necessary to consign, and they pay on-the-spot for all accepted items. Check policies on the website in advance for tips on what they can and cannot consider for consignment.

Red Beans & Rice
14th St. NW, DC
www.redbeanchildren.com
Red Beans and Rice really IS the only boutique of its kind in Washington, DC. They carry both new and consigned children's clothing at great prices – in addition to books, games, toys, and gifts. They host fantastic end-of-season clearance sales (think 40 to 50 percent off!), and everything they stock is of high quality. And the breadth of their inventory is impressive, given the shop's cozy space. Red Beans and Rice also hosts children's events and performances.

Wiggle Room
Downtown Bethesda, off Old Georgetown Rd.
www.wiggleroom.biz
Love Wiggle Room! New on the scene since the first edition of this book was published, this downtown Bethesda shop is a gem. They carry a large selection of maternity wear, baby and children's clothing (up to size 6) and accessories, and all the gear you need – strollers, soft carriers, bouncy seats, high chairs, as well as eco-friendly specialty products for little ones and mamas. Never fear the parking situation: In addition to metered spaces on the street, a garage is located right across the street (with free parking on weekends). Wiggle Room regularly hosts special events and sales. Sign up for their email list to get early notice of special deals!

Annual "Dani's Duds" Consignment Sale
www.danisduds.com
Open one week every spring and one week every fall at different NoVa locations, offering a super-sized selection of gently used children's toys and clothing – toys, books, videos, CDs, software, coats, clothes, furniture for infants through age 12. Sign up for email notification on their website.

JLW's Annual "Tossed & Found" Sale
www.jlw.org/jlw/fundraisers_tossed.htm
For more than 15 years, this huge rummage sale sponsored by the Junior League of Washington has offered super-inexpensive stuff for babies and kids. Typically held in April. Check the website for dates and location. Proceeds benefit the Junior League's literacy projects throughout the DC metro area.

TotSwap
http://totswap.net
The huge and ever-expanding TotSwap events are held in Gaithersburg and Timonium, MD several times a year. A great way to sell – and buy – new and gently-used maternity, baby, and children's items! TotSwap features children's clothing, shoes, accessories, gear, toys, indoor/outdoor play equipment, books, DVDs, sports equipment, maternity goodies, and more. Over 300 families typically sell their items at each TotSwap event – in addition to DC-area retailers who offer their new merchandise at kiosks throughout the sale.

Craig's List, DC
http://washingtondc.craigslist.org/bab/
Check out the "For Sale: Baby & Kids" section on the Craig's List Washington, DC site. Great place to buy (and sell) gently-used baby and kids' furniture, gear, and even clothing.

> *author's note:*
> For the inside scoop on many more seasonal consignment events specializing in baby and children's goodies, register at the Our Kids website and benefit from their extensive, continually updated listings, covering sales throughout the DC area: www.our-kids.com.

DC'S FAVORITE CHILDREN'S BOOKS

Hooray for Books
Old Town Alexandria, 1555 King St.
www.hooray4books.com
After the sad demise of A Likely Story in November 2007, we're thrilled that a new children's bookstore has opened in the same space, founded and managed by two former A Likely Story staffers, Ellen Klein and Trish Brown. Hooray for Books opened its doors in spring 2008 and is off to a great start. Hooray for Books is building a strong selection of titles for all ages – from baby board books to young adult fiction – as well as a carefully selected offering of puzzles, toys, and gifts. We also appreciate

that Hooray for Books is eager to special order any title you're looking for that's not currently on the shelf, with such orders usually arriving within a week. They host regular storytimes (many of which have fabulously imaginative themes), as well as special events ranging from appearances by costumed characters to author signings to craft events and magicians' workshops. We also love that they've launched a blog where customers are encouraged to share tips and reviews of their favorite children's titles. It has the potential to become a great resource for those of us who love to read with our kids.

Aladdin's Lamp Children's Books
N. Arlington/Falls Church, 2499 N. Harrison St.
We're big fans! This lovely independent children's bookstore – a longtime local favorite - is tucked away in the basement level of the Lee Harrison Plaza in Arlington. What we most admire about Aladdin's Lamp is its ample and diverse stock of books for all ages, from toddler board books to young adult fiction and nonfiction – and beyond. They keep a superb selection of classics and new releases on the shelves – so chances are good they'll have what you are looking for! And if they don't have it in stock, Aladdin's Lamp will be quick to order it for you, whether a children's book or an adult title. The staff is knowledgeable and courteous, and Aladdin's Lamp regularly hosts free storytimes, children's sing-along performances, workshops for parents, and other family-oriented events. The only thing we'd love to see them do is launch a website, which would allow those of us who trek from neighboring communities to more easily keep up with their in-store calendar!

Booktopia Books & Gifts for Children
Bethesda, Shops at Sumner Place on Sangamore Rd.
Booktopia offers a wide variety of children's books, specialty toys, cool science kits, and arts and crafts for all ages. They also host storytimes and offer nice perks like gift wrapping. Like Aladdin's Lamp, we'd love to see Booktopia launch a website, allowing busy parents to keep up with their latest offerings and in-store events!

Politics & Prose children's section
Chevy Chase, NW DC
www.politics-prose.com
Politics & Prose is a Washington institution. They have an excellent

breadth of stock, they provide above-and-beyond customer service, and they are a hub for book-related events. The children's section at Politics & Prose is no exception – well-stocked with both classics and new releases for all ages, backed by knowledgeable staff. We really appreciate their frequently updated website, with its "Kidz Page" section highlighting new releases, award-winning titles, and in-store events. The Politics & Prose storytimes are wildly popular with families who live in upper NW, and they even sponsor a Teen Book Group for the older set.

The Story Tellers
Occoquan, VA historic district
www.3storytellers.com
Located near the waterfront in the historic district of Occoquan (between Fairfax and Prince William Counties) is a brand-new bookstore focused on children's and young adult titles. They opened their doors in spring 2008, and as of press time for this book are preparing to launch an online storefront. The Story Tellers focuses on award-winning, school-approved, and culturally-diverse books. They also have a full lineup of activities for kids of all ages (and some for adults), including readings, book signings, writing seminars, and art classes.

LOOKING FOR MORE STORYTIMES?
Check out storytime offerings at **Kinder Haus** in Clarendon, Arlington (www.kinderhaus.com), **Olsson's** in Old Town (www.olssons.com) and **The Pajama Squid** in Takoma Park (http://shop.thepajamasquid.com) – as well as your **public library system**:

DC, www.dclibrary.org
Montgomery County, www.montgomerycountymd.gov
Fairfax County, www.fairfaxcounty.gov/Library
Prince George's County, www.prge.lib.md.us
Alexandria, www.alexandria.lib.va.us
Arlington, www.arlingtonva.us
Loudon County, http://library.loudoun.gov

SHARING THE WEALTH:
Where to Donate Gently-Used
Clothing, Furnishings, Gear, Toys, & Books

We've often heard local parents ask where to donate gently-used clothing, furniture, accessories, and gear when it has been outgrown. Selling to consignment shops is one good way to rid your house of clutter and recycle playthings. Donating to a worthy cause is another option, and here are a few suggestions.

Consider involving your child as you pack up items for donation and take them to the drop-off – Teaching by doing is the best way to instill the family values of gratitude and giving. It can also be a therapeutic way for your kids to willingly "let go" of the playthings they've outgrown. By cleaning out your closets and the playroom once or twice a year, you can make a big difference in the life of local families in need.

A Wider Circle, which provides basic home furnishings to individuals transitioning out of homeless shelters, is working overtime to keep up with the significant needs of local children whose parents are being served by the program. Most recently: In an effort to give every child in metro DC a bed, they've launched a new campaign, "A Bed for Every Child." *DC Baby* reader and A Wider Circle volunteer Malia tells us, *"There is a desperate need right now for some items that we might have just sitting around, such as cribs, portable cribs, bassinets, infant car seats,, strollers, etc. If you have things that are just lying around - not awaiting a next child - please think about contributing. Or please keep it in mind for when you are done with these items in the future, as there is an ongoing need."* For more info about the program and their drop-off facility, go to www.awidercircle.org.

Children's Inn at NIH has a need for toys (*new only*, in this case) for ages birth through teens. To donate, call 301.496.5672. www.childrensinn.org

Mary's Center for Maternal and Child Care in Northwest DC, which serves the health needs of Spanish-speaking low-income women and their babies, needs children's and childcare books, pregnancy and birth books, and other relevant items. Call 202.483.8319 for information or visit www.maryscenter.org

The Healthy Babies Project in Northeast DC needs new and gently used toys and books for newborns to age eight. Contact 202.396.2809 to donate. www.healthybabiesproject.org

The Campagna Center in Alexandria has a need for new and gently used toys and books for ages three to 12. Call 703.549.0111 to donate. www.campagnacenter.org

Healthy Families Montgomery in Gaithersburg needs new or gently used toys and books for newborns to age three. Call 301.840.2000, ext. 222 to donate.

The Naomi Project in Arlington County, which pairs trained volunteer mentors with high-risk pregnant women and young mothers, helps support consistent prenatal and pediatric care. Volunteers are their biggest demand, but they also need donated cribs, strollers, and other baby gear that is gently used or new. Items like pregnancy and childcare books, books appropriate for newborns through toddler age, self-care items for the mamas, baby gifts, etc. may also be accepted. For information, call 703.860.2633 or visit www.naomiproject.org.

The **Center for Child Protection and Family Support** in Southeast DC needs new or gently used toys and books for ages four to 16. Contact Mary McLaughlin at 202.544.3144 to donate.

The Child Development Center of Northern Virginia needs new and gently used toys and books for newborns to age five. Call 703.534.5353, ext. 100 to donate.

My Sister's Place, a DC shelter for battered women and their children, needs new or gently used blankets, twin-size sheet sets, and pillow cases. Call 202.529.5991 to donate. www.mysistersplacedc.org

Suited for Change accepts clean, gently used clothes and accessories (belts, briefcases, purses) from professional women and donates them to low-income women who are trying to enter the workforce. When a woman completes a job-training program at any of 40 local agencies, a Suited for Change volunteer helps her pick out two outfits for job interviews. If she gets a job, she has access to more outfits to begin work.

You can drop off items to curbside volunteers on the second Saturday of every month between 9 a.m. and noon at 1531 P St. NW. Receipts are available. Call 202.232.1097 for more info. www.suitedforchange.org

The Family Crisis Center of Prince George's County serves 125 children a year who are abandoned, orphaned, or escaping abuse. Clothing, diapers, bottles, and toys are accepted. Call 301.779.2100, ext. 10 for information.

United Cerebral Palsy of Washington and NoVa has an Early Head Start program for infants and toddlers. They always need more diapers, wipes, toys, and clothes. Call 703.360.2060, ext. 225 to help.

Reston Youth Club Bike Shop, Burke Earn-a-Bike Program, and Urban Rangers in Adams Morgan and Columbia Heights are programs that help kids and teens earn their own bikes by doing repair work and community service. These are kids who would not otherwise be able to afford a bicycle. To donate a bike, call 703.689.4433 for the Reston program, 703.239.2125 for the Burke program, and contact Katie Davis at 202.332.0774 for the Urban Rangers program.

Northern Virginia Family Service works through the schools to reach low-income families, including infants, school-age children, and adults. They have a need for school supplies, including pens and pencils, crayons, paper, dictionaries, calculators, scissors, and gear like backpacks. Call 703.533.9727 to donate. www.nvfs.org

Boys & Girls Clubs' Group Homes and Shelters house more than 300 children a year at 10 locations. If you have extra or unused tickets to sporting or children's entertainment events, consider donating them to these youngsters. Call Joy Hill at 301.587.7875. www.bgcgw.org

Salvation Army thrift stores accept baby and children's clothing, furniture, gear, and toys in gently-used condition. In Alexandria (6528 Little River Turnpike) you can do the easy drive-through drop-off six days a week, Monday through Saturday. In Hyattsville (3304 Kenilworth Ave.), call the store for drop-off hours: 301.403.1704. For information about pick-up of items for donation in the DC area, call 1.800.95.TRUCK. www.uss.salvationarmy.org

Goodwill accepts baby and children's clothing, furniture, gear, and toys in gently-used condition. Policies on what they can accept and drop-off times may vary by location. They also offer home pick-ups throughout most of the DC metro area. Drop-off locations include NE DC, Rockville, Gaithersburg, Arlington, Springfield, Sterling, Vienna, and Manassas. www.dcgoodwill.org/donate/where_to_donate.htm

CHAPTER 9
Food & Dining Out

A LIFESAVER: THE SIX O'CLOCK SCRAMBLE

The Six O'Clock Scramble has saved our sanity – especially after adding a second child to the family. This subscription weekly e-newsletter produced by DC-area mama, chef, and cookbook author Aviva Goldfarb is worth every penny – and more. Family-friendly recipes and an easy-to-print grocery shopping list are delivered to your inbox every week. Menus change by the season and are never dull – offering something tasty for the parental palate while also taking into consideration the dietary needs and occasionally picky palates of children. Many of the recipes are vegetarian-friendly (or adaptable with suggested substitutions). Prep and cook time estimates are included with each recipe – with many of the dishes taking 30 minutes or less to prepare. Dietary info helps you keep tab, if you're counting calories. A subscription runs about $26.50 for six months, or about $47.50 for a full year. Makes a great gift for expectant parents and families! Earn additional subscription time when you refer a friend. See the website for sample menus and lots more: http://thescramble.com.

THE LATEST & GREATEST: COOK-AHEAD SERVICES

Since I wrote the first edition of this book in 2005, cook-ahead services have proliferated like mad, with new franchises opening throughout suburban DC. A helpful option for busy families, these places support home-cooked meals that you heat and eat at home – but you assemble them ahead of time and they do the menu planning, grocery shopping, and some of the prep for you.

Here's how it works: You book a time in advance (online or by phone), show up, and in their state-of-the-art, fully stocked kitchen assemble anywhere from six to 14 meals for your family. The process takes about two hours on-site. (Adults only, due to health code regulations.) At home you freeze the meals, heating them up individually when you're ready to serve.

There's room to individualize – for example, to adjust the spiciness of a recipe, or to make two meals of the chicken cacciatore because your family won't eat the shrimp tacos. Cost-per-serving ranges from about $2.70 to $3.75 – so it's more economical than eating out (and possibly healthier, as well). Some of the services offer special perks like doing all the prep work for you at an additional charge, or splitting portions (especially appealing to couples with one baby or toddler who is not yet eating full portions).

Let's Dish, www.letsdish.net
The Kentlands, Gaithersburg
11401 Woodglen Rd., Rockville
The Snowden Center, Columbia
9602 Deereco Rd., Timonium
Amyclae Business Center, Bel Air
Cameron Chase Village Center, Ashburn
6550 Little River Turnpike, Alexandria
Cameron Chase Village Center, Ashburn
11215 Lee Hwy., Fairfax
705 E. Market St., Leesburg

> *"I just tried Let's Dish! for the first time and… I loved it. The ingredients were fresh and the recipes are really good. This could simplify my life, and I'm going again soon."*
>
> *- Katie*

Dream Dinners, www.dreamdinners.com
720 Cloverly St., Silver Spring
1701 Rockville Pike, Rockville
12162 Darnestown Rd., Gaithersburg
2601 Salem Church Rd., Fredericksburg
COMING SOON: Arlington

Thyme Out, www.thymeout.com
As of this book's press date, Thyme Out has plans to move into new digs at the Kentlands in Gaithersburg, and an additional location in Rockville. Check the website for the full scoop.

DC'S FAVORITE GROCERY DELIVERY

There are several popular options in the DC area, including:

Washington's Green Grocer, www.washingtonsgreengrocer.com
Washington's Green Grocer, founded by longtime Washingtonians Zeke and Lisa Zechiel, delivers a selection of fresh fruits and vegetables, organic dairy products, and specials (e.g. fresh herbs, peppers, pastas) to homes throughout the DC metro area. Once a week you can have the absolute freshest in-season items plunked down at your doorstep. And the process is easy. A Monday email and voicemail posting each week announces the choices. Twelve to 14 different types of fruits and veggies are available to choose from each week, plus the specials and all of the organic milks, cheeses, eggs, and plain yogurts. You let them know what you want, and poof – you're done. You can also customize your weekly box by volume – They offer a small box geared for a single person (or a couple who eats out a lot), and the standard box, which is designed for a couple or small family. The smaller box weighs 12 to 15 pounds, while the standard box weighs 18 to 25 pounds. You can choose from a combo of organic and conventional produce, or go for 100 percent organic. Perhaps best of all, there are no contracts or iffy obligations with this service. If you go out of town, you can cancel for any given week. You don't even have to be home to receive it, since you can pay by credit card and designate a place to leave the box (porch, garage, etc.).

Peapod Delivery, www.peapod.com
In the DC metro area, Peapod is affiliated with Giant grocery stores. It's an easy-to-use system that allows you to "shop" online at the Peapod website, placing your order and having it delivered to your front door. You can even provide specs for some of your items, such as yellow or green bananas and thin or thick-sliced deli meats. The service is used by many area families – especially those in which both parents work full-time outside the home and those who have a new baby.

Safeway Delivery, www.safeway.com
Safeway now offers online ordering and home delivery of groceries, serving the District and the suburbs of Maryland and NoVa. With many features similar to what Peapod offers, you can shop by aisle, create and

save an "express list" for yourself, and access special members-only features like a recipe center and articles on wellness and nutrition.

DC'S FAVORITE HEALTHY MEALS-TO-GO

Trader Joe's, www.traderjoes.com
1101 25th St. NW, DC
6831 Wisconsin Ave., Bethesda
10741 Columbia Pike, Silver Spring
12268-H Rockville Pike, Rockville
18270 Contour Rd., Gaithersburg
612 N. St. Asaph St., Old Town Alexandria
5847 Leesburg Pike, Bailey's Crossroads
9464 Main St., Fairfax
11958 Killingsworth Ave., Reston
6394 Springfield Plaza Rd., Springfield
7514 Leesburg Turnpike, Falls Church
Trader Joe's has a great selection of fresh-prepared takeaway entrees, soups, and side dishes, ready to take home and heat quickly in the oven or microwave. Many come packaged in individual servings, but others will serve more than one as a side dish. Our favorites: the Chinese Chicken Salad, the Organic Black Bean and Corn Enchiladas, the Bouillabaisse Seafood Stew, and the gallon-jug of their Southern Iced Tea.

Whole Foods, www.wholefoods.com
1440 P St. NW, DC (Logan Circle)
2323 Wisconsin Ave. NW, DC (Glover Park)
4530 40th St. NW, DC (Tenley)
5269 River Rd., Bethesda
316 Kentlands Blvd., Gaithersburg
1649 Rockville Pike, Rockville
833 Wayne Ave., Silver Spring
2700 Wilson Blvd., Arlington
1700 Duke St., Old Town Alexandria
8402 Old Keene Mill Rd., Springfield
4501 Market Commons Dr., Fairfax
7511 Leesburg Pike, Falls Church
11660 Plaza America Dr., Reston
143 Maple Ave. E., Vienna

I'm a big Whole Foods fan, since I first shopped at the tiny original WF Market in Austin, Texas as a college student in the early 1990s. They still have friendly and helpful staff, great produce, and a big selection of fresh-prepared entrees, sides, soups, sandwiches, and desserts. Fabulous salad and pasta bar in some locations, as well as a hot-foods bar that is equally good for take-out or for a sit-down meal in the store (where high chairs are also available). Great for busy families, workday lunches, or packing a picnic. Our favorites: the cheese and jalapeno tamales, Maryland crab cakes, grilled salmon fillets, and corn fritters.

> **MOM MADE FOODS: A LOCAL SUCCESS STORY**
> When you purchase those yummy, healthy Mom Made baby and toddler foods in the frozen section at Whole Foods, Balducci's, Super Targets, and Wegmans, you're part of a DC success story. Mom Made Foods was founded by Alexandria mompreneur Heather Stouffer just a few years ago, and has taken off like a rocket. These organic foods for children have been featured by The Washington Post, the Wall Street Journal, the Oprah Winfrey Show, and many others. Mom Made regularly hosts tastings and nutrition classes throughout the DC area, and its website features dietician-authored Q&As you'll want to check out. Congrats to Heather and her team for taking Mom Made all the way – and for providing us with a product we love to feed our kids!

ULTIMATE TREAT: A PERSONAL CHEF

That's right, a personal chef. A gift certificate makes a great gift for expectant and new parents – Especially for those who already have another child (or two) to care for, or those who don't have a strong support network of family and friends nearby. They can customize according to dietary restrictions or preferences, vegetarian, etc. Here are a few recommendations:

Lynn McKee at Lynn's Meals in Minutes
240.476.1669
www.lynnsmealsinminutes.com

Fine Dining Solutions
703.869.1242
www.finediningsolutions.com

Lauren Mobley at Purple Mango
301.581.9667

Linda Berns at Custom Kosher
301.581.0422
www.personalchef.com/customkosher.htm

**HEALTHY SNACK TIPS FROM A LOCAL
NUTRITIONAL COUNSELOR (& MOM!)**

Katherine Sumner, CHC, AADP, is a holistic health and nutritional counselor and an Alexandria mama who consults with our daughter's preschool on integrating healthier eating habits. One of the best resources she's shared with us and other families in the preschool is an "idea list" of healthy snacks - Great for posting to your frig as a reminder when you're brainstorming a grocery list, packing a bag for the playground, sending snacks to school, or looking to put together something quickly for cranky children, under the duress of a busy schedule. Katherine suggests:

seasonal organic fruit

rice cakes with seed butters (e.g., sunflower butter)

raw veggies (baby carrots, celery sticks, cucumber, sugar snap peas, baby tomatoes, green beans) with hummus or white bean dip

yogurt mixed with granola, seasonal organic fruit, and seed
 trail mix with seeds and unsulphered dried fruit
organic yogurt

whole grain or sprouted toast with butter and/or raw organic honey

chips (rice chips, quinoa chips, organic corn chips) with salsa or guacamole

homemade baked goods – carrot muffins, pumpkin muffins, banana bread, herb bread

organic cheese sticks

yogurt cheese with veggies or pita bread

rice crackers with dip

dehydrated veggies and fruits

For more about Katherine's consulting and her workshops for parents, visit www.pureandsimplehealth.org and contact her at: kat4sumner@yahoo.com or 703.474.4055.

DC'S FAVORITE CHILD-FRIENDLY RESTAURANTS
WASHINGTON, DC:

2 Amys Pizza
3715 Macomb St. NW (Cleveland Park/Cathedral)

author's note:
We love this gourmet pizza, and the kid-accommodating environment. One warning to the uninitiated: 2 Amys can get super-crowded at peak times, such as weekends and Friday nights. Bring a snack from home, in case you end up hanging out on the sidewalk for a few minutes, waiting for a table.

American City Diner
5532 Connecticut Ave. NW (Chevy Chase), www.americancitydiner.com

> **author's note:**
> The first thing your child will notice upon arriving at American City Diner: The coin-operated horsie out front (friendly and eager to serve). Inside: The miniature automated train that runs constantly on an elevated track around the main entry and seating area. (Ask the hostess to blow the train's horn, if you really want a thrill.) Next: The oversized toy and candy machines at the entry (We tried to bypass them, but it didn't work). And then: The old-fashioned mini-jukeboxes at most booths. Followed by: The abundance of greasy kid favorites on the menu – Grilled cheese, burgers, traditional breakfast favorites, chicken fingers, sandwiches, hot dogs, you name it. And the milkshakes are to die for. We're not talking health food here – American City Diner is a greasy spoon. But there are a few attempts at healthier fare thrown in. For example, you can get applesauce as a child's side item, and you can order a fruit smoothie if you want to skip the ice cream. American City Diner has a tradition of screening free movies outside in the warmer months.

Austin Grill

The Lansburgh, 750 E St. NW
NOTE: The Glover Park location on Wisconsin Ave. is (sadly) no more.
www.austingrill.com

> **author's note:**
> The downtown DC Austin Grill is convenient to several family-friendly outing spots, including the Verizon Center, National Theater, and the National Gallery of Art's sculpture garden.

Baja Fresh

1333 New Hampshire Ave. NW (Dupont Circle)
1990 K St. NW (Eye St.)
www.bajafresh.com

Bella Roma

3155 Mt. Pleasant St. NW (Mt. Pleasant)

Ben's Chili Bowl
1213 U St. NW, www.benschilibowl.com

> ***author's note:***
> A DC institution, if there ever was one! You've got to eat at Ben's at least once while living in or visiting Washington. And since it's as laid-back as can be, no reason not to bring the kids for a famous chili dog or chili burger. Don't expect healthy. It's a decadent splurge!

Bertucci's
1218 Connecticut Ave. NW (Dupont Circle)
2000 Pennsylvania Ave. NW (Foggy Bottom)
www.bertuccis.com

Bua (Thai)
1635 P St. NW (Dupont Circle)

Buca di Beppo
1825 Connecticut Ave. NW (Dupont Circle)

Cactus Cantina
3300 Wisconsin Ave. NW (Cleveland Park/Cathedral)
www.cactuscantina.com

Café Deluxe
3228 Wisconsin Ave. (Cathedral)
www.cafedeluxe.com

California Pizza Kitchen
1260 Connecticut Ave. NW (Downtown), www.cpk.com

California Tortilla
728 7th St. NW (Chinatown)
3501 Connecticut Ave. NW (Cleveland Park)
www.californiatortilla.com

> **author's note:**
> Yummy, fresh, casual Cal-Mex food with healthy options in a counter-service setting. Great option for kids!

Capitol City Brewing Co.
1100 New York Ave. at 12th St. NW (MCI Center), www.capcitybrew.com

> **author's note:**
> Capitol City has a good children's menu that offers a healthy option. You can drop the fries and add veggies on any children's item – no extra charge.

Chef Geoff's (AU Park location)
3201 New Mexico Ave. NW, www.chefgeoff.com

> **author's note:**
> Love the AU Park Chef Geoff's patio seating, shaded by trees and set back slightly from the street. Plenty of highchairs, crayons, a kids' menu. . . But the adults get to eat well, too. We really like the Sunday brunch, complete with live jazz. An especially popular weekend gathering spot for families who live in the AU Park, Tenley, and Friendship Heights neighborhoods.

> *"My mother, daughter, and I had very nice dinner tonight [at Chef Geoff's in AU Park], but when we left the restaurant I noticed I had a flat tire. It was about 90 degrees outside, and I'm embarrassed to admit I don't know how to change a tire. So I went back into the restaurant to see if I could find someone there to change my tire for a small fee. The first waiter who heard my story said he would find someone to help. When I said I was willing to pay someone $10 to change it, he said 'Oh no. We'll just do it because it's the right thing to do.' Imagine that!*
>
> *He went to find a manager to help. In the meantime, a gentleman asked me if I needed a table, and when I explained about my flat tire, without hesitation he said, "I'll do it." He went outside and changed my tire and was*

> *extremely pleasant through the whole thing, even talking very sweetly to my daughter and asking how we enjoyed our dinner as he unscrewed lugnuts! Of course I thanked him and offered to give him some money, but he refused. Turns out my good Samaritan was Damien LaRuffa, President of Operations. As he walked away, my three-year-old daughter said, 'He's a wonderful man.' That was an understatement."*
>
> *- Molly*

Chez Antoine
2427 18th St. NW (Adams Morgan)

The Diner
2453 18th St NW

Ella's Coffee
1500 block N. Capitol at P St. NW

Ella's Wood-Fired Pizza
Penn Quarter - Ninth St. NW, between F and G Sts. - www.ellaspizza.com

> *author's note:*
> Since I wrote the first edition of this book, Ella's has opened their patio for outdoor seating! A lovely way to enjoy their yummy Neopolitan pizzas and kid-friendly attitude when the weather is nice. Ella's is also a good option for family dining before or after a visit to the National Portrait Gallery/Museum of American Art, Verizon Center, or the National Theater.

Faccia Luna Pizzeria
2400 Wisconsin Ave. NW (Glover Park / Upper Georgetown)

Firehook Bakery
3411 Connecticut Ave. NW (Cleveland Park/Woodley)
www.firehook.com

Guapo's
4515 Wisconsin Ave. NW (Tenleytown), www.guaposrestaurant.com

> **author's note:**
> On weekend nights Guapo's is a major meeting hub for neighborhood families, many of whom have young kids who attend Janney's Elementary. Cheap, loud, child-friendly, and crowded.

Heritage India
1337 Connecticut Ave. NW (Dupont Circle)

Jaleo
480 7th St. NW (Chinatown/Gallery Place), www.jaleo.com

> **author's note:**
> Jaleo is one of our favorite "nicer" restaurants in DC, and eating tapas-style is inherently family-friendly. And they do welcome children, offering high chairs and smiles. However, I do warn against taking young kids on Friday and Saturday nights during the happy hour and dinnertime. Extra loud and extra crowded, with a demographic that leans toward singletons and couples who aren't necessarily thrilled to party with the tots.

Johnny's Half-Shell
2002 P St. NW (Dupont Circle), www.johnnyshalfshell.net

Lebanese Taverna
2641 Connecticut Ave. NW (Cleveland Park), www.lebanesetaverna.com

Legal Sea Foods
Seventh St. NW, 202.347.0007
K St. NW, 202.496.1111
www.legalseafoods.com

Lex Cajun Grill

2608 Connecticut Ave. NW (Woodley Park)

Melting Pot
1220 19th St. NW
www.meltingpot.com

Mt. Everest Restaurant
1805 18TH St. NW

> *"Every time we've eaten there, the wait staff at Mt. Everest have been really good with our daughter, and they're flexible about our special requests. We actually feel welcome there with a toddler."*
>
> *- Michelle*

Nam Viet
3419 Connecticut Ave. NW (Cleveland Park)

National Museum of the American Indian, Café/Food Court
On the National Mall, inside the museum

> *author's note:*
> Our favorite place to have lunch with our daughter when visiting the Mall. So many delicious choices – and healthy ones – for both children and adults. Try to grab a table near the big wall of glass overlooking the outdoor rock waterfall. A mesmerizing view for little ones!

Radius Pizza
3155 Mt. Pleasant St. NW

Rosemary's Thyme Bistro
1801 18th St. NW (Dupont Circle)
http://rosemarysthyme.com

Sala Thai

3507 Connecticut Ave. NW (Cleveland Park)
www.salathaidc.com

Thai Room
5037 Connecticut Ave. NW (Chevy Chase)

Third & Eats
500 Third St. NW (Capitol Hill)

Tono Sushi
2605 Connecticut Ave. NW (Woodley Park)

White Tiger (Indian)
301 Massachusetts Ave. at Third St. NE (Union Station)

MARYLAND SUBURBS:

Austin Grill
7278 Woodmont Ave., Bethesda
919 Ellsworth Dr., Silver Spring
www.austingrill.com

> **author's note:**
> We are Austin Grill aficionados, and I can vouch that it's
> among the kid-friendliest of DC-area restaurants. Austin Grill
> has a good children's menu (applesauce or rice and beans,
> instead of fries!), they supply crayons and drawing paper
> when you arrive, and they bring kids' drinks in a spill-proof
> kiddie cup. There's plenty of outdoor seating at the Bethesda
> location to enjoy when the weather's nice, and it's fun to
> people-watch at this busy downtown Bethesda spot – near
> shopping, two blocks from a playground, and one block from
> the entrance to the Capitol Crescent trail. Parking in the
> metered public lot directly behind the restaurant.

Baja Fresh
4930 Elm St., Bethesda
1607 Rockville Pike, Rockville
301 King Farm Blvd., Rockville

8515 Fenton St., Silver Spring
622 Center Point Way, Gaithersburg
www.bajafresh.com

BD's Mongolian Barbecue
7201 Wisconsin Ave., Bethesda
www.bdsmongolianbarbeque.com

Bertucci's
11919 Rockville Pike, Rockville
www.bertuccis.com

> *"Bertucci's gives out crayons and a ball of dough to play with. And they have a good children's menu. They've always been friendly and accommodating with my son."*
>
> *- Andrea*

Café Deluxe
4910 Elm St., Bethesda
www.cafedeluxe.com

> **author's note:**
> We've had a couple of slow waits for food at the Bethesda location of Café Deluxe, but other than that annoyance they have been very child-friendly. We consider this restaurant a decent training ground for future outings to "white tablecloth" venues! Good food for the adults, reasonable prices, highchairs and crayons for the children. We like their sidewalk seating when the weather is good.

California Pizza Kitchen
Montgomery Mall, Bethesda
136 Boardwalk Place, Gaithersburg
www.cpk.com

California Tortilla
4862 Cordell Ave., Bethesda

7727 Tuckerman Ln., Potomac
199 E. Montgomery Ave., Rockville
3941 Evergreen Pkwy., Bowie
7419 Baltimore Ave., College Park
19847-O Century Blvd., Germantown
18101 Village Center Dr., Olney
www.californiatortilla.com

> *"We like the kids' items on the menu at California Tortilla and how laid-back the place is. Our child can make a mess or make noise and no one really notices or cares. The 80s music is fun to listen to and the people who work there are friendly."*
>
> *- Meredith*

Cheeburger Cheeburger
14921 Shady Grove Rd., Rockville
www.cheeburger.com

Chevys Fresh Mex
668 Clopper Rd., Gaithersburg
7511 Greenbelt Rd., Greenbelt
www.chevys.com

Eggspectations
923 Ellsworth Dr., Silver Spring

Glory Days Grill
18050 Mateney Rd., Germantown

Guardado's
4918 Del Ray Ave., Bethesda
www.guardadosnico.com

Hard Times Café & Chili Parlor
4920 Del Ray Ave., Bethesda
4738 Cherry Hill Rd., College Park
1117 Nelson St., Rockville

1003 W. Patrick St., Frederick
1021 Washington Blvd., Laurel
www.hardtimes.com

Hot Breads Bakery & Café
301.977.1919, 70 Market St. (Kentlands), Gaithersburg
www.hotbreadsmddc.com

Joe's Crab Shack
221 Rio Blvd., Gaithersburg
www.joescrabshack.com

Ledo Pizza
5245 River Rd., Bethesda
www.ledopizza.com

> *author's note:*
> We love their square-shaped pies! And the Bethesda location is a neighborhood institution. Gets packed on the weekends by Bethesda families. Nice outdoor seating when the weather is good helps with the overflow.

Mayorga Coffee
8040 Georgia Ave., Silver Spring

Melting Pot
9021 Gaither Rd., Gaithersburg
www.meltingpot.com

Mi Rancho
8701 Ramsey Ave., Silver Spring

Original Pancake House
7700 Wisconsin Ave., Bethesda

> *author's note:*

> Crowded on the weekends, especially at breakfast/brunch. A longtime family-friendly favorite for Bethesda and Chevy Chase families.

Old Hickory Grille
1093 Seven Locks Rd., Potomac
www.oldhickorygrille.com

Old Georgetown Grille
7755 Old Georgetown Rd., Bethesda

Olney Ale House
2000 Sandy Spring Rd., Olney

Parkway Deli
8317 Grubb Rd., Silver Spring

Potomac Pizza
19 Wisconsin Circle, Chevy Chase
9812 Falls Rd., Potomac
9709 Traville Gateway Dr., Rockville
625 Center Point Way, Gaithersburg
www.potomacpizza.com

Rainforest Café
Towson Town Center, Towson, www.rainforestcafe.com

> ***author's note:***
> It's loud in the rainforest. The colors are loud. The music is loud. And loudest of all are the kids who love Rainforest Café. This is, as their slogan says, "A wild place to eat." I don't mean to scare you off. For the most part, it's a manageable noise level at Rainforest Café. It won't cause you to pull your hair from its roots like, say, Chuck E. Cheese. But it won't be the most tranquil dining you've ever done, either. That's why most young children love this place. There's lots to see and hear, with nary a dull moment.

Rio Grande Café

4870 Bethesda Ave., Bethesda
231 Rio Blvd., Gaithersburg

Rock Bottom Brewery & Restaurant
7900 Norfolk Ave., Bethesda
www.rockbottombethesda.com

> *"I like that the child's macaroni-and-cheese at Rock Bottom comes with fruit as a side dish. That kind of thing is hard to find. The grown-up food is good too. We order a steak, ribs, or the beer-sautéed chicken."*
>
> *- Sam*

Sala Thai
4828 Cordell Ave., Bethesda
www.salathaidc.com

Silver Diner
11806 Rockville Pike, Rockville
www.silverdiner.com

Savory
7071 Carroll Ave., Takoma Park

Tandoori Nights (Indian)
106 Market St., Gaithersburg
www.tandoorinights.com

Udupi Palace (Indian)
1329 University Blvd., Takoma Park

NORTHERN VIRGINIA:

Ariagato Sushi
11199 Lee Hwy., Fairfax

Artie's Restaurant
3260 Old Lee Hwy., Fairfax

Austin Grill
801 King St., Old Town Alexandria
8430 Old Keene Mill Rd., Springfield
www.austingrill.com

> *author's note:*
> In 2007 the City of Alexandria approved outdoor sidewalk
> seating for more restaurants along King St. in Old Town – an
> overdue and welcome change! Now you and your little ones
> can sit outside, enjoy the fresh air, and people-watch when
> the weather is nice.

Baja Fresh
3231 Duke St., Alexandria
7003 Manchester Blvd., Alexandria
1101 Joyce St., Arlington
1100 Wilson Blvd., Rosslyn
1116 W. Broad St., Falls Church
2815 Clarendon Blvd., Clarendon
11690 Plaza America Dr., Reston
12150 Fairfax Town Center, Fairfax
3011 Nutley St., Fairfax
www.bajafresh.com

Bertucci's
725 King St., Alexandria
2700 Clarendon Blvd., Arlington
13195 Parcher Ave., Herndon
6525 Frontier Dr., Springfield
1934 Old Gallows Rd., Vienna
www.bertuccis.com

Big Bowl
2800 Clarendon Blvd., Arlington
11915 Democracy Dr., Reston

Bubba's Bar-B-Q
7810-F Lee Hwy., Falls Church

Buzz Bakery & Coffee
901 Slaters Ln., Alexandria, www.buzzonslaters.com

> **author's note:**
> We're fans of Buzz, and so are lots of other parents of young children. This hip and welcoming neighborhood bakery and coffee shop has plentiful outdoor seating and a child-sized table indoors, next to a child-sized kitchen set. They play good music. They offer free wifi access. Not to mention that the staff is friendly and the pastries are out of this world!

Caboose Café & Bakery
2419 Mt. Vernon Ave., Del Ray, Alexandria, www.caboosebakery.com

California Pizza Kitchen
1201 S. Hayes St., Arlington (Pentagon Centre)
4200 Fairfax Corner West, Fairfax
7939 L. Tysons Corner, Mclean
www.cpk.com

California Tortilla
2057 Wilson Blvd., Arlington (Courthouse)
Fair Lakes Promenade Shopping Center, Fairfax
www.californiatortilla.com

> *"California Tortilla has healthy choices, good food, and is affordable, with no worries about your kids being too loud or making a mess. Gotta love the 80s music, too."*
>
> *- Mandy*

Casa Grande
9534 Arlington Blvd., Fairfax

Cassatt's

4536 Lee Hwy., Arlington
www.cassatts.com

> "Cassatt's has a great deal Wednesday nights. Parents have dinner at the restaurant upstairs, and children paint with watercolors downstairs under adult supervision provided by the restaurant. The kids also dine while they draw and paint -- chicken nuggets, veggies, cheese, fruit, etc. My boys (aged 4 and 2) lasted over an hour before coming to find us upstairs... It gives parents with young children a great break to actually talk with one another!"
>
> - *Vicki*

Cameron Perks
4911 Brenman Park Dr., Alexandria, www.cameronperks.com

> ***author's note:***
> The favorite hang-out for Cameron Station families. Friendly and kid-friendly, they serve good coffees, treat, and lunches. They also regularly host children's musicians for casual weekday performances. Check their website to find out the current lineup.

Coastal Flats
11901 Grand Commons Ave., Fairfax Town Center

Connaught Place (Indian)
10425 North St., Fairfax

> *Connaught Place is so nice to families! They'll make special orders and small portions for children, and there are always babies and toddlers there – even though it's really a nice restaurant. They bring naan bread out while you're waiting for your food, so kids can snack if they get restless."*
>
> *-Jamie*

Coyote Grill

10266 Main St., Fairfax

The Dairy Godmother
2310 Mt. Vernon Ave., Del Ray, Alexandria, www.thedairygodmother.com

> *author's note:*
> *Delish frozen custard, root beer floats, and other nostalgic*
> *treats make this a neighborhood meeting spot. Our daughter*
> *loves the sparkly "magic wands" they sell at the checkout*
> *counter for $2 each.*

Don Pablo's
3525 Jefferson Davis Hwy., Alexandria
13050 Fair Lakes Shopping Center, Fairfax
10691 Davidson Place, Manassas
46280 Potomac Run Plaza, Sterling
2840 Prince William Pkwy., Woodbridge
www.donpablos.com

Esposito's Pizza
9917 Lee Hwy., Fairfax

The Wharf
119 King St., Old Town Alexandria

> *author's note:*
> The Wharf has good (if basic) seafood, a kids' menu, and
> reliable service in a kitschy setting that is plenty relaxed for
> children. A great place to go if you've got children in tow but
> want to stroll the Old Town waterfront and get a decent
> meal.

Generous George's Positive Pizza
3006 Duke St., Alexandria, 703.370.4303
www.generousgeorge.com

> *author's note:*
> So much to enjoy at Generous George's. We love their vintage kitschy décor, the vintage circus props and campy memorabilia. We love the neon signage and the giant toy soldiers out front. We love the fact that they bring our daughter a balloon. We love their recent renovation, including the greatly-improved family restroom. We love their pile-it-on, gooey, make-a-big-mess pizzas, and their ridiculously large mugs of beer for mamas and daddies (designate a driver, folks). We love their kids' menu of indulgent comfort foods, their spill-proof children's cups, and their 1950s tables that take me back to my great-grandmother's kitchenette. They also do birthday parties and catering. Sign up for Generous George's email list to get coupons and announcements of special events.

Fireflies
Del Ray, Alexandria

> *author's note:*
> Our favorite time to visit Fireflies is for Sunday morning brunch, when the visiting bluegrass band entertains. There's space in front of the stage for the kids to get up and dance – and they frequently do.

Grounded Coffee Shop
6919 Telegraph Rd., Alexandria
www.groundedcoffeeshop.com

Jammin' Java
227 Maple Ave. E., Vienna, www.jamminjava.com

> *author's note:*
> Though their weekday kids' concerts are no longer free, Jammin' Java in Vienna is still very much a mini-Mecca for mini music lovers. Jammin' Java regularly hosts the hottest kids' musicians in the DC area, and it's a regular gathering

place for mamas, daddies, and their tots. Jammin' Java also happens to have great coffee and treats, a nice aesthetic, and a comfortable décor. Their café fare includes excellent dips and sampler plates, gourmet chilis, salads, sandwiches, and sweets. Jammin' Java has received glowing reviews from the likes of USA Today, the Washington Post, Washingtonian, and Dirty Linen. Visit their website for the current calendar of children's performances.

Juke Box Diner
7039 Columbia Pike, Annandale

Hard Times Café & Chili Parlor
1404 King St., Old Town Alexandria
3028 Wilson Blvd., Arlington
428 Elden St., Herndon
6362 Springfield Plaza, Springfield
14389 Potomac Mills Rd., Woodbridge
www.hardtimes.com

Layalina (Lebanese)
5216 Wilson Blvd., Arlington

Los Tios
2615 Mt. Vernon Ave., Del Ray, Alexandria, www.lostiosgrill.com

author's note:
We've had great experiences here. Fresh, yummy Mexican food in a kid-friendly setting. Enjoy the patio tables when the weather is good, then stroll across the street to the playscape at the Mt. Vernon School.

Mancini's Café & Bakery
1508 Mt. Vernon Ave., Del Ray, Alexandria, www.cateringbymancinis.com

Melting Pot
1110 N. Glebe Rd., Arlington
11400 Commerce Park Dr., Reston
www.meltingpot.com

Mexicali Blues
2933 Wilson Blvd., Arlington, www.mexicali-blues.com

> ***author's note:***
> Love their Salvadoran and Mexican food! Nice atmosphere in
> a great neighborhood, with highchairs and crayons for the
> kids, to boot. The meals on the children's menu are all priced
> at an attractive $3.50.

Milano Pizza & Pasta
1015 Dranesville Rd., Herndon
www.milanosonline.com

Mango Mike's
4580 Duke St., Alexandria
www.mangomikes.com

Metro 29 Diner
4711 Lee Hwy., Arlington

Monroe's
Del Ray, Alexandria

PJ Skidoos
9908 Lee Hwy., Fairfax
www.pjskidoos.com

Rio Grande Café
1827 Library St., Reston

> *"Rio Grande gives kids a big dough ball to play with while you're waiting for your food. It sounds weird, but actually it's a really nice distraction!"*
>
> *- Amy*

St. Elmo's Coffee Pub
2300 Mt. Vernon Ave., Del Ray, Alexandria

Sala Thai
2900 N. 10th St., Arlington
www.salathaidc.com

Silverado
7052 Columbia Pike, Annandale

Southside 815
815 S. Washington St., Alexandria, www.southside815.com

Sweet Water Tavern
3066 Gatehouse Plaza, Falls Church
45980 Waterview Plaza, Sterling
14250 Sweetwater Ln., Centreville

Tandoori Nights
2800 Clarendon Blvd., Arlington
www.tandoorinights.com

author's note:
We are Indian food fans, for sure! And Tandoori Nights is a great spot for getting your Indian fix, whether it's date night or a family dinner. Try one of the pakora or rice dishes for finicky kids. Tandoori Nights is located upstairs near Crate & Barrel in the Market Commons shopping area in Clarendon, which means you can visit the playground and the fountain with the little ones before or after your meal. Marylanders: They also have a Gaithersburg location!

Taqueria Poblano
2400-B Mt. Vernon Ave., Alexandria
2503-A N. Harrison St., Arlington
www.taqueriapoblano.com

> ***author's note:***
> Taqueria Poblano is not only tasty and exceedingly kid-friendly, but it also specializes in my husband's favorite -- CHEAP. Our favorites are the soft tacos with grilled shrimp, red onion, and avocado, chiles rellenos, and the fresh limeade. Child plates include mini-portions of cheese quesadillas, burrito, or taquitos.

Union Street
121 S. Union St., Old Town Alexandria, www.usphalexandria.com

> ***author's note:***
> Just nice enough to take out-of-town guests, and just casual enough to bring a three-year-old child. Union Street has a children's menu and plenty of highchairs, and we have always been well received with friendly service. Great seafood and a very pleasant atmosphere, complete with real tablecloths!

Viet House
6226 Richmond Hwy. (Rt. 1), Alexandria

> *"Viet House has great food and plenty of room to get around with all the baby stuff you have to lug when you go out to dinner. We can even bring a stroller in with no problem. The waiters are so nice and they give lollipops to the kids after the meal."*
>
> *- Sharon, Alexandria mama*

Whitlow's on Wilson
2854 Wilson Blvd., Arlington

author's note:
The fact that it gets crazy crowded on weekends at brunch/lunch attests to the appeal of this longtime Clarendon favorite. Extremely kid-friendly, with plenty of classics on the menu. Outdoor seating when the weather is mild.

CHAPTER 10
Children's Health Care Providers

The District's Favorite Pediatricians

Chevy Chase Pediatrics
5225 Connecticut Ave. NW, 202.363.0300

Children's at Adams Morgan
1630 Euclid Street NW, 202.884.5580

Children's at Shaw
2220 11th Street NW, 202.884.5500

Children's at Spring Valley
4900 Massachusetts Ave. NW, 202.966.5000

> *"We go to Sheila Shanahan at the Spring Valley practice. She has been seeing our son since he was born. She is very attentive to detail and was just named in the Washingtonian as a 'top doctor.' She has morning call hours for non-emergency issues, which I've found very helpful. Also, every doctor in the practice has one nurse they work with regularly, who you can talk to during office hours if the doctor isn't available. (She also takes time during lunch to meet with parents of potential new patients.) I have heard good things about other doctors in the practice, too. They don't take insurance, though, so you have to do the paperwork yourself."*
>
> *- Unice*

Dr. Francis Palumbo
4900 Massachusetts Ave. NW, 202.966.5000

Drs. Hamburger, Kaplan, Paulson, Ratner, Schoonover, & Wagner
2141 K St. NW (Foggy Bottom), 202.833.4543

Drs. Hudson, Simrel, & Rainey
2600 Naylor Rd. SE, 202.582.6800

Pediatric Village
4910 Massachusetts Ave. NW, 202.244.1553

Dr. Ioana Razi
3537 R St. NW , 202.333.1774

> *I'm not even pregnant yet, but I hear excellent things about Dr. Razi. She's a homeopathic pediatrician with training in both traditional medicine and alternative health care. She doesn't handle insurance, so you'd have to pay out-of-pocket. And I hear she's quite in demand.*
>
> *- Susan*

NoVa's Favorite Pediatricians

Children's Medical Associates
6303 Little River Turnpike, Alexandria
10657 Braddock Rd., Fairfax
www.cmanva.com

> *"We like everything about the Children's Medical Associates office in Alexandria. They do all kinds of things that make it easier on families when their kids are sick, and the staff is great."*
>
> *- Stacy*

Farrell Pediatrics
11349 Sunset Hills Rd., Reston, 703.435.0808

Dr. Matt Irwin
517 Wythe St., Alexandria
703.780.1261

> *"Dr. Irwin is kind of new on the scene but he's an awesome family practitioner, and I especially like how he relates to children. He is trained as an MD and also as a master's family counselor, and his approach is very holistic. He often takes the homeopathic treatment route when it's appropriate. He also prescribes when it's called for. He works alone as a small, private practice, so no crowds or chaos. He even makes home visits on occasion. He's also just a very sincere doctor with a great bedside manner. He doesn't take insurance, so you'll want to think ahead about payment."*
>
> *- Anonymous Alexandria mama*

Dr. Jasmine Moghissi
527 Maple Ave E., Vienna
703.281.5560

Dr. Laurence Murphy
5212 Lyngate Ct., Burke
703.503.9100

Dr. Isabel Ramaswamy
3801 N. Fairfax Dr., Arlington, 703.522.4780

Kidz Docs
1451 Belle Haven Rd., Alexandria, 703.765.6093
www.thekidzdocs.com

> *"A lot of Old Town families go to Kidz Docs, and we really like it. They have separate waiting areas for sick kids and well kids, which is nice, and fun panda-themed décor that helps distract anxious children. Their nurse practitioners are great."*
>
> *- Kristy*

> **author's note:**
> Kidz Docs has taken excellent care of our children's health for the past several years. They've seen our daughter through annual well-child visits, immunizations, referrals to specialists, and run-of-the mill childhood illnesses. They also cared for our newborn son after his birth at Inova Alexandria Hospital. We have always encountered professionalism and care at Kidz Docs, as well as courtesy from the office staff. And we like both the physicians and the nurse practitioners. If you find that you "click" with a particular provider, you can request that individual for future appointments.

Lake Ridge Pediatrics
4660 Kenmore Ave., Alexandria
703.212.6600

Northern Virginia Pediatric Associates
107 N. Virginia Ave., Falls Church
703.532.4446

> *"We've always been treated courteously by the staff at NoVa Pediatric Associates, and our worried phone calls have been answered promptly. My kids' favorite pediatrician is Dr. Atiyeh. I like that they keep some Saturday times open for sick calls."*
>
> - J.C.

Reston Pediatrics
11130 Sunrise Valley Dr., Reston
703.262.0100

Drs. Shapiro & Perez
10801 Lockwood Dr., Silver Spring
301.593.5566

Sleepy Hollow Pediatrics
2946 Sleepy Hollow Rd., 3B, Falls Church
703.534.1000

> *"We moved too far away to go there anymore, but I like that Sleepy Hollow has a neighborhood feel. We really felt like we knew them and that they knew us."*
>
> *- Kimmy*

Vienna Pediatrics
410 Maple Ave W., Vienna
703.359.5160

Virginia Pediatric Center
3700 Joseph Siewick Dr., Fairfax
703.758.7100

Whole Child Pediatrics
20925 Professional Plaza, Ashburn
703.723.8900

> *"Whole Child has a holistic approach and they incorporate therapies like homeopathy into their pediatrics practice. They also offer home visits for newborns, instead of having them come into the office setting when they're so small."*
>
> *- Maria*

Suburban Maryland's Favorite Pediatricians

Drs. Berkowitz, Feldman, Burgin, Glaser, & Delaney
6201 Greenbelt Rd., College Park, 301.345.1900

Drs. Bernstein, Paxton, Witkin, Feldman, & Buckley
344 University Blvd. W., Silver Spring, 301.681.6730

Drs. Brasch, Goldstein, & Filie
4601 N. Park Ave., Chevy Chase, 301.656.2745

Dr. Dinea Desouza
19251 Montgomery Village Ave., Gaithersburg
301.926.3633
19501 Doctors Dr., Germantown
301.540.0555

Capitol Medical Group
8401 Connecticut Ave., Chevy Chase, 301.907.3960

> *"We like that Capitol Medical Group has monthly meetings for pregnant women and their partners, where you can get the tour of the office and talk about your questions and concerns. They also have a lactation consultant and even an osteopath on staff."*
>
> *- Anne*

Children First Pediatrics
10301 Georgia Ave. NW, Silver Spring, 301.681.6000
2401 Research Blvd., Rockville, 301. 990.1664

Drs. Cohen, Eig, & Madden
10313 Georgia Ave., Silver Spring, 301.681.7020

Dr. Gary Brecher (MD & FAAP)
20528 Boland Farm Rd., Germantown, 301.972.9559

Drs. Schwartz, Plotsky & Burgett
10810 Darnstown Rd., Potomac, 301.294.9242

Dr. Hsuan Huang
121 Congressional Ln., Rockville, 301.468.6161

Dr. Pam Parker
12301 Old Columbia Pike, Silver Spring, 301.625.2800

Kensington Pediatrics
10400 Connecticut Ave., Kensington, 301.949.8860

> *"I plan to use Dr. June Fusner at Kensington Pediatrics for my daughter's care. She is a pediatrician who also incorporates homeopathy. Her physician's assistant is also great, and they are both big breastfeeding supporters.*
>
> *- Katie*

Pediatric Care Center
5612 Spruce Tree Ave., Bethesda, 301.564.5880

Primary Pediatrics
9811 Mallard Dr., Laurel
301.776.8000
2415 Musgrove Rd., Silver Spring
301.989.0085

Shady Grove Pediatric Associates
10400 Connecticut Ave., Kensington, 301.942.2212

Drs. Smith, Guarinello, & Pellicoro
9692 Pennsylvania Ave., Upper Marlboro
301.599.7300
Rte. 301, Waldorf Medical Center, Waldorf
301.645.0300

Dr. Alan Vinitsky
902 Wind River Ln., Gaithersburg, 301.840.0002

DC's Favorite Pediatric Dentists

Children's Hospital Pediatric Dentistry
111 Michigan Ave. NW, 202.884.2160

Maryam Mohamaddi, DDS
Beverly Pediatric
2440 M St. NW, 202.331.3474

Dana Greenwald, DMD & Partners
5028 Wisconsin Ave. NW (Friendship Heights), 202.966.0045

> *"I cannot express how much we love Dr. Greenwald for our kids! She's a natural. She makes what could be a very bad experience a very good one. We wouldn't dream of going to any other pediatric dentist."*
>
> *- Meghan*

Stan Shulman, DDS (Family dentist, but extra-great with kids)
5002 Massachusetts Ave NW, 202.966.3100

NoVa's Favorite Pediatric Dentists

Arlington Smile Center
www.arlingtonsmilecenter.com
5015 Lee Hwy., Suite 202, Arlington, 703.525.0023
Offers both pediatric and family dentistry, with some appointments early as 7 a.m. and some Saturday hours.

Girish Banaji, DDS, PC
8505 Arlington Blvd., Fairfax, 703.849.1300

Brite Smiles Pediatric Dentistry
6116 Rolling Rd., Springfield, 703.451.2195

Jayne Delaney, DDS
50 S. Pickett St., Alexandria, 703.370.5437

> *author's note:*
> We really like Dr. Jayne Delaney. She's been our daughter's dentist since 2005, and has made those early dentistry experiences positive and pleasant for all involved. The

receptionist at Dr. Delaney's office is exceptionally pleasant and helpful, and the waiting room has plenty of toys and books. The staff is good with even fearful, squirmy toddlers, the exam rooms are uniquely outfitted for kids, and the patients get special perks (like a treasure-treat at the end of the appointment, and cool sunglasses they can wear while under the lights in the exam chair).

Granato & Crandall, DDS, P.C.
8719 Stonewall Rd., Manassas, 703.368.1000

Christine Reardon-Davis, DMD
801 N. Quincy St., Arlington , 703.778.7610

Pediatric & Adolescent Dentistry
10875 Main St., Fairfax, 703.352.4121

Michael Ternisky, D.D.S.
Cris Ann Ternisky, D.D.S.
6711 Whittier Ave., Mclean, 703.356.1875

Suburban Maryland's Favorite Pediatric Dentists

Berg & Lawrence
4201 Northview Dr., Bowie, 301.262-0242 or 301.262.2896

Bethesda-Potomac Children's Dental & Ortho Care
9800 Great Falls Rd., Potomac, 301.299.4400
4405 East-West Hwy., Suite 102, Bethesda, 301.654.3012

Dr. Camps Pediatric Dental Center
2415 Musgrove Rd., Silver Spring, 301.989.8994

Shailja Ensor, D.D.S.
11301 Rockville Pike, Bethesda, 301.881.6170

Drs. Morgenstein & Levy, P.A.
11301 Rockville Pike, Rockville, White Flint Mall
301.881.6170

Amy Light, DMD
9812 Falls Rd., Potomac, 301.983.9804

Metropolitan Pediatric Dentistry
5530 Wisconsin Ave., Chevy Chase, 301.718.1012

Pediatric Dental Center
19847 Century Blvd., Germantown, 301.540.9366

Ricardo Perez, DDS, PC
5530 Wisconsin Ave., Chevy Chase, 301.718.1012

Ronald Starr, DMD
3304 East-West Hwy., Bethesda, 301.654.3011

Carol Orlando, DDS
10401 Old Georgetown Rd., Bethesda, 301.581.1100

CHAPTER 11
Safety

Safety isn't the sexiest topic, but it's as important as any of the other planning and prepping you do for your DC baby. Safety considerations will also change (constantly) as your child grows, so it's a journey, not a destination. And if you're like us, you need all the help you can get.

A FEW FAVORITE RESOURCES

Safe Start Baby
888-240-SAFE
www.safestartbaby.com
We really like Safe Start Baby and its owner, Michele Spahr. Michele is a real pro, not a pushy salesperson, who knows her stuff when it comes to babyproofing and child safety. She will help you prioritize what you need and what you can afford. And she'll help you make your house a safer place for young children, without turning it into a forbidding fortress.

Safe Start offers home assessments, safety product sales, and professional installation throughout the Washington, DC metro area. They also provide private and group Red Cross-authorized baby/child CPR classes and first aid classes. And their online store allows for quick and easy orders on a wide range of safety products.

A gift certificate to Safe Start Baby makes for a baby shower gift that will continue to be used long after Junior outgrows a newborn onesie. It's also a nice option for grandparents who want to treat the new family to a present they can't and won't refuse. If you host a "Safe Start Party" in your home for friends and neighbors, you earn a free consultation (a savings of roughly $75). Go to the website to sign up for their free e-newsletter, which alerts you to special offers and sales.

Babyguard
703.821.1231
www.babyguard.com

Mclean-based Babyguard provides consultation and professional childproofing in your home, as well as selling home safety products direct to customers and through their online storefront. Offering in-home installations throughout the DC metro area, they have a 17+-year track record of local success. Check out their frequent specials and their child safety tips on the website.

Children's Safety Care
301.977.8334
www.childrenssafetycare.com
Gaithersburg-based Children's Safety Care was founded 12+ years ago by a team of PhDs who saw a need for affordable and simple safety prevention devices that could help both city and suburban parents keep kids of all ages safe. Children's Safety Care has a loyal following of families in the DC area – many of whom are repeat customers, coming back for help and products each time they move homes or welcome a new baby to the family.

CHILD SAFETY CLASSES OFFERED BY:

American Heart Association
www.americanheart.org

American Red Cross
www.redcross.org

Columbia Reston Hospital
www.restonhospital.net

Holy Cross Hospital
www.holycrosshealth.org

Georgetown University Hospital
www.georgetownuniversityhospital.org

George Washington University Hospital
www.gwhospital.com

INOVA Hospitals
www.inova.com

Potomac Hospital
www.potomachospital.com

Sibley Memorial Hospital
www.sibley.org

Washington & Shady Grove Adventist Hospitals
www.adventisthealthcare.com

Washington Hospital Center
www.whc.mhg.edu

YMCA of Metropolitan Washington, DC
www.ymcawashdc.org

CAR SEAT INSPECTIONS

Where to go in the District and suburbs if you want to have an expert check for proper installation of your child safety seat? Though it should be simple to correctly install a seat, it's not. And though most of us think we've done it correctly, studies show that most of us haven't. You could save your child's life by learning how!

Be sure to call before you go! Days and times are likely to change. Also, be sure to install the car seat yourself *before* you show up…These are inspections and educational instruction, not installation services.

Children's National Medical Center & Safe Kids DC offer free car seat inspections on a drop-in basis at the main hospital campus, 111 Michigan Ave. NW at the back drive of the hospital. Hours are typically Wednesday through Friday, 10 a.m. to 1 p.m. and 2 to 4 p.m. CALL FIRST: 202.884.4993.

More DC locations for car seat inspections:

DMV Inspection Station
1001 Half St. SW, 202.645.4300

Second District Police Station
3320 Idaho Ave. NW, cps.checks@dc.gov
NO walk-ins. Appointment only.

Department of Fire & EMS
Engine #24, 5101 Georgia Ave. NW
Engine #33, 101 Atlantic St. SW
202.727.1778
Must call for appointment: 202.727.1778

Virginia Child Safety Seat Hotline Recording: 703.280.0559
For VA child passenger safety laws and guidelines on correct safety seat usage:
www.safetyseatva.org

Alexandria Cares, City of Alexandria
For upcoming seat-check dates and locations: 703.924.9294
Check upcoming events or find out how to make an appointment at the website: www.alexandriacares.org
Alexandria Cares also sponsors a program that gives free child safety seats to low-income residents. Call the number above for details.

Arlington County Fire Department
The ACFD offers an educational program for parents and caregivers, teaching them how to install their own child safety seats. For details or to register, call 703.228.2229. Low-income residents in need of a child safety seat may contact Arlington's Department of Health and Human Services at 703.228.1350.

Fairfax County Police Stations, Car Seat Inspections
You must call ahead for an appointment!
Fair Oaks District Station, 703.591.0966, press #8
Franconia District Station, 703.922.0889
Mclean District Station, 703.556.7750, ext. 5417
Mt. Vernon District Station, 703.360.8400, ext. 5500
Reston District Station, 703.378.0904, ext. 5208
Sully District Station, 703.814.7000, ext. 5140
W. Springfield District Station, 703.644.7377

City of Falls Church Car Seat Inspections
Call for appointment: 703.248.5111

Town of Herndon Car Seat Inspections
Call for appointment: 703.435.3134

Town of Vienna Car Seat Inspections
Call for appointment: 703.255.6396

Prince William County Car Seat Inspections
Call hotline for information: 703.792.4636, message 401

Montgomery County Car Seat Inspections
To make an appointment for a child safety seat inspection in Montgomery County, call 240.777.2223. There is often a two to three week wait for an appointment, so plan accordingly. Both weekday and weekend appointments are available, at two locations in Gaithersburg and a third location in Aspen Hill.

Montgomery County Child Passenger Safety Hotline:
240.777.2222

A MUST-KNOW RESOURCE:
THE POISON CENTER, 1.800.222.1222
www.poison.org
Each year, The Poison Center in DC receives 55,000 phone calls from residents and health professionals in the metro area – Most of them from mothers whose children have gotten into household products and who are panicked about what to do. The Poison Center is a nonprofit, non-government organization providing medical guidance in poison emergencies. Their services are free, and they are open all day, every day, providing confidential information. They even provide translation services for parents and childcare providers who don't speak fluent English. Every household with children in the DC area should have their

phone number posted on the fridge, along with other emergency contacts.

SAFETY RESOURCES ONLINE

Consumer Product Safety Commission
www.cpsc.gov
Recent product recalls, safety news, to report an unsafe product, and to sign up for email announcements.

SAFE KIDS USA
www.usa.safekids.org
For information, resources, referral.

Maryland Kids in Safety Seats (KISS)
www.mdkiss.org
Online guide to buying the appropriate seat for your child, how to install, Maryland safety laws, and upcoming seat check / seat help events.

Bike Walk Virginia
http://bikewalkvirginia.org
For safe biking with babies and children.

Bikes & Helmet Safety, DC
http://mpdc.dc.gov, go to the "Family Safety" section or do a search for the key terms. The site includes the DC helmet law, details about the bicycle helmet distribution program, and safety tips.

National Highway Traffic Safety Administration
www.nhtsa.gov or www.safercar.gov
For information on child safety seats and booster seats, reporting defective child safety seat products, as well as the latest car safety news.

SAFE KIDS Coalition of Virginia
www.vcuhealth.org/virginiasafekids

Main site for the 10 SAFE KIDS coalitions in Virginia. Go to the "Education Information" link to learn about seatbelt and child safety laws in the state.

District of Columbia, Sex Offender Registry Database
www.mpdc.dc.gov

State of Maryland Sex Offender Registry Database
www.dpscs.state.md.us/onlineservs/sor

State of Virginia Sex Offender Registry Database
http://sex-offender.vsp.state.va.us

CHILD FINGERPRINTING PROGRAMS

Child Fingerprinting Program, DC Metro Police Department
Youth and Preventive Services Division, 202.576.6768

Child Fingerprinting Program, Fairfax County Police Department
Mount Vernon District Station, 703.360.8400
McLean District Station, 703.556.7750
Mason District Station, 703.256.8035
Reston District Station, 703.478.0904
Franconia District Station, 703.922.0889
West Springfield District Station, 703.644.7377
Fair Oaks District Station, 703.591.0966
Sully District Station, 703.814.7000

Child Fingerprinting Program, Montgomery County Police Department
757.229.0507

CHAPTER 12
DC's Favorite Photographers
for Pregnancy, Children, & Families

Meet the *DC Baby* Photographer!

Elizabeth Dranitzke, PHOTOPIA
www.photopiadc.com
202.550.2520

Meet the official DCB photographer, who took the author photo on the back of this book! We are clients – and huge fans – of photographer Elizabeth Dranitzke, who has shot some of our all-time favorite portraits of our daughter and our family. We first fell in love with her online portfolio when working on the first edition of this book in 2005. Since that time, we have become full-fledged devotees.

Dranitzke, Capitol Hill mama of two, has a true artist's eye and a great sense of style. Writing about Elizabeth's photography is like dancing about architecture – It can't really do justice. But her website has many fabulous samples from her portfolio, and it's a must-see. Dranitzke, who has been featured in the *Washington Post and the Lilaguide DC*, among others, draws praise for her "instant rapport with children," her flexibility and sensitivity to the ever- changing moods of little ones, and her selection of unique and fun locations for photo shoots. We've found her blessedly patient and so good with young children – including reticent kids who are slow to warm up to a new person wielding a camera.

More things to love about Dranitzke's approach: She works with available light, which allows for the greatest flexibility in shooting and the most flattering results. She takes her time meeting with clients to toss around ideas and locations in advance, and works in both outdoor and indoor settings. She does both color and black & white, shooting in formats that offer a good deal of versatility. She shares lots of tips with clients that can help you come prepared and relaxed. And perhaps best of all, Elizabeth knows and loves this city, skillfully using Washington as a backdrop – Among her favorite locations are the National Arboretum, the East Wing of the National Gallery, the National Botanic Gardens, Bartholdi

Park at the Botanic, the Sculpture Garden, the Haupt Garden, and the many neighborhood playgrounds and hideaways that dot the city.

Dranitzke holds a B.A. in photography from Sarah Lawrence College and an M.F.A. in photography from the California College of Arts and Crafts. She has worked as a photographic educator with arts institutions, schools, and community groups including The Friends of Photography/Ansel Adams Center, The California Academy of Sciences, and The Crossroads School and the L.A. County Museum of Art in Los Angeles. Dranitzke's work has also been exhibited in San Francisco, Los Angeles, and here in Washington. Elizabeth works in a hip and kid-friendly space near Eastern Market, making the task of going over proofs and orders at her office a pleasure in itself. Be sure to check out her new blog, at www.photopiadc.com/blog.html.

GETTING PICTURE-READY:

Elizabeth Dranitzke of PHOTOPIA shared some of her tips for photo session success with the *Washington Post* in 2003. Among them:

"I suggest people dress their babies in outfits they love... Be comfortable and casual. Don't try to be someone else. If it's a group, I say no plaids, polka dots, stripes, and logos. They become more dominant than faces."

"If you are in your house, clear the clutter. And use as much natural light as you can. Use environments that make your kids happy, where they're going to be themselves."

"Engage with each other while posing."

"Make sure your baby is rested and fed, ready to play. Bring toys, a blanket, and snacks. I always tell people to bring extra clothes; kids can get trashed in a second."

MORE OF DC'S FAVORITE FAMILY PHOTOGRAPHERS

We love photos, especially good ones, and especially of our children! Elizabeth is our family's photographer, so we're able to give her the first-hand recommendation that comes from a satisfied client. But there is SUCH an abundance of photographic talent in and around DC – and the following photographers are those whose work we admire and who have been repeatedly recommended to us. We encourage you to look at portfolios online, read (or request) plenty of referrals, compare pricing and services, and ultimately to go with the photographer whose style and personality captures your fancy.

Rashmi Pappu Photography
703.838.0330
www.rpappuphotography.com

Oh Baby! Photography, Liz Vance
703.731.4592
www.ohbabyphoto.com

> *"We had a wonderful experience with our pregnancy photos (and our recent newborn and family photos) with Liz Vance. This has been the most exciting project for us and we are thoroughly enjoying working with Liz... She is very much the professional when it comes to artistic talent, but very personable when it comes to your individual photos. She actually came to our house to shoot the pregnancy photos, since I had been on bed rest, but she also has a studio."*
>
> *- Danielle*

Studio Diana, Diana Adams
703.691.1661
www.studiodiana.com

> **author's note:**
> Since the first edition of this book in 2005, Diana Adams has enjoyed some high-profile assignments, including

photographing an event hosted by HRH Princess Anne at Buckingham Palace. But she's also still right at home taking beautiful portraits of the DC-area's own little princes and princesses, in addition to a thriving wedding portraiture business.

Susan Braswell Photography
703.549.5030
www.susanbraswellphotography.com

Karen London Photography
202.615.1969
www.karenlondonphotography.com

Golden Photography, Kristy Golden
301.656.4786
www.kristygolden.com

Thomas Van Veen
301.758.3085
www.thomasvanveen.com

"Thomas does his photography solely by 'house calls,' not in a studio. His philosophy is that pictures of children and families should be in the setting where they are most comfortable and natural."

- Kimberly

Brett Cordeau Photography
www.cordeauphoto.com

Erin Rexroth Photography
www.erinjphoto.com

"Erin did a great job of capturing our family's personality. I have two very energetic girls who are not easy to photograph, but Erin did a great job...The whole experience

> was stress-free and fun, and that really comes across in the pictures."
>
> *- Lisa*

The H.I.P. Studio, Stephanie Zbinden
703.624.3058
www.thehipstudio.com

Nancy de Pastino, Little Prints Portrait Photography
www.littleprintsphoto.com

> **author's note:**
> Nancy de Pastino takes a unique approach to doing business as a photographer. You get to keep the rights to your own photos, and you can print what you like – whenever you like – forever. She also offers professional prints, if you want to get the full-service treatment.

Bellies & Births, Karen Colbert
410.788.5605
www.belliesandbirths.com

Kaileen Galhouse Photography
410.245.7333
www.galhousephotography.com

> "I am especially impressed by how easy Kaileen is to work with, for both adults and children. For the adults, she was extremely accommodating in setting up the photo shoot and delivering the photos... She worked with my son to coax smiles and laughter out of a cranky three-year-old, showing him how the camera worked and even letting him take pictures. I would work with Kaileen again in a heartbeat."
>
> *- Katy*

Stacey Vaeth Photography
202.276.2481
www.staceyvaeth.com

Adelaide Photography, Kristin Callahan
301.616.2229
www.adelaide-photography.com

Jeff Lubin Photography
703.356.3535
www.jefflubin.com

---

author's note:
Each spring, portrait photographer Jeff Lubin puts his skills to
work for a great cause, offering discounted sessions of
children's portraiture to benefit the Lombardi Cancer Center
at Georgetown University. Here's how it works: You write a
check for a set fee (as of the publication date of this book,
this tax-deductible fee was $150), and in return you get a
sitting of your child featuring multiple poses, and one 8x10
print. Proceeds go to the Lombardi Center. As you might
imagine, this is a major discount on a professional sitting fee
and an 8x10 print, to boot. We've heard from Jeff Lubin's
clients, and they really adore his work.

Rebecca S. Weiner Photography
703.963.3631
www.rswphotography.com

---

*"We had a terrific photo shoot in Old Town Alexandria with
Rebecca. She was patient and playful with our daughters,
and was so creative in capturing both posed and candid
shots. When we stopped for a snack break and our youngest
ended up with a mouthful of Oreo crumbs, Rebecca
immediately captured the moment as a testament to the*

> *unbridled joy of a four-year-old. It's one of our favorite photos!"*
>
> *- Cathy & Brent*

Simply Create Photography, Johanna Waisley
571.223.1938
www.simply-create.com

> *"We have used Johanna Waisley of Simply Create Photography for the last four years and she is an incredible artist!"*
>
> *- Jennifer*

CHAPTER 13
DC's Favorite Children's Entertainers

"Mr. Knick Knack" (a.k.a. Steve Rossi)
703.598.6173
www.mrknickknack.com
Mr. Knick Knack is the real deal, sharing a sweet, fun mix of stories and songs with young audiences. He's a familiar favorite at spots like Jammin' Java in Vienna, Noodles & Noggins in Clifton, Wren & Divine in Mclean, Tysons Corner, Reston Town Center, and White Flint – in addition to seasonal festivals, special events, and children's birthday parties. We've been in Mr. Knick Knack's audience more than once, and we love his sincere, down-to-earth way with the kids and his no-costumes, no-gimmicks simplicity as a performer. Mr. Knick Knack's themes of unconditional love and self-expression are good for what ails us these days. His version of "Old McDonald" rocks! And his signature ballad, "My Heart Is Like a Family," will melt yours – guaranteed.

"Oh Susannah!" (a.k.a. Susan McNelis)
301.933.2006
susannahparties@aol.com, susannahconcerts@aol.com
www.susannahmusic.com
We love Oh Susannah!, and had such fun at her performance during the launch party for the first edition of this book, back in fall 2005. Not only is she a consummate professional and a strong vocalist with a great lineup of kid-friendly songs, but we really get a kick out of her punky, spunky performance persona! A local favorite for toddlers through young school-age kids, Oh Susannah! performs regularly at venues throughout the DC area and also hosts highly-recommended kids' parties, where she provides percussion instruments to make it a real sing-along. Susannah can also do balloon animals and face painting, in addition to the music. Check out her repertoire and her children's CDs at the website. Her second CD won an iParenting Media Award.

Lilo Gonzalez
301.346.9322, lilo@erols.com
Lilo Gonzalez, who plays guitar and sings in both English and Spanish, comes so highly recommended from local moms and educators whose

reviews I really appreciate, including founder of Jonah's Treehouse Vicki Gersten and the folks at The Lowell School, the Levine School of Music, the Latin American Youth Center, and the Latin American Montessori Bilingual Charter School – all of whom love and know him as a familiar performer! Lilo is very interactive and great with young children, and is available for children's birthday parties. I'm told young kids love his songs and warm up to his style immediately!

The Great Zucchini
202.271.3108
www.thegreatzucchini.com
Our daughter is a huge fan of kids' magician The Great Zucchini. She and her classmates first fell for him when he performed at her preschool, where I'm told the kids were wild with giggles throughout the performance. He performs regularly at Arlington Cinema & Drafthouse, as well as at area daycares, schools, and camp programs. Zucchini also does birthday parties! Options include a basic package with a 40-minute magic show for children ages two to six, with lots of audience participation and the birthday child as the star. At the end of the show, kids learn a magic trick. A more elaborate birthday party package includes all that plus an addition 30 minutes of Zucchini-directed games.

"The Banjo Man" (a.k.a. Frank Cassel)
fcassel@aol.com
www.banjomanfc.com
The Banjo Man does shows at special events throughout the metro, area and also performs at children's parties. He performs lots of traditional kid favorites, and even brings streamers and maracas for the kids to join the fun. Check his website for more info and CDs. You can catch his live performances regularly at spots including the Takoma Park Farmers Market, Jammin' Java in Vienna, and twice monthly at the Silver Diner in Rockville.

Rocknocerus
info@rocknocerus.com
www.rocknocerus.com
This rockin' children's duo mixes it up with both standards and originals that both kids (ages one to nine) AND their parents love. Rocknocerus'

Coach Cotton and Willibob will captivate all ages. They perform regularly at venues like Jammin' Java, and have developed quite the cult following among families with kids of all ages. Find out more about their children's parties by sending an email.

Bob Brown Puppet Productions
703.319.9102
www.bobbrownpuppets.com
Bob Brown Puppet Productions does school productions, special events, and children's birthday parties. Their two birthday shows, "Clowning Around" and "Kaleidoscope," are geared toward ages three to seven, with a variety-show-style format (rather than a narrative, which tends to be harder for young, hyped-up party attendees to sit still for). Bob and his puppet friends regularly perform at Fairfax County Parks events and at Wolf Trap's summer shows.

"BanjerDan" (a.k.a. Dan Mazer)
dan@banjerdan.com
www.banjerdan.com
BanjerDan is a solo acoustic performer who is a popular children's musician and plays banjo, guitar, mandolin, and Dobro. Kids adore him! You can catch BanjerDan at the Silver Spring Farmers Market, the Green Meadows Petting Farm in Jessup, the National Theatre, and with J.B. Beverley and the Wayward Drifters – as well as at seasonal festivals, special events, and children's parties. His CD, "Old Stuff," is available for purchase online at CDBaby.

"Broccoli the Magic Clown"
703.768.7352
www.broccolithemagicclown.com
Broccoli has been named among the favorite children's entertainers since 2003 by *Washington Families* magazine. He has entertained everyone from babies to senior citizens for 25 years, and his children's shows include magic, balloon sculpture, audience participation, and comedy. Broccoli also works with fun colleagues including "Cookie the Clown" and "Jake the Musician," both of whom are available for children's parties.

Carousel Puppets

703.444.9426

www.carouselpuppets.com

Susan Wall's Carousel Puppets incorporates audience participation into lively shows featuring music and large, colorful marionettes and hand-puppets. They can provide goodie bags for children's parties, and they also offer puppet-making workshops. The birthday party variety show includes singing frogs, a disco-dancing dog, and juggling clowns – with plenty of audience participation, as kids are invited to come forward and help with the puppets.

Charley Montroll

301.530.6786

www.folksinging.tv

Charley Montroll is a kids' musician who plays the guitar, banjo, and ukelele in the folk tradition, has lots of songs in his repertoire, and brings instruments for the kids to play. His performances are suitable for all young children, but especially geared toward the toddler set – and I hear he puts on a fabulous toddler birthday party. The party repertoire is a musical journey that also includes magic, with percussion instruments for the kids to play. Check out audio clips from his three CDs at the website.

Christian & Co. Entertainment

703.425.6663

www.gr8shows.com

This local entertainment agency has been around since the 1970s, and they offer a number of entertainers for kids' parties, schools, and special events. Among their lineup: magicians, acrobats, clowns, puppeteers, jugglers, story-tellers, caricaturists, face-painters, hula lessons, seasonal characters, and doodle-artists. They provide references you can contact prior to hire, and their rates are competitive.

Greta Gonzalez

703.765.0727

http://gretagonzalez.com

We've seen face painting artist Greta Gonzalez in action (she painted our daughter's face at Baby Loves Disco in DC), and what a talent! Greta's great with children, and adjusts the speed and detail of her work to the attention spans of her young subjects. She also does glitter tattoos, henna, and body painting. Greta is available for children's parties and special events – Be sure to call early, before she books up for your preferred date.

Kaydee Puppets
703.385.4543
www.kaydeepuppets.com
The Kaydee Puppeteers have been touring metro DC since 1972, doing shows at libraries, schools, rec centers, the Smithsonian, and the Library of Congress' 125th anniversary celebration, as well as children's parties. Their 30- to-45-minute performances allow for audience interaction, and their large, moving-mouth puppets are perfect for ages two+. Birthday party show options include The Princess and the Pea, Rapunzel, The Frog Prince, The Ugly Duckling, Jack & the Beanstalk, The Three Little Pigs, The Three Billy Goats Gruff, and Little Red Riding Hood.

"Mister Don," a.k.a. Don Bridges
703.449.0817
www.donbridgesongs.com
Mister Don's sing-alongs for young children cover territory such as sibling rivalry, strange pets, and caring for the planet. His interactive shows allow the kids to play their own instruments and incorporate plenty of hand motions and singing. Mister Don plays regularly at Jammin' Java in Vienna. He won a 2004 Wammie Award for best children's vocalist, and was nominated in 2004 for Wammie's best contemporary folk recording.

Peter McCory
funmusic@petermccory.com
www.petermccory.com
Peter McCory of Warrenton, VA is a one-man-band for kids age two to 10. He plays familiar children's songs, nursery rhymes, folk songs, and his own original tunes. There aren't many among us who can sing, strum guitar, banjo, or ukulele, AND toot a harmonica, kazoo, or whistle, WHILE playing drums, cymbals, and a cow bell with our feet. Truly a sight to behold!

Milkshake
410.662.8392
www.milkshakemusic.com

Milkshake is the Baltimore-based duo of Lisa Mathews (vocals) and Mikel Gehl (acoustic guitar), both members of the rock group Love Riot. Their "Bottle of Sunshine" received a Parents' Choice Recommended Award in their 2005 Best Audio category. Two of their videos air on the Noggin network, between cartoons, as part of the Move to the Music program. And you've also probably seen their short performance video in between programs on PBS Kids.

CHAPTER 14
DC'S Favorite Children's Cakes

Amphora Bakery
301 Maple Ave. W., Vienna, 703.281.5631
1151 Elden St., Herndon, 703.925.0505
www.amphorabaker.com

> *"Amphora's Elmo cake is too cute. It was the best- looking and -tasting one I found, and my son loved it."*
>
> *- Kirsten*

Christina at Simply Sweet Bakery
703.660.6206, info@simplysweetbakery.com
www.simplysweetbakery.com

> *"Christina created two very artistically detailed superhero birthday cakes for my sons (age 4 and 5) that matched their party theme of Batman and Spiderman. The quality of her cakes impressed and satisfied both children and parents alike."*
>
> *- Monique*

Blue Iris Bakery
703.395.5824, blueirisbakery@email.com
www.blueirisbakery.com

> *"Jen Rudolph at Blue Iris is great to work with and the cakes are pretty and not too expensive. She even does delivery in NoVa. And she does a free individual cake for the birthday boy or girl."*
>
> *- Anonymous Arlington mama*

Chantel's Cakes & Pastries
703.709.1488, 506 Shaw Rd., Sterling
http://pages.loudouncounty.com/food/chantels.htm

> *"Chantel's does really cute and yummy kids' cakes. And I loved that they delivered to our house, which made the day of my daughter's birthday party so much easier!"*
>
> *- Amy*

Costco
1200 South Fern St., Arlington (Pentagon City)
7373 Boston Blvd., Springfield
4725 West Ox Rd., Fairfax
10925 Baltimore Ave. (Rt. 1), Beltsville
21398 Price/Cascades Plaza, Sterling
10701 Sudley Manor Dr., Manassas
880 Russell Ave., Gaithersburg
www.costco.com

> *"If you want a big, basic sheet cake that tastes good and is really cheap, Costco is the place."*
>
> *- Beth*

Creative Cakes
301.587.1599, 8814 Brookville Rd., Silver Spring
www.creativecakes.com

> *"Creative Cakes has lots of sizes for kids' cakes, and lots of different themes. Really cute and the cakes are moist and delicious."*
>
> *- Angie*

Custom Cake Design
301.216.1100, 8535 Ziggy Ln., Gaithersburg
www.customcakedesign.com

> *"I went to a Bar Mitzvah where there was a delicious cake made by Custom Cake Design. They do party cakes with different themes, as well as lots of wedding cakes. We're going to use them for my daughter's next birthday."*
>
> *- Addie*

Heidelberg Bakery
703.527.8394, 2150 N. Culpeper St., Arlington
www.heidelbergbakery.com

> *"Heidelberg's has a binder full of pictures of their children's cakes, and if you have a desire for something different they will work with you. They have great customer service."*
>
> *- Denise*

Heller's Bakery
202.265.1169, 3221 Mt. Pleasant St. NW
www.hellersbakery.com

> *"Heller's makes good-tasting and cute birthday cakes, especially for girls."*
>
> *- Katie*

Hot Breads Bakery & Café
301.977.1919, 70 Market St. (Kentlands), Gaithersburg
www.hotbreadsmddc.com

> *"We highly recommend Hot Breads for cakes and pastries. We use them for our parties!"*
>
> *- Andrew, founder/owner of Andy's Parties*

Just Ask Mo
703.359.5055
www.justaskmo.com

> **author's note:**
> We chose Monique Roberts of Just Ask Mo to do our daughter's third birthday cake, and we couldn't have been more pleased. Monique worked with us to make an "Angelina Ballerina" edible image for our sheet cake – which absolutely thrilled our Angelina-obsessed birthday girl. Not only did the cake look stellar, but it was moist, rich, and got raves from the party guests. We went with a yellow cake finished in vanilla buttercream, with raspberry filling. YUM. Monique serves the DC metro area, including NoVa, the District, and Maryland, and offers delivery for a reasonable extra fee.

Stella's Bakery

301.231.9026, 11510 Rockville Pike, Suite D, Rockville
www.stellasbakeryonline.com

> *"Everyone loves Stella's cakes. They are so popular! It's a family-owned Greek bakery and they do great-tasting and great-looking cakes. The cakes aren't cheap, but they're so worth it."*
>
> *- Ashley*

CHAPTER 14
DC'S Favorite Children's Haircuts

Aponte's Barber & Salon
2505 N. Harrison St., Arlington
703.237.5698

> *"Aponte's has been around forever. They're quick and affordable and good with squirmy kids. They also give a lollipop!"*
>
> *- Ellen*

Bradlee Barber Shop
3638 King St., Alexandria
703.998.9830

> *"Bradlee is cheap, and they have a car and horse the kids can sit on. They will take a picture for your child's first haircut. Also lollipops after kids' cuts. My husband likes to go there for his haircuts, too."*
>
> *- Lee*

Bradley Barber Shop
6918 Arlington Rd., Bethesda
301.907.7870

> *"Bradley Barber Shop is an old-fashioned kind of place where they really take care of people. Great customer service and good with kids.*
>
> *- Deena*

Bubbles
201 Massachusetts Ave. NE (Capitol Hill)
202.546.7343
2020 K St. NW (Foggy Bottom)
202.659.5005

Cartoon Cuts
1619 Rockville Pike, Rockville
301.816.3098
701 Russell Ave. (in Lakeforest Mall), Gaithersburg
301.948.7020
11784 Fair Oaks Mall, Fairfax
703.359.2887
21100 Dulles Town Center, Sterling
703.433.1400
6686 Springfield Mall, Springfield
703.719.9791
www.cartoon-cuts.com

> *"Cartoon Cuts might not be a great place for a child who gets easily overstimulated, but for my kids the TVs, the toys in the waiting area, and the noise are good distractions."*
>
> *- Tricia*

Eclips Kids
1373 Beverly Rd. (at Fair Lakes Shopping Center), Mclean
703.356.0064
www.eclipshair.com

> *"Eclips Kids has some of the same stuff as Cartoon Cuts, like the TVs and toys in the waiting area, but I find it quieter and less manic-feeling than Cartoon Cuts. My daughter had a hard time holding it together at Cartoon Cuts, but does great at Eclips."*
>
> *- Stacy*

Hair Cuttery
1645 Connecticut Ave. NW (Adams Morgan)
202.232.9685
www.haircuttery.com

Kids Cuts
8300 Sudley Rd. (at Manassas Mall), Manassas
703.368.7366

Uzuri Braids
122 Kennedy St. NW
202.291.1118

"If you need someone to do your child's coarse/African American hair, go to Uzuri. They do the most beautiful braids and it's all natural without a lot of chemical relaxers. They're really good with my daughter."

- Kim

The Yellow Balloon
255 Market St. W., Gaithersburg
240.243.0573

author's note:
This full-service Gaithersburg salon is loaded with sights and sounds that will make haircuts easier for many kids. There are the actual yellow balloons. Then there are the racecar chairs. And the video games. And the rides. And the popcorn. You can even host a "glamour birthday bash" on-site. Brilliant!

Notes

Notes

Notes